Magic and Witchcraft

Magic and Witchcraft

From Shamanism to the Technopagans

with 205 illustrations, 61 in color

Nevill Drury

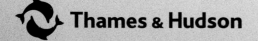
Thames & Hudson

Contents

Pages 2-3:
Shaman Mongush
Lazo performs *camlanie*,
meaning 'the ritual',
purifying with flame.
Tuva, Siberia, 2002.

Page 4: Love's Enchantment,
a young witch applies
magic ointment.
Flemish,
15th century.

© 2003 Thames & Hudson Ltd,
London
Text © 2003 Nevill Drury

First published in hardcover in the
United States of America in 2003
by Thames & Hudson Inc.,
500 Fifth Avenue,
New York, New York 10110

thamesandhudsonusa.com

Library of Congress Catalog
Card Number 2003102191
ISBN 0-500-51140-3

Printed and bound in Singapore
by Star Standard

Introduction

Magic is as old as humanity itself. From the earliest animist concepts of a universe alive with potent spiritual forces to the emergence of Wicca and contemporary Neopaganism, magic has helped invest the cosmos with sacred meaning. For the practitioner, the magical arts provide a sense of power and purpose in an essentially mysterious world.

Magic uses sacred and personal symbols to convey spiritual significance. From a magical perspective, symbols provide a meaningful bridge between the familiar world and the much less predictable world governed by gods, spirits and unseen forces. In Carlos Castaneda's *Journey to Ixtlan* (1972) the Yaqui shaman, don Juan Matus, explains the paradox of the magical world in these terms: 'For me the world is weird because it is stupendous, awesome, mysterious, unfathomable....' And yet, for don Juan, this also helps define the nature of the magical challenge itself, for the role of the shaman is to gain a sense of self-empowerment and sacred meaning within the context of an essentially mysterious universe. 'My interest,' don Juan tells Castaneda, 'has been to convince you that you must assume responsibility for being here, in this marvellous world...in this marvellous time.'

Don Juan's approach to shamanic magic differs greatly from the more widespread perception of magic as a form of superstition based essentially on ignorance and fear. Following the lead of the anthropologist Sir James Frazer in *The Golden Bough* (1911–15), magical thought has been commonly regarded as a form of pre-science – an earlier and less sophisticated phase of human intellectual development. Indeed, elements of this perception are reinforced by popular folklore with its black cats, and magic spells cast by wicked, toothless crones. With the exception of the ancient use of magical amulets as a form of protection, however, the sort of magic described in this book has little to do with superstition. As I hope to demonstrate, in all phases of human history the concept of magical consciousness relates much more to the concept of *will* or *intent* – to the idea that one can bring about specific effects or changes within one's personal sphere of awareness. There is also an implicit understanding within most forms of magical practice that magic itself should be taken seriously and accorded profound respect. Through the ages magic has been regarded as an *esoteric* tradition which, by its very nature, involves the exploration of hidden or unknown human potentials.

It is in relation to the issue of *will* that magic differs from mysticism and the more mainstream forms of world religion. The magician, unlike the mystic or religious devotee, draws not so much upon the concept of grace bestowed by God as on the idea that one may alter one's state of consciousness magically at will – that the gods or spirits will respond to certain ritual procedures. It may be that the magician dresses ceremonially to capture the very nature of a particular deity and in so doing invokes its sacred or symbolic energy. Perhaps sacred god-names are uttered – as in the Kabbalah, in the pagan traditions of witchcraft and in certain Gnostic formulations. Here the core idea is that the name of the god or goddess embodies the very essence of the deity, and that by invoking the sacred vibration one is not only tuning in to the archetypal level of awareness associated with these sacred beings, but actually attaining mastery over them.

As will become evident in this book, the idea of *will* is vital to the magical attitude. We find it in the ancient world where the magician creates a figurine of another person and then treats that figurine lovingly or aggressively in order to produce a specific and tangible result. We find it in Gnostic transcendentalism, where knowledge of sacred god-names ensures that a particular deity or archon will act in a way intended by the theurgist, and we find it in shamanic accounts, where the magical apprentice has to whirl his spirit-catcher near a sacred water hole and concentrate on the 'spaces' within the conjured sounds in order to *will* a magical 'ally' to appear. Similarly, in the modern ritual magic of the Hermetic Order of the Golden Dawn, it is through focused intent that the magician is able to rise through the planes of 'inner space' – through the symbolic and mythological realms associated with the Kabbalistic Tree of Life. In all of these instances the idea of magical will is central to the activity in question. And although it has been commonplace to equate magic with superstition and ignorance, since the time of the Renaissance magic has frequently been associated with spiritual or metaphysical purpose. Indeed, Gareth Knight, in his *History of White Magic* (1978), has defined magic as a means of assisting the 'evolution of spiritual will'.[1]

All of this, of course, is quite foreign to most established religious traditions. Prayer and supplication, offerings of thanks to a saviour god, and acts of worship in a church, are in no way intended to capture the god. Quite the reverse, in fact. Western religious devotion is an attitude of mind where worshippers humbly submit themselves to God in the hope that He will bestow grace and salvation. There is no implied act of control or mastery here. The supplicant waits, passively, until grace is received.

The magical attitude, on the other hand, is clearly more active – and often more assertive. The magician, shaman and witch are at the centre of their own particular universe. With their sacred formulae, ritual invocations and concentrated willpower they believe they can bring certain forces to bear. The magician believes that he or she can *will* to effect.

In a modern context the 'primitivism' of this approach has been legitimized by existentialist philosophy and the rise of the human potential or 'personal growth' movement. In the twentieth century it became common for interpreters of the Western magical tradition to regard the gods of High Magic as emanations of the creative imagination, or as forces of the transcendent psyche. The noted authority on modern Western magic, the late Dr Israel Regardie (1907–85), employed Carl Jung's model of the archetypes of the collective unconscious to explain to his audience what he meant by invoking a god. For him it was a ritual means of channelling into conscious awareness a specific archetypal energy-form from the universal or 'collective' psyche. British novelist and occult writer Colin Wilson has similarly related his long involvement with European existentialism to a study of Western magic in order to show that such an approach offers both a transcendental and an optimistic goal – that human beings can overcome their feelings of isolation by engaging with universal aspects of awareness and connectedness.

It is true, however, that many magicians, witches and occultists in different periods of history have viewed their respective gods and goddesses as existing in their own right – as beings beyond the human psyche, as entities belonging to another plane of existence. These practitioners regard the magical arts as a vital means of communication with the sacred powers that sustain the universe itself. Magicians throughout the ages have tended to share one feature in common, and that is the notion of a hierarchy of supernatural beings or 'powers' with whom they can interrelate. These powers in turn provide sacred knowledge and wisdom – wisdom that allows the magical devotee special insights into the dynamics of the universe and the sacred potentials of humanity. Especially within the modern context – for example, among Neopagans and Goddess worshippers – magic is regarded as a wisdom-path leading to personal growth and renewal on an archetypal level of being. For them, magic transforms their perception of the world from one that is profane and devalued to one that is sacred and universal. It is about vision, and deep, insightful spiritual knowledge.

I should mention at this point that my principal focus in this book is on those forms of magic in which the practitioner utilizes sacred formulae, ritual invocations and personal willpower to produce specific results – to master the gods and spirits and even to become like them. The Afro-Caribbean traditions of magic, which include Voudou, Macumba and Santería, utilize states of trance in which magical devotees become possessed by gods and spirits and do not themselves exercise control of the outcome. Such forms of magic, while undoubtedly fascinating, have not substantially shaped the Western magical

A vision of the
Divine Names – *Faust in his
Study,* an etching by Rembrandt
van Rijn, *c.* 1652–53.

tradition, which is the main subject of this overview. For this reason I have not
included them here.

As I hope to show in this book, one of the central aims of magic involves the
quest for personal transformation – the quest to be at one with the spirits, gods
and goddesses of the magical realms: to act like them and, at times, to gain mastery
over them. Magicians in all periods of history have sought to tap the mysterious
forces of the universe and to utilize these powers for their own purposes – whether
for good or for evil. As I see it, such intentions lie at the very heart of all forms of
magic. Considered in this light, magic is a particular approach to gaining metaphysical mastery in a mysterious and unpredictable world.

Chapter One

Shamanism: The Oldest Magical Tradition

Shamanism is a hunter-gatherer tradition, an ancient visionary practice of utilizing altered states of consciousness in order to contact the spirits who rule the forces of the natural world. As a cultural form dating back to Neolithic times, shamanism can claim to be the world's oldest magical tradition. By its very nature, it opens us to the very heart of a magical universe alive with the potent forces of good and evil — forces of healing, destruction and renewal that involve visionary powers of transformation.

The term 'shaman' brings to mind the enigmatic image of a medicine man or sorceress — one who enters a trance state to undertake a vision-quest of the soul. This quest involves journeying to sacred places and reporting back on matters of cosmic intent. It may be, within any given community, that the shaman is a healer able to conquer the spirits of disease, a sorcerer skilled in harnessing spirits as allies or a sort of psychic detective able to recover lost possessions. At other times the shaman may seem priest-like — an authoritative figure who acts as a sanctioned intermediary between the gods of Creation and the more familiar realm of everyday domestic affairs. Whatever the shaman's specific role within the community, he or she commands awe and respect through the ability to journey to other worlds and return with revelations from the gods. In the twentieth century there has been a strong revival of interest in shamanism and indigenous spirituality, and this will be explored in Chapter 12.

The classic source literature on shamanism focuses especially on Siberia, and consequently the term 'shaman' itself has entered our language, via the Russian, from the Tungusic word *saman*. Many shamanic societies can still be found in different regions of the world, however, and by looking at the earliest forms of religious expression, we can provide a context for the rise of shamanic practices in different hunter-gatherer communities.

Siberian shaman Mongush Lazo performs a purifying ritual to appease ancient spirits angered by an archaeological dig. Valley of the Kings, Tuva, south-central Siberia, February 2002.

BEGINNINGS

Intimations of religious awareness have been found in Middle Palaeolithic cave sites in Europe and Central Asia. The partial skeleton of a Neanderthal child was discovered at Teshik-Tash in Uzbekistan, encircled with ibex horns, which were arranged vertically in pairs, the pointed ends driven into the ground. It might have

Drawing depicting
the sacrifice of a bison bull
and an entranced or prostrate
shaman. Lascaux,
c. 13,000 BCE.

Drawing of a disguised
hunter pursuing his prey.
Les Trois-Frères, Ariège,
c. 13,000 BCE.

been to protect the body from scavenging animals, or it could have had a deeper significance. In another Neanderthal site, in a cave at Le Moustier in France, a dead youth was lain as if asleep with his head resting on his right arm, supported by a pillow of flint flakes. His body seems to have been strewn with red ochre, and burnt animal bones were scattered around him. It is possible that the Neanderthals believed in spirit beings and some sort of afterlife.

Although such a conclusion is, of course, speculative, with the advent of the Upper Palaeolithic Era, there is a clear indication that Cro-Magnon man had begun to think magically. The noted scholar Abbé Henri Breuil, referring to the prehistoric cave art of Western Europe, wrote: 'Animals are represented pierced with symbolical arrows (bison and ibexes at Niaux; horses at Lascaux), clay models are riddled with spear marks (at Montespan, a headless lion and bear, which seem to have received new skins at various times) – facts which evoke the idea of sympathetic magic. The numerous pregnant women and men closely pursuing their women suggest the idea of fertility magic. The deliberate alteration of the essential features of certain animals seems to indicate taboos. Human figures dressed up in animal or grotesque masks evoke the dancing and initiation ceremonies of living peoples or represent the sorcerers or gods of the Upper Palaeolithic.'[1]

One of the most characteristic examples of magical cave art was discovered in the Franco-Cantabrian cave of Les Trois-Frères. Dated to *c.* 13,000 BCE, the cave drawing depicts a hunter-sorcerer, armed with a bow and disguised as a bison, in a herd of wild beasts. Another drawing found at the same site shows a sorcerer wearing horned headgear, presumably to deceive his prey. From earliest times, religion, art and magic have been intertwined. Traditionally the hunter-sorcerer has always been regarded as a master of wild animals – able to control their fate through his hunting magic, adept at disguises and a practitioner of animal sacrifice. Very early on, he learned to mimic the animals and based his dances on their movements. He may also have felt some sort of psychic bond with them. The Upper Palaeolithic hunter-sorcerer can be seen as a precursor of the archetypal shaman with his animal familiars and clan totems. The powerful psychic connection between shamans and different animal species may also have led to the belief that some shamans could transform their human consciousness into an animal form.

ANIMISM AND THE BELIEF IN SPIRITS

The pioneering English anthropologist Sir Edward Tylor (1832–1917) gave a name to the earliest phase of magical and religious thinking, calling it 'animism', after the Greek word *anima*, meaning 'soul'. According to Tylor, the idea of a soul, or spirit, seemed already at this stage to be universal, and prehistoric humans apparently believed that not only did they have a soul but so did animals and plants. Stones, weapons, food and ornaments could also have souls, and a person's spirit could enter into the bodies of other people, animals or objects through an act of possession. Tylor believed that the origin of animism probably lay in the experience of dreams, which seemed to show that a man could exist independently of his physical body. Today, certain indigenous peoples still use a common word for 'shadows', 'spirits' and 'ghosts', reflecting the belief in man's dual existence. The Algonquin, for example, call a man's soul his *otahchuk*, or 'shadow'; the Quiché say *natub* to denote a 'shadow' or 'soul', and the Zulu use the term *tunzi* for a shadow, spirit or ghost.

Tylor considered that once prehistoric human beings had come to conceive of two selves – the waking self and the phantom – it was a logical progression to the belief that the soul could undertake spirit journeys beyond the body or into an afterlife. Early evidence for this is found in the remains of funeral rites in which servants were sacrificed to serve deceased high-ranking officials in the afterworld, thus perpetuating the social order beyond death. Tylor also believed that tribesfolk – 'savages' or 'rude races' as he disparagingly called them – continued to reflect such animism in their everyday behaviour. It was animism, the belief in spirits, that would lead them to converse with wild beasts, seeking their pardon prior to slaying them in the hunt, or to form the conviction that animals could have souls which in earlier lives had occupied the bodies of other human beings – possibly deceased friends or ancestors.

An antler-headed god or shaman holding a torque and serpent among a cluster of animals. Detail from the Gundestrup cauldron, Denmark, 1st or 2nd century BCE.

Tylor's overall concept is still highly regarded today, although it has not gone unchallenged. The distinguished French sociologist Emile Durkheim (1858–1917), who undertook a broad survey of cultural patterns, believed that the earliest type of human society consisted of undifferentiated hordes. Later, the hordes formed themselves into clans – a unit Durkheim believed to be more basic than the family. He was not impressed by Tylor's essentially psychological idea that magical and religious thinking originated from dreams. He believed that the clan came to be seen as the overriding social unit and became 'sacred' simply because it represented a higher, more all-embracing reality than the individual. Indeed, he pointed out that when the clans acquired totem animals as symbols of differentiation such totems were even more sacred than the animals themselves. Durkheim looked for evidence of this development in the Australian Aborigines, the best documented of the hunter-gatherer tribal people still surviving in modern times.

According to Durkheim, among Australian hunter-gatherers the totem animal or plant not only identified the clan but helped define patterns of kinship, since all clan members considered that they were related to each other. Durkheim also noted that Central Australian tribes like the Arunta, or Aranda, had ritual objects – *tjurunga* or *churinga* – that were sacred to the clan, and whose names were never revealed to strangers.

Today the distinction between Tylor's and Durkheim's way of thinking continues. Anthropologists evaluating shamanism from a psychological perspective tend to be more interested in the altered states of consciousness accessed through trance, in the visionary origins of the shaman's magical and religious beliefs, and in other factors such as epileptic seizures, schizophrenic behaviour patterns and the use of psychedelic substances, all of which are associated with shamanism. Functionalists on the other hand, are more inclined to ignore the experiential side of the shaman and his metaphysical world, concentrating instead on the role the shaman plays in society by interpreting tribal customs and taboos, reinforcing the beliefs underpinning the social structure and providing guidelines for the tribe.

It seems to me that there is no escaping the inner dimension, the awesome magical realm that in the shaman's cosmological system parallels the everyday world and fills it with significance. If we did not consider the role of familiar spirits, initiatory visions, the experience of magical dismemberment and rebirth, and the transformative projection of consciousness into other living forms like animals and birds, we would have a very one-sided understanding of shamanism. We could also hardly explain its mystique or account for the continuing interest in shamanic states of consciousness in the modern personal growth movement.

With these factors in mind we can now ask: who exactly is the shaman, how does he or she become one, and what is 'the journey of the soul' that seems to be so central to the shamanic process?

Sacred 'men's business' – an Aboriginal men's ceremony or *corroboree*, central Australia. The men's bodies are decorated with personal totemic markings.

The flight of the soul. Late Pueblo-style drawing of the shaman's spirit-journey, from a rock carving in Idaho.

The Siberian Underworld. Ostiak-Samoyed drawing showing a horned shaman, animals and birds, 1920s.

BECOMING A SHAMAN

Shamanism is really a form of applied animism, or animism in practice. Because Nature is alive with gods and spirits, and because all aspects of the cosmos are perceived as interconnected — the universe consisting of a veritable network of energies, forms and vibrations — the shaman is required to operate as an intermediary between different planes of existence. The idea of a universe alive with spirits is brought home in the journals of Danish explorer and anthropologist Knud Rasmussen (1879–1933), who undertook an epic three-year journey in the American Arctic regions and whose own grandmother was part-Inuit. An Iglulik shaman told him: 'The greatest peril of life lies in the fact that human food consists entirely of souls. All the creatures that we have to kill and eat, all those that we have to strike down and destroy to make clothes for ourselves, have souls, souls that do not perish with the body and which must therefore be pacified lest they should revenge themselves on us for taking away their bodies.'[2]

We can define a shaman as one who is able to perceive this world of souls, spirits and gods, and who, in a state of ecstatic trance, is able to travel among them, gaining special knowledge of the supernatural realm. He or she is ever alert to the intrinsic perils of human existence, of the magical forces that lie waiting to trap the unwary, or that give rise to disease, famine or misfortune. But the shaman also takes the role of an active intermediary — a negotiator in both directions. As

American anthropologist Joan Halifax points out: 'Only the shaman is able to behave as both a god and a human. The shaman then is an interspecies being, as well as a channel for the gods. He or she effects the interpenetration of diverse realms.'[3]

Shamans are called to their vocation in different ways. In some cases it seems almost as if the spirits have chosen the shaman. These are the 'greater shamans', called spontaneously through dreams or mystical visions. The 'lesser shamans', those who have simply inherited their role, or who seek initiation from one already established as a shaman, have a lower status, especially among the peoples of Siberia and Arctic North America.

As children or young adults, shamans are often of nervous disposition and may seem strangely withdrawn from society. Anthropologist Ralph Linton notes: 'The shaman as a child usually shows marked introvert tendencies. When these inclinations become manifest they are encouraged by society. The budding shaman often wanders off and spends a long time by himself. He is rather anti-social in his attitudes and is frequently seized by mysterious illnesses of one sort or another.'[4] The Chukchee peoples of Siberia believe that a future shaman can be recognized by 'the look in the eyes which are not directed towards a listener during conversation but seemed fixed on something beyond. The eyes also have a strange quality of light, a peculiar brightness which allows them to see spirits and those things hidden from an ordinary person.'[5] Waldemar Bogoras, who studied the Chukchee at first hand, provides a context for this occurrence: 'The shamanistic call may come during some great misfortune, dangerous and protracted illness, sudden loss of family or property. Then the person, having no other services, turns to the spirits and claims their assistance.'[6]

Much has been made of the idea that shamanism is born of crisis and disease – it has even been compared with schizophrenia. Julian Silverman, a leading advocate of this view, feels that the main difference between schizophrenics and shamans is that shamans are 'institutionally supported' in their state of mental derangement while modern society, for the most part, regards schizophrenia as an aberration. He believes that there is a striking parallel between the two phenomena, and quotes a psychiatric description of schizophrenic states to make his point: 'The experience which the patient undergoes is of the most awesome, universal character; he seems to be living in the midst of struggle between personified cosmic forces of good and evil, surrounded by animistically enlivened natural objects which are engaged in ominous performances that it is terribly necessary – and impossible – to understand.'[7] While shamans and schizophrenics share the ability to move in and out of different mental states, however, the shaman has learned how to integrate the different realms of consciousness. As Mircea Eliade (1907–86), philosopher of religion, observed in *Shamanism* (1964): '...the primitive magician, the medicine man, or the shaman is not only a sick man; he is, above all, a sick man who has been cured, who has succeeded in curing himself. Often when the shaman's or medicine man's vocation is revealed through an illness or epileptoid attack, the initiation of the candidate is equivalent to a cure.'[8] Eliade elaborates in *Birth and Rebirth* (1964): 'The shamans and mystics of primitive societies are considered, and rightly, to be superior beings; their magico-religious powers also find expression in an extension of their mental capacities. The shaman is the man who *knows* and *remembers*, that is, who understands the mysteries of life and death.'[9]

Clearly there is more involved here than just psychological aberration or disease. Because epilepsy and schizophrenia are regarded in ancient societies as manifestations of the spirit world, it is not surprising that people suffering from these conditions are capable of later becoming worthwhile shamans. But it is because they are open to the world of spirits that they are special, not simply because they are sick. Harnessing the power is everything – the crisis, or disease, thus becomes an initiation. Shamans are expected to exhibit control of the supernatural powers that interfere with human life. This includes procuring game animals at times when the hunt appears to be failing, driving away evil spirits, obtaining good weather and curing the sick.

MYTHIC DISMEMBERMENT AND REBIRTH

An initiatory theme of dismemberment and rebirth occurs in several forms of shamanism, and sometimes distinguishes strong shamans from lesser shamans in their respective communities. A typical tale describing mythic dismemberment is found among the Avam Samoyed of Siberia. A neophyte who wished to be a shaman was told that he would receive his 'gift' from the Lords of the Water. The neophyte was sick from smallpox at the time, and it was said that 'the sickness troubled the water of the sea'. The candidate climbed a mountain, where he met a naked woman and began to suckle at her breast. She said he was her child and introduced him to her husband, the Lord of the Underworld, who provided him with animal guides to escort him to the subterranean region. There he encountered the inhabitants of the Underworld, the evil shamans and the lords of epidemics, who instructed him in the nature of the diseases plaguing mankind.

After his heart was ritually torn out and thrown into a pot, the candidate travelled to the land of female shamans where his throat and voice were strengthened, and then to an island where the Tree of the Lord of Earth rose into the sky. The Lord gave him certain powers, among them the ability to cure the sick. He then continued, encountering magical stones that could speak, women covered with hair like a reindeer's and a naked blacksmith, working the bellows over a huge fire in the bowels of the earth. Again the novice was ritually slain and boiled over the fire in a cauldron 'for three years'. The blacksmith then forged the candidate's head on one of three anvils ('the one on which the best shamans were forged') and told him how to 'read inside his head', how to see mystically without his normal eyes and how to understand the language of plants. Having mastered these secrets, and having had his body constituted anew after immolation, the shaman awoke 'resurrected' as a revivified being.[10]

It is clear from this account that the Avam Samoyed shaman has both a social and an individual role to play in his shamanizing function. His trance experiences reveal the source of illness and disease that affect everyone, but he also gains for himself, via a spiritual rebirth process, impressive supernatural powers. The shaman becomes a special figure because he has been reconstituted by the god at the anvil; his gift of magical sight and communication are born of heaven and not of earth. Occasionally, in fact, the shaman demonstrates his ongoing relationship with the heavenly domain by taking spirit wives from that dimension. The Buryat of Siberia believe that the children of such unions are semi-divine.[11]

The dismemberment-rebirth theme is not exclusively associated with Siberian shamanism and also occurs, for example, among Australian Aboriginal 'men of

Aboriginal clansmen's ground-painting of the tracks of the mythical emu around the waterhole birthplace of the ancestor Karora, entered by the shaman at initiation.

high degree'. In western South Australia the would-be shaman is put into a waterhole where a mythical snake swallows him and then ejects him in the form of a baby – a sign perhaps that the shaman is still 'new' to the spirit world. The head medicine-man now recovers him, but treats him as if he were a corpse by ritually breaking his neck, wrists and joints. Into each mark and cut he inserts *maban*, a life-giving shell which is believed to cause rejuvenation and fill a person with power. In this way the 'dead' Aborigine is reborn to the world of magical knowledge. [12]

The Aborigines around the Munja Cattle Station at Walcott Inlet had similar initiatory patterns. Dreams would reveal to a would-be 'doctor man' that the high god Unggud wished him to become a *banman*, a shaman. Unggud would 'kill' him near a waterhole but his essence would rise up – visible only to medicine men. At the same time he would observe a giant snake with arms, hands and a crown of feathers. Unggud would then lead him to a subterranean cave where he would begin to transform him into a man of knowledge: 'Unggud gives him a new brain, puts in his body white quartz crystals which give secret strength, and reveals to him his future duties. He may remain unconscious for some time, but when he awakes he has a great feeling of inner light. He is certain of being equal to Unggud. Instruction, guidance and experience follow for many months, even years.'[13] The shaman now has special magical powers. With his inner eye he is able to see past and future events and also able to send his *ya-yari*, or dream familiar, out of his body in search of information. According to the late Professor A. P. Elkin, a specialist in Aboriginal supernaturalism, 'the psychic element in these talents is clearly all pervasive. It is termed *miriru* and comes from Unggud. Fundamentally it is the capacity bestowed on the medicine man to go into a dream state or trance with its possibilities. Indeed, *miriru* makes him like a Wandjina, having the same abilities as the heroes of "creation times".'[14]

THE JOURNEY OF THE SOUL

A distinguishing feature of shamanism in all cultures is the journey of the soul. Because the shaman can travel in his spirit-vision to other realms he is regarded as a 'technician of the sacred' or a 'master of ecstasy'. In his role as an intermediary between the physical and metaphysical worlds the shaman gains privileged and sacred knowledge from the gods or spirit-beings with whom he interacts, and his capacity to return with sacred information for the benefit of society becomes all-important.

In a sense, the shamanic journey of the soul can be regarded as a controlled act of mental dissociation, and this state can come about in many ways. Sometimes sacred psychedelic plants provide the impetus, but at other times the spirit-quest is

Two Inuit shamans in a flying race; one is in the air, and the other has fallen back. From Knud Rasmussen, *Eskimo Folk Tales*, 1921.

Sedna, Goddess of the Ocean and guardian of all sea-creatures, suckling her offspring. Inuit stone-cut print, 1961.

associated with periods of fasting or sensory deprivation, with chanting and the beating of drums, or with a particular response to a powerful visionary dream.

Among the Menangkabau peoples of Indonesia, it is considered that the life-force, or *sumangat*, leaves the body in dreams or during states of sickness, and that the task of the *dukun*, or shaman, is to counteract the hostile influence of evil spirits during the out-of-the-body state. The *dukun* summons friendly spirits through a smoke offering, lies down on the ground covered by a blanket, trembles physically and then projects his consciousness into the spirit world. In the Mentawei Islands near Sumatra, shamans dance until they fall into a state of trance. They are then borne up into the sky in a boat carried by eagles where they meet sky spirits and ask them for remedies for disease.

Traditional Inuit shamans work themselves into a state of ecstasy by utilizing the energy of a drumbeat and invoking helper spirits. Some Inuit lace their arms and legs tightly to their bodies to hasten the release of the inner light-force on the 'spirit flight', or *ilimarneq*. In his *Report of the Fifth Thule Expedition 1921–1924*, Knud Rasmussen described a metaphysical journey to the Sea Goddess. Here the shaman's role is to intercede on the community's behalf, travelling in his spirit body to the bottom of the sea. At the beginning of the ceremony, members of the adult community gather around the shaman and observe him while he sits in meditative silence. Soon, feeling he is surrounded by helper spirits, he declares that 'the way is open' for his journey. Various members of the household sing in chorus while the shaman undertakes his difficult task, carefully avoiding three large, rolling stones on the sea floor and slipping nimbly past the Goddess's snarling watchdog. 'He almost glides as if falling through a tube so fitted to his body that he can check his progress by pressing against the sides, and need not actually fall down with a rush. This tube is kept open for him by all the souls of his namesakes, until he returns on his way back to earth.'[15] The shaman meets the Sea Goddess who, he can see, is nearly suffocating from the impurities of human misdeeds. As the shaman strokes her hair to placate her, the Sea Goddess tells him in spirit-language, that there have been secret miscarriages among the women, and boiled meat has been eaten in breach of taboo. When the shaman returns in due course, it is this message he brings and the offenders are sought out to explain their wrongdoing.

We can see from this account that the spirit-journey is not undertaken as an indulgence. There is always a clear task involved – to counteract sickness, to under-stand the nature of breached taboos, to recapture a lost or tormented soul, or to help restore harmony to the different planes of the cosmos. This, essentially, is the role of the shaman – to journey to other worlds and to use revealed knowledge for a positive outcome. In this way the shaman is an intermediary between the gods and mankind.

A Siberian shamanic healing ceremony. The shaman beats his drum, indicating that the spirit-journey has commenced.

REMNANTS OF TRADITIONAL SHAMANISM

Siberia

Siberia is vast – stretching from the Urals in the west to the Altai Mountains in the south and the Arctic Ocean in the north – encompassing tundra, fertile plains and rugged mountain systems. Here the shaman is both a healer and ecstatic who undertakes journeys to the sky and the Underworld in search of the fugitive souls that are responsible for illness. Shamans in this region also utilize divination and clairvoyance, and are sometimes capable of handling fire-coals without being burned. Siberia is the home of many diverse peoples, including the Buryat and Goldi; the nomadic reindeer-herding Chukchee of the north-east; the Turkic-speaking Kirghiz, Yakuts, Uighurs and Altaians; and the Evenks and other neighbouring tribes in the Tungus-speaking region near the Yenisey and Lena rivers.

Buryats distinguish between 'white' shamans who liaise with the gods and 'black' shamans who summon spirits, while Yakuts contrast the gods 'above', regarded as passive and comparatively powerless, with the gods 'below' who have closer

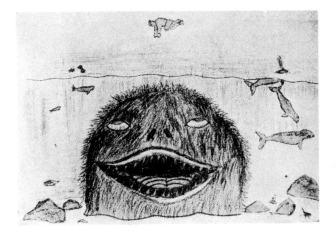

A Chukchee shaman descends into the sea. His task is to appease the ferocious god Anky-Kele, lord of the ocean. North Siberian, c. 1945.

ties with the earth. Yakuts believe they have obtained mastery of fire from Ulu-Toyan, who dwells in the west in the third heaven. This god also created birds, woodland animals and the forests.

The Altaian shaman sacrifices a horse, addresses the Master of Fire, fumigates his ritual drum, invokes a multitude of spirits, and then calls to the Markut, the Birds of Heaven. After a complex ceremony of purification, he beats his drum violently indicating that he is 'mounting' into the sky accompanied by the spirit of the dead horse. After ascending through several heavens in his visionary consciousness, he converses with the creator god Yayutsi and also bows before the Moon and Sun in turn. Finally he arrives at the celestial abode of Bai Ulgan, where he learns details of future weather patterns and the outcome of the harvest. The shaman then collapses in a state of ecstatic release. Mircea Eliade notes that Bai Ulgan seems to be a god of the 'atmosphere' and it is not uncommon among Indo-European shamans to sacrifice horses to a god of the sky or storms.[16]

The Chukchee believe that spirits may be contacted in dreams and that the shaman can utilize them to recover the lost souls of sick patients. The shaman is said to 'open' the patient's skull and replace the soul, which he has just captured in the form of a fly or bee. Goldi shamans, on the other hand, specialize in funerary activities, guiding the deceased into the realms of the Underworld. The Goldi shaman calls on his helper-spirits for guidance as he accompanies the dead person, who is mounted on a sled with food for the journey, towards the land of the departed. He subsequently locates relatives of the deceased in the Underworld so that the newly departed soul is safely accepted in the nether realms. Only then does the shaman return.

North America

Shamanism is found in Alaskan Inuit society among the Tlingit of the north-west coast; among the Paviotso hunters, fishers and gatherers from western Nevada; the Mescalero and Chiricahua Apache hunters of Texas, Arizona and New Mexico; the Lakota Sioux of Dakota; the Nez Perce of New Mexico and Arizona; Ojibwa, also known as Chippewa from Northern Minnesota; Zuni of New Mexico and Arizona ; and Twana of Washington State. Shamanic traditions still survive among such Pacific Coast tribes as the Pomo and Salish; the Chumash, who formerly occupied the region around Ojai; and tribes like the Yurok, Wintun and Karok of north-western California.

A funerary vessel from New Mexico, c. 1100–1250 CE, showing a masked coyote dancer. The central hole allows the spirit inside to be 'killed'.

Shamans sometimes travel in their spirit-vision by transforming into animal forms. An Inuit shaman's wooden mask from Nunivak, south Alaska, early 20th century.

Paviotso shamans enter trance states and fly in the spirit-vision to retrieve lost souls and effect healing cures, and on occasion also hold shamanic ceremonies to control the weather — bringing rain when needed, halting clouds or melting river-ice. The Paviotso Dick Mahwee has described how he obtained his first shamanic visions during a dream in a cave near Dayton, when he was fifty years old. In a state of seemingly 'conscious sleep', Mahwee had a mystical encounter with a tall, thin Indian holding an eagle tail-feather, who taught him ways of curing sickness. Mahwee now utilizes trance states: 'I smoke before I go into the trance. While I am in the trance no one makes any noise. I go out to see what will happen to the patient. When I see a whirlwind I know that it caused the sickness. If I see the patient walking on grass and flowers it means that he will get well; he will soon be up and walking. When I see the patient among fresh flowers and he picks them it means that he will recover. If the flowers are withered or look as if the frost had killed them, I know that the patient will die. Sometimes in a trance I see the patient walking on the ground. If he leaves footprints I know that he will live, but if there are no tracks, I cannot cure him. When I am coming back from the trance I sing. I sing louder and louder until I am completely conscious. Then the men lift me to my feet and I go on with the doctoring.'[17]

Central America

Home to many shamanic cultures, Central America has a notably high incidence of psychedelic shamanism since this region is especially rich in hallucinogenic plants. The Yaquis of northern Mexico ritually smoke the yellow *Genista canariensis* flowers containing cytisine, and the Huichols conduct their peyote pilgrimages in sacred country in the north-central

A Maya Lord's shamanic double (or *way*) in snakeskin trousers performs an ecstatic dance with a boa constrictor. Vase painting, Guatemala, 8th century CE.

Mexican desert. The Tarahumara Indians of Chihuahua sometimes add *Datura inoxia* to the fermented maize drink *tesguino*, and several Mexican Indian tribes consume sacred mushrooms as part of their vision quest, including the Mazatecs, Chinantecs, Zapotecs and Mixtecs, all from Oaxaca.

South America

There are various healing practices in this region, not all of them shamanic. The distinction between a *curandero* and shaman is not always clear, and there are also various spiritist traditions that are unrelated to shamanism. For example, the practices of French spiritualist Allan Kardec (1808–69) have been very influential in Brazil, as has Macumba — a magical religion similar to Haitian Voudou, which combines native folk superstitions, African animism and aspects of Christianity.

As in Mexico, shamanism in South America tends to be psychedelic, making frequent use of tropical plants that contain hallucinogenic alkaloids. The *Banisteriopsis* vine is widely used by shamans in the forests of the Upper Amazon, for the visions

A female *machi* (shaman) has ascended to the seventh level of her *rewe*, or notched pole, in order to complete her skyward journey. Beating her drum has helped her climb the World Tree. Mapuche region, Chile.

Back view
of a shaman-dancer
assuming the spirit-form
of a jaguar. He wears
jaguar skins and a
feather headdress.
Matto Grosso,
Brazil.

it produces are believed to represent encounters with supernatural forces. This is the case with the Jivaro of Ecuador, the Shipibo-Conibo, Campa, Sharanahua and Cashinahua of eastern Peru, and the Sione Indians of eastern Colombia.

Australia

Among many Australian Aboriginal groups the shaman or medicine-man is known as the *karadji*, or 'clever man'. Aboriginal culture extends back at least 40,000 years, and it is thought that the Aborigines probably migrated to Australia from southern India, reaching Cape York via the Malay Peninsula and the East Indies. Today the principal regions where the traditional Aboriginal religion is still found are Arnhem Land, in central North Australia, and in the Central Australian desert — although there are scattered communities in other regions. For the Australian Aborigines, illness, death and accidents are caused by magical or animistic actions. Magicians also know how to 'sing' a person to death and 'point the bone' – a type of projective magic where a kangaroo bone or carefully prepared stick is pointed at the intended victim.

The shamanic aspect of Australian Aboriginal culture becomes more obvious when we consider the initiation of medicine-men. Among the Arunta, or Aranda, the candidate goes to the mouth of a particular cave where he is 'noticed' by the spirits of the Dreamtime. They throw an invisible lance at him, which pierces his neck and tongue, and another which passes through his head from ear to ear. Dropping down 'dead' he is now carried by the spirits into the cave, and his internal organs are replaced with new ones and with magical quartz crystals upon which his 'power' will later depend. When he rejoins his people as a person 'reborn', he has a new status as a healer-shaman, although he will not normally perform as a *karadji* for a year or so. Among the Wiradjeri of western New South Wales the power of the crystals stems from the fact that they are believed to embody the essence of Baiame, the All-Father or Great Sky-God of the Australian people. The Wiradjeri describe Baiame reverently as a very great old man with a long beard, sitting in his camp with his legs resting under him, and one of their legends has a clearly shamanic aspect. Two great quartz crystals extend from his shoulders to the sky above him, and Baiame sometimes appears in their dreams, causing a sacred waterfall of liquid quartz to pour over their bodies, absorbing them totally, and they grow wings instead of arms. Later the dreamer learns to fly and Baiame sinks a piece of magical quartz into his forehead to enable him to see inside physical objects. Subsequently an inner flame and a heavenly cord are also incorporated into the body of the new shaman.

Indonesia and Malaysia

Menangkabau shamans seek their visions by travelling deep into the jungle or to the top of high mountains, while among the Iban, shamans undertake a fast, sleep near a grave, or travel to a mountain top until magical powers are obtained from a guardian spirit. The Iban also refer to the initiation of shamans through a metaphysical 're-structuring' process which has strong parallels with Aboriginal initiations: 'they cut his head open, take out his brains, wash and restore them, to give him a clear mind to penetrate into the mysteries of evil spirits and the intricacies of disease; they insert gold dust into his eyes to give him keenness and strength of sight powerful enough to see the soul wherever it may have wandered; they plant barbed hooks on the tips of his fingers to enable him to seize the soul and hold it fast; and lastly they pierce his heart with an arrow to make him tender-hearted and full of sympathy with the sick and suffering.'[18]

Dyaks also refer in their legends to shamanic journeys to the sky. The god Tupa-Jing noticed that the Dyaks were on the verge of exterminating themselves because they had no remedies for sickness and were cremating ill people as their only solution. He therefore saved a woman from the funeral pyre as she ascended in clouds of smoke, took her to heaven and instructed her in the skills of medicine. She was able to return to earth and pass on the precious knowledge.

These notions of spirits and sickness parallel those found in other shamanic cultures. The Sumatran Kubu believe that sickness arises when a person's soul is captured by a ghost. Shamans, known here as *malims*, are called in to effect an exorcism. During the seance the *malims* dance, fall into a trance, and the chief *malim* is then able to 'see' the patient's soul and retrieve it.

Among the Dyaks, the *manang*, or shaman-healer, falls into a trance state during a *belian*, or curing ceremony, and journeys to the Underworld to retrieve a soul that has been captured by a spirit. Sometimes it is necessary for the *manang* to lure the evil demon back to the patient's house and kill it.

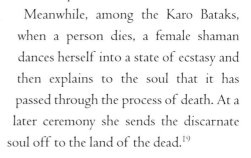

Meanwhile, among the Karo Bataks, when a person dies, a female shaman dances herself into a state of ecstasy and then explains to the soul that it has passed through the process of death. At a later ceremony she sends the discarnate soul off to the land of the dead.[19]

A shaman's grimoire, or 'book of spells' from Sumatra, Indonesia. Made from folded strips of bark and bound in wood, the grimoire contains secret rituals for invoking spirits and unleashing forces.

Eastern Asia

Here shamanism and animism pre-date the more familiar mainstream religious philosophies, such as Buddhism and Confucianism. In Tibet, Bon shamans speak of a sacred rope that in times past linked the priests with the celestial dwelling of the gods, and even today they are believed to use their drums to propel themselves through the air. Healers undertake the search for the patient's soul if this is perceived as a cause of sickness.

The Lolo of southern Yunnan also believe that in earlier times men moved more freely between heaven and earth. The shaman-priest officiates in funerary rituals, 'opening the bridge to heaven' and helping the deceased find their way across mountains and rivers to the Tree of Thought and other post-mortem regions beyond. Influenced by Chinese magic, the shamans of Yunnan practise divination and undertake visionary journeys on horseback to retrieve lost souls.

American anthropologist Larry Peters, in his 1987 account, describes how the Nepalese practise an authentic form of shamanism, which, though drawing on

In this Balinese Tjalonarog dance, the witch-doctor Rangda has snatched the body of a dead child.

In Tibet, pre-Buddhist Bon-Po shamanic dances opened a path to the spirit-world. Now monks don masks and ornate costumes to perform seasonal Bon-Po/Buddhist ceremonies.

elements of Hinduism and Buddhism, appears to pre-date them. Peters' key informant, Bhirendra, was the son of a *bombo*, or shaman, and when he was thirteen he experienced a spontaneous state of demonic possession which led to his initiatory calling. Under the guidance of his father and the spirit of his deceased grandfather, Bhirendra learned to enter trance states voluntarily, and in due course to activate the spiritual light between the eyes – a condition leading to magical out-of-body flight. Bhirendra described a vision in which he journeyed to the highest heaven to meet the supreme shaman deity, Ghesar Gyalpo: 'I walked into a beautiful garden with flowers of many different colours. There was also a pond and golden glimmery trees. Next to the pond was a very tall building which reached up into the sky. It had a golden staircase of nine steps leading to the top. I climbed the nine steps and saw Ghesar Gyalpo at the top, sitting on his white throne which was covered with soul flowers. He was dressed in white and his face was all white.

He had long hair and a white crown. He gave me milk to drink and told me that I would attain much *shakti* to be used for the good of my people.'[20]

Shamanism is also found in isolated regions of Japan, which is not surprising since it seems likely that Tungusic and Altaic-speaking tribes exerted a cultural influence on Japan, prior to the advent of Buddhism, in the third or fourth centuries BCE. Female shamans, or *miko* — more common than male shamans — are still found in small villages where they utilize trance, telepathy, mediumship and fortune-telling, and communicate with guardian deities or spirits of the dead. In the larger cities, however, the role of the female shaman has been absorbed by Shinto ritual.

SHAMANISM AND MEDIUMISM

In Japan especially, but essentially everywhere divinatory practices are found, shamanism overlaps with mediumism. Both practices involve trance states but the focus is clearly different. Shamanism tends to be active, while mediumism is more passive: shamanism involves a going-forth of the spirit, whereas mediumism involves a coming-in of the sacred force, as with the Pythian oracle at Delphi, who made divinely inspired pronouncements in trance at the Temple of Apollo. Some forms of modern spiritualism — referred to in contemporary Western culture as 'channelling' — also belong in this category, and here ancient sages are believed to communicate with the living through the medium. Also in this category, although quite different in terms of content and mythic imagery, is Haitian Voudou, where the 'Divine Horsemen', or *loa* divinities, are believed to 'descend' on the trance subjects during their ecstatic dance rituals and 'ride' them into a state of inspired frenzy. In all forms of mediumistic trance, however, subjects are passive channels for the revelations — they do not recall their visionary episodes.

In the shamanistic traditions, on the other hand, the ecstatic retains full consciousness of the altered state, and takes full responsibility for what transpires during the visionary journey. From ancient times up to the present, shamanism has always involved the conscious pursuit of magical powers — powers capable of transforming not only the shaman but also those within his sphere of influence. Essentially, magic is all about employing metaphysical forces to achieve specific outcomes. These outcomes in turn reflect the magician's intent, whether for good or ill.

Chapter Two

Magic in the Ancient World

Magical beliefs and practices were widely dispersed throughout the ancient world – the spiritual legacy of a shamanic tradition of a universe alive with both hostile and beneficent forces. The word 'magic' itself comes from the Greek *mageia* and the Latin *magia*, meaning the art of the magician or magus. These derive in turn from ancient Persia, where the *magos* was a priest or religious practitioner. Herodotus (*c.* 490–25 BCE) refers to the *magoi* – the secret Persian group responsible for royal sacrifices, funeral rites and the interpretation of dreams. By the time of Plato (427–347 BCE), however, the term *magoi* had acquired a negative connotation, denoting beggar priests and diviners who would come to wealthy households and claim special powers of healing bestowed by the gods.

ANCIENT GREECE AND ROME

We can divide ancient Greek sources into three broad categories. The first is associated with Homer's epic poetry, the second with the Hellenistic period – namely the three centuries before the birth of Christ – and the third with Roman imperial rule – an era of considerable magical syncretism and diversity.

Odysseus with the renowned sorceress Circe, who prepares a magic potion in her cauldron. Boetian black-figure vase painting, late 5th century BCE, Thebes.

The earliest reference to a magical operation recorded in the Greek language is in Book 10 of Homer's *Odyssey* (late eighth century BCE). Odysseus, returning from the Trojan War, encounters Circe, a beautiful sorceress who lives on the island of Aeaea. The daughter of the sun god Helios and Perseis, she has been banished to Aeaea after murdering her husband. She is renowned for her knowledge of magic and poisonous herbs, and is also able to predict the future. But while Circe can change Odysseus' companions into swine, she has no power over Odysseus himself because he is protected by a magical herb called *moly*, given to him by Hermes. Nevertheless, Odysseus is seduced by Circe's charms, and she bears their son. In Book 11 of the *Odyssey*, Odysseus follows Circe's magical instructions, digging a trench and making an offering to the dead of honey, milk, water and wine. He slaughters two black sheep, catching their blood in his trench, which attracts the ghosts of the dead. When they drink it, they can, for a short time, communicate with the living.

Orpheus, said to be a Thracian, playing his lyre and singing to a group wearing distinctive Thracian cloaks and fox-skin headgear. Attic red-figure vase painting, *c.* 440 BCE.

In the sixth century BCE, we find references to *magoi*, or miracle-workers, renowned for their magical powers. One was a historical figure: the mathematician and metaphysician, Pythagoras. Another was Orpheus, a type of latter-day shaman – whose mythic origins predate this period but who inspired the Orphic Mysteries, a cult that flourished in the sixth century BCE.

Orpheus was portrayed in legends and poems and also on vase paintings as a singer who played a lyre given to him by Apollo. His songs were so enchanting that rivers ceased to flow and wild animals were at peace with one another – indeed, all Nature was charmed by him. Whether Orpheus was based on a historical person we have no way of knowing, but in Greek legend he is described as the son of Apollo and Calliope (the muse of epic poetry). Like a shaman on a spirit-journey, Orpheus ventured into the Underworld to recover his beloved wife Eurydice. Moved by his sad song, Hades, Lord of the Underworld, agreed that she could return with Orpheus as long as he did not look back at her during their journey. Orpheus did look back, and she was then lost to him forever. According to legend, Orpheus was torn apart by women in a bacchanalian frenzy and his head was thrown into the river Hebrus, but Zeus placed his lyre in the heavens. Orphic initiates affirmed the divine nature of the human soul and believed that spiritual liberation could be achieved through ascetic practices and rites of purification.

Pythagoras was born on the island of Samos *c.* 569 BCE. According to some sources he visited Egypt around 535 BCE, engaging in learned discussions with various priests, and may have also acquired his knowledge of geometry at this time. Around 518 he migrated to the city of Croton in southern Italy, and founded a philosophical school there. Pythagoras maintained that all aspects of reality were fundamentally mathematical, that philosophy was a vehicle for spiritual purification and that the human soul could reach union with the Divine. His inner circle of

The oracular head of Orpheus floated down the Thracian river Hebrus, and, still singing, reached the island of Lesbos. In this Attic red-figure cup painting, Apollo looks on as the prophecy is recorded, *c.* 400 BCE.

A bronze head, thought to be that of Pythagoras. Copy of a Greek original of *c.* 300 BCE, found at Villa dei Pisoni, Herculaneum.

followers were known as *mathematikoi* and followed a code of secrecy. After his group in Croton was attacked in 508, Pythagoras went to nearby Metapontium, and it is thought that he died there *c.* 475 BCE.

Various miracles or mystical powers were ascribed to Pythagoras, perhaps with the intention of presenting him as a superhuman figure. It was claimed that on one occasion he was seen in two different cities at the same time. It was also said that he had a golden thigh and had been King Midas in an earlier life. He converted a wild bear to a vegetarian diet, a river called out, 'Hail, Pythagoras!' and he predicted that a dead man would be discovered on a certain ship as it entered a harbour. On another occasion he bit a poisonous snake to death. Pythagoras was undoubtedly considered a 'divine man' — *theios aner* — a magical human being capable of transcending the normal restraints of time and space.

Much of our detailed knowledge about magical practices, however, dates from more recent times. Fragments of magical recipe spell-books from Graeco-Roman Egypt, many of them instructional texts relating to the prevention and treatment of illness, have survived and have been translated. Rather like modern cooks, magical practitioners preserved their painstakingly accumulated secrets in their own private notebooks, which contained specific recipes, hints, notes and ideas — some of them borrowed or adapted, some independently developed. Each recipe would be tested and then improved, and the formula written down. A key collection of spell-books is Preisendanz's *Papyri Graecae Magicae*, which several scholars believe is of comparable significance to the Nag Hammadi Gnostic scriptures (see Chapter 3). The *Papyri Graecae Magicae* date from the second century CE, but many of these texts would have been much older secret writings handed down from father to son.

Some scholars believe that Greek magical papyri derived from Egyptian religion, but Fritz Graf, who has worked on ancient Greek religion, believes that by the second century Egyptian religion had become absorbed in what he calls 'the vaster fabric of Graeco-Roman paganism'. Graf thinks there were many sources — Greek, Jewish, Assyrian, Babylonian and Sumerian — and that collectively they contributed to what he calls 'late pagan syncretism'.[1]

According to Graf there were changing perceptions of the magician in ancient Greece and Rome. The figure known as the *magos* is also linked to the *goes* — a type of ritual ecstatic healer or diviner, regarded as an intermediary between the gods and humankind, and reminding us of the traditional shaman. The term *goes* would later give rise to the word *goetia*, which in the Middle Ages was specifically associated with black magic.

Even in ancient Greece some magicians were accused of summoning the spirits of the dead and bewitching through incantations. Plato regarded magicians and sorcerers as dangerous because they threatened 'the just relationship that normally unites humans and gods', and he made an important distinction between magic, which was intended to persuade the gods to follow a certain course of action, and religion, which allowed the gods a free choice. Graf maintains that the word *magos* first gained widespread use around the beginning of the fifth century BCE, but at this time it was also used to describe what he calls 'outsider activity'. As outsiders, magicians would in all likelihood, be found among the ranks of one's enemies, rather than one's friends, and they were thought to be responsible for unwanted outcomes in everyday life. It was commonplace to accuse one's neighbours of engaging in acts of sorcery.

Similarly, there were varying concepts of the 'magician' in ancient Rome. During the republican era the term *goes* was generally applied to soothsayers or diviners, and *magus* did not refer to a practitioner of magic but to the Persian priesthood with its traditional rites and divination. Cicero (106–43 BCE), for example, regarded the Magi simply as the wise men and scholars from Persia who had interpreted the dreams of King Cyrus, even though he was well aware of people who practised necromancy – the act of summoning spirits of the dead. By this time the Romans already had laws in place against what would later become known as black magic – for example, no one was allowed to curse a neighbour's harvest with *mala carmina*, or harmful spells – and they recognized the healing powers of positive *carmina*, incantations. It is not until the rule of Augustus (first emperor of Rome in 27 BCE) that the magus is specifically associated with the sorcerer.

The Magi (in their Phrygian caps) following a bright star in the heavens and bearing gold, frankincense and myrrh. Mosaic in the church of Sant'Apollinare, Ravenna, 5th or 6th century CE.

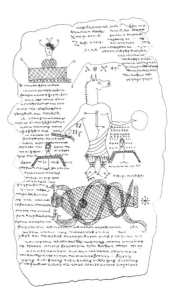

Drawing of a Roman *defixio*, or cursing tablet. The mummified figure attacked by two coiled snakes is the intended victim of the sorcery, in this case a rival jockey. Late 4th century CE.

Figurine made to an old recipe preserved in *Papyri Graecae Magicae*, found with a *defixio* in a clay pot, Egypt. The intention was to bind this young woman in love through all her senses. 3rd or 4th century CE.

A century after Cicero, however, quite different attitudes to the magical arts emerged. Pliny the Elder refers in his voluminous *Natural History*, published after his death in AD 79, to 'vain beliefs in magic', and he clearly associated magic with deceit and fraud. Pliny recognized the validity of spiritual healing, which he termed *medicina*, but, like Plato, he was critical of healing methods that claimed a sacred origin, and magic seemed to him to belong in this category. Pliny traced magic back to Persia at the time of the prophet Zoroaster (Zarathustra *c.* sixth century BCE), and regarded magic as distinctly un-Roman. For Pliny the defining quality of magic was divination. So it appears that the Roman conception of magic developed in two stages. During the republic, the Romans recognized the existence of ritual incantations but did not specifically call them *magia*. Later, by the time of Pliny, *magia* had come to encompass both medicine and astrology, and also included acts of divination.

With regard to the more pragmatic and assertive aspects of ancient magic, it is clear that so-called binding or cursing tablets have been a feature of magical practice for a very long time. They seem to be a specifically Greek invention, dating as far back as the fifth century BCE, and spreading to other regions of the Mediterranean world. Known in Greece as *katadesmoi* and in Rome as *defixiones*, the earliest binding tablets were thin sheets of lead on which the victim's name had been scratched. These were then thrown into graves, pits or wells, with the intention of consigning the victim's fate to various demons or to the ghosts of the dead. Cursing and binding tablets increasingly used longer texts and more elaborate designs. Their preparation would also be accompanied by complex rituals in which clay, wax or lead dolls were bound, pierced or burnt to simulate the intended impact on the victim.

Essentially *katadesmoi* and *defixiones* were intended to subject another person to one's own will or desire. Sometimes binding tablets were intended to arouse wild, erotic love in the person pursued, while others were directed against legal or economic competitors. Aggressive magic even applied to chariot-racing. In an ancient stadium in Carthage, archaeologists discovered curse tablets buried a metre or so beneath the track. They were made of strips of lead etched with a curse; each had been folded and driven into the ground with a long nail. One sought to curse a chariot driver with blindness, another to strike down a horse with gout. It is likely that few riders in these sporting events would have begun a race without burying counter-spells of their own, or without at least wearing amulets to counteract the curse tablets buried beneath the track.[2]

Magical figurines were also commonplace in the ancient world, from classical Greece through to late Egypt. Sometimes these figurines were distorted, with the head or feet turned backwards, and sometimes they were pierced with needles. For the person who created it, the sculpted image (even when not strictly representational) and the actual person were one and the same, and damage inflicted upon the figurine was believed to have an effect on the person symbolized by it.

Amulets, on the other hand, were protective. A very ancient tradition, they were often worn on the body or placed next to other objects to ward off various forms of evil. Almost anything could serve as an amulet – a red string wound around the wrist, a stone carried in a small pouch around the neck, or a piece of iron tied to one's bed.

EGYPTIAN AMULETS AND MAGIC

Most forms of Egyptian magic that have survived are concerned with protection and healing.[3] Egyptian amulets were famous throughout the ancient world and were widely exported and copied. Permanent amulets were worn as jewelry, and a perennial favourite was the famous *wedjat* eye, or 'eye of Horus'. In Egyptian cosmology it was Thoth who restored the eye of Horus, thereby making it into a symbol of wholeness and health. We know from artefacts held by the Kelsey Museum at the University of Michigan that around 250 CE an Egyptian woman named Helena placed a simple charm written on papyrus into a small metal tube. This tube was probably worn on a string, and the surviving scrap of papyrus inside it reads: 'Heal Helena from every illness and every shivering and [fever], ephemeral, quotidian, tertian, quar[tan]'.[4] Another Egyptian charm in the same collection and dating from the same era or slightly later, was made from reddish bloodstone and was worn by a woman to obtain divine aid for conception or childbirth. The charm included a motif of a god holding a key, signifying his power to safely 'open' and 'close' the woman's womb.

The rooster-headed and serpent-legged deity Abraxas, of Persian origin, featured extensively on Egyptian and Near Eastern amulets from the second century CE onwards, and such amulets would often display a whole range of cultural and linguistic influences. It would not be uncommon, for example, for an amulet depicting Abraxas to show him wearing a Roman tunic and surrounded by an Egyptian ouroboros – a snake devouring its tail – which symbolized regeneration and eternity. Such amulets might also be inscribed with various Greek letters as well as the names of the Jewish archangels Michael, Raphael, Gabriel and Ouriel. Abraxas (also known as Abrasax) was a popular binding deity on amulets because the numeric value of each letter of his name totalled 365, the number of days in a year, and therefore rites of 'binding' would endure through the passage of time and perhaps last forever. It is likely that incantations invoking his name gave rise to the magic words 'abracadabra'. The 'words of power' inscribed upon these amulets were, of course, central to their efficacy. In the Egyptian *Pyramid Texts*, and

Drawing of Abraxas, a Gnostic deity. The numerical value of his name in Greek letters was 365, the number of days in the year. An amulet (below) with the magical formula 'Abracadabra', derived from Abraxas.

Egyptian amulets (above) in the form of the *wedjat* eye, or 'eye of Horus', early first millennium BCE.

A funerary papyrus of *c.* 1350 BCE (right) shows Hunefer, the deceased, brought by Anubis to the Hall of Judgment where his heart will be weighed against the feather of truth of the goddess Maat.

the later funerary texts known collectively as the Egyptian Books of the Dead, the term *hekau* was used to denote 'a possessor of magic' but the word is also used to denote magical 'words of power' themselves. Texts like the *Theban Recension of the Book of the Dead* and also *The Book of Gates* and *The Book of the Am-Tuat*, were descriptions of the underworld regions through which the soul would pass after death, accompanied by the Sun-god Ra. The Sun-god's knowledge of *hekau* guaranteed that the forces of light would prove victorious over evil and darkness. Not surprisingly 'words of power' found their way on to many protective amulets, and have featured in Western ceremonial magic ever since.

MAGIC IN MESOPOTAMIA

Although the ancient Greeks and Romans regarded Persia and Egypt as the cradle of specialist magical knowledge, several scholars regard Mesopotamia as the main source of binding magic involving figurines. Burning or melting figurines was a common magical practice. Generally they were made from clay or such substances as tallow, wax, cedarwood or dough, and they frequently included items associated with the intended victim — strands of hair, drops of saliva or semen, scraps of clothing or even dust from footsteps.[5] Often these figurines would be burnt in an oven, dissolved in water, trodden on, or left in a place where they would be exposed to the influence of dangerous demons, such as a graveyard or a polluted drain.

Mesopotamian painted terracotta plaque of the goddess Lilitu (prototype of the Hebrew Lilith), Queen of the Demons, early 2nd millennium BCE. Lilitu brought death to children, and amulets provided protection.

Babylonian protective figurines for burial in walls and floors.

As Marie-Louise Thomsen has noted in her essay on the subject (2001), using magical figurines to 'give a person to the demon Lamastu, who afflicts children, or to Ereskigal, the queen of the land of the dead, or to the Fire god was, in each case, simply a metaphor…indicating that what happened to a figurine was transferred to the person it represented.'[6] It was, of course, necessary to protect oneself from such potent sorcery, and for this the Mesopotamians used magical amulets. Amulets have been found invoking Ninurta, the Mesopotamian counterpart of Sirius, to protect babies from demons, and they would be placed across the baby's neck or hung at the head of its bed.

Amulets could also have a proactive aspect, and it was common to use love charms. In formulating his incantations, a young man might compare the woman of his desires to the great goddess Inanna, and he might also produce a figurine of the beloved. Surviving text-fragments provide clues about how this was done: 'If that woman does not come, you take *tappinnu*-flour [and] throw [it] into the river to King Ea; you take clay from banks of the two rivers, from the far side [of the Tigris] and the far side [of the Euphrates]; you make a figurine of that woman, you write her name on its left shoulder. Facing Samas you recite the incantation: "The Beautiful Woman" over it. At the outer gate of the West Gate you bury it…she will walk over it. You recite the incantation "The Beautiful Woman" three times [and] that woman will come to you [and] you can make love to her.'[7]

DIVINATION AND ORACLES

Binding spells or curses focus on achieving specific outcomes and on gaining power over another person or situation. Acts of divination, in contrast, seek information relating to future events without actually manipulating the events that will later come to pass.

Homer's *Iliad* and *Odyssey* provide us with the earliest references to oracles and divination in the ancient world, and describe the interpretation of the behaviour, flight and cries of birds, and the interpretation of dreams. Indeed, from Homer through to the Christianized world of later antiquity, the interpretation of dreams remained a major source of information relating to the intentions of the gods and the flow of forthcoming events. Homer tells us in Book 19 of the *Odyssey* that visions come to humanity from the Gates of Ivory and Horn in the Underworld. The dreams that come through the Gate of Ivory are sent to delude us with their empty promises but those from the Gate of Horn refer to events that will really take place.

Sacred communications from Zeus could also be received through oracles. The site of the earliest known oracle, dating from the eighth century BCE, was at Dodona in north-west Greece. Here, it was said, Zeus gave counsel from his sacred 'high-foliaged oak'. These oracles seem also to have involved priestesses – Peleiads – whose activities included impersonating doves. The shrine and oracles at Delphi had a reputation unsurpassed in the ancient world. It was here that Themistocles sought divine guidance before the battle of Salamis and here too that King Croesus asked whether he should go to war against Persia. The oracles were transmitted from Apollo through the Pythia, or Pythoness, Apollo himself being regarded as the mouthpiece of his father, Zeus. The Pythian oracle at Delphi was always a woman 'past the age of child-bearing',[8] and her role involved entering the inner sanctuary, or *adyton*, where she would sit upon a tripod in the same way that Apollo was said to have done. The enquirer would pay a fee and then sacrifice a goat, which would be declared suitable only if it shivered when dowsed with water. Then, as the seance proceeded, the specific enquiry was written down or spoken, the Pythia would enter a state of trance, and her utterances would be subsequently interpreted and translated into hexameter verse by her officiating priest. An Attic vase dating from approximately 440 BCE shows the Pythia seated on the tripod gazing into a flat dish while holding a sprig of laurel in her right hand. The dish contained lots – black and white beans – which the Pythia would use to indicate 'yes' or 'no'. Oracular responses were received on the seventh day of the month, except during the three months of winter when Apollo was believed to be absent. Depending on demand, there were sometimes two Pythias working at the shrine, with one in reserve. The Greeks of the late fourth

The earliest known oracle, dating from the eighth century BCE, was in Dodona in north-west Greece. Here Zeus, father of the gods and lord of Olympus, communicated through his sacred oak. Bronze statue of Zeus, from Dodona, *c.* 470 BCE.

Attic red-figure vase,
c. 440 BCE, showing the
Pythian oracle at Delphi.
She sits on the Pythian tripod,
holding a sprig of laurel sacred
to Apollo, the black and white
beans in the dish deciding
'Yes' or 'No'.

Apollo attacks the python
to win the Pythian tripod.
Silver coin, Croton,
c. 420 BCE.

century BCE became convinced that the possession of the Pythian priestess at Delphi was caused by vapours rising from fissures in the rocks, but there is no geological evidence that the limestone rocks there could have produced such vapours and no cleft has ever been found.

BECOMING A MAGICIAN

In the ancient world, as today, the most potent forms of magic involved the acquisition of secret sources of power. Well formulated rituals and a knowledge of secret barbarous names could sway the lesser gods in the *magos's* favour, but to become a magician in the first instance involved initiation, and this in itself was perceived as a gift from the gods. As magicians in the ancient world became ever more knowledgeable, they aspired not only to gather an effective collection of binding spells and curses but also a thorough knowledge of the names of those divinities on whom to call for special assistance. Knowing the secret name of a god was to hold sway over that god, for the sacred name itself was considered an attribute of divinity. Divulging what took place during rites of initiation was strictly forbidden and, increasingly, a knowledge of secrets became the mark of the magician. It is possible that the 'secret' aspects of ancient Greek magic may have come

Zeus aiming a thunderbolt at Typhon, demon of the whirlwind, the counterpart of Seth, the Egyptian god of chaos. Drawing based on a bronze shield band panel from Olympia.

originally from Egypt where the scribes wrote the names of herbs on the statues of the gods so that the masses would not learn their real names for practising magic.

Some forms of Greek magic were thought to provide the magician with a *parhedros* — a superhuman or divine assistant similar to the magical ally of the traditional shaman. The Christian bishop of Lyons, Iranaeus (130–202 CE), claimed that the Gnostic Marcion possessed one, and that this daemon helped him with prophecy. A *parhedros*, or magical ally could be used to 'bring on dreams, to couple women and men, to kill enemies, to open closed doors and to free people in chains, to stop the attack of demons and wild animals, break the teeth of snakes and put dogs to sleep. It could also bring forth nourishment, e.g. water, wine, bread, oil, vinegar, and could help organize banquets.'[9] The pagan Celsus (*c.* 170 CE) considered Jesus a magician because he could do some of these things.

Some magical rituals, however, were not so much about achieving specific pragmatic outcomes as transforming the actual magical practitioner. A ritual known as *Sustasis to Helios* was believed to turn the individual into *a lord of divine nature*, and it can be summarized as follows: 'At sunrise the future magician goes to the highest part of his house and unfolds a sheet of pure white linen. At noon, the magician crowns himself with black ivy, undresses, and stretches out on the sheet, with eyes "covered with an all-black band" and wrapped up like a corpse; with eyes still closed but turned to the sun, the magician recites a long prayer to the god Typhon. At the end, a sea falcon will appear and touch the recumbent body with its wings. This is the central act. After that, the magician rises, dresses all in white, makes a fumigation with incense, thanks the god, and comes down from the roof.'

According to Fritz Graf, the magician undertaking this ritual is assuming the role of Seth-Typhon, who in this context is a form of the Sun God, in order to experience ritual death and resurrection, a theme we will also encounter in our exploration of modern Western magic. The roof is used because it is closer to the Sun; the sheet of white linen represents the purified space necessary for a magic ritual; the wrapping and the black ivy symbolize death; resurrection follows contact with the divine represented by the wing of the falcon; and the fresh clothes are a sign of the initiate.[10]

ANCIENT MYSTERY CULTS

Celebration of the Mysteries was found in different regions of the Mediterranean world from the sixth century BCE onwards,[11] and there seems to have been an overlap with magical initiation. Magic, however, is essentially individualistic — it is the *magos* himself who initiates proceedings. The Mysteries, on the other hand, were communal — secret religious gatherings initiating participants in the sacred attributes of a god or goddess. The Mysteries celebrated not only deities from the

Mithras slaying the bull. Of Persian origin (shown by his cap), Mithras was a god of light and fertility. He was associated with Taurus, the constellation entered by the sun at the beginning of spring. Rome, early 2nd century CE.

Greek pantheon but from other cultures as well — among them the gods of Egypt, Syria, Anatolia and Persia. The Greek word *mysterion* derives from the verb *myein*, meaning to close the lips and eyes, and initiates of the Mysteries were not allowed to divulge the secrets that had been revealed to them. Most initiates (*mystai*) kept their vows of secrecy, and as a consequence we possess few details of these ceremonies. It is likely, however, that in most of the Mystery cults certain aspects of the central myth would have been translated into performances, and the initiates would have probably worn masks and costumes to enact the sufferings and triumphs of the cult god or goddess. Food and drink were also part of the celebration.

The famous Mysteries at Eleusis were dedicated to Demeter and her daughter Persephone (also known as Kore, or daughter) who were revered as goddesses of the grain. The Mysteries sacred to Dionysus celebrated the powers of Nature in cultivated crops, such as grapes, as well as the wild vegetation of the woods and mountains. The Mysteries of Hera — derived from the Syrian goddess Atargatis — honoured fertility, just as the Mysteries of the Egyptian god Osiris focused on the life cycles in Nature and the connections between rebirth and fertility.

Demeter and her daughter Persephone sending the gift of corn to humanity. Attic drinking cup, *c.* 490–480 BCE.

In agrarian Greece, the Mother Goddess embodied the fertility of the earth and the universal source of life, and there can be little doubt that the Mysteries sacred to Demeter, Hera and Isis were to some extent a rebuff to the Olympian dominance of Zeus. There were Mysteries in the ancient world with a male focus, however. The Mithraic cult initiated only men and attracted many Roman soldiers and officers. The initiatory

grades included Miles (Soldier), Leo (Lion) and finally Pater (Father), and the initiatory contests celebrated the manly virtues of courage and fortitude.[12]

A characteristic theme of the Mystery cults was that of death and rebirth. Initiation involved 'dying' to one's former identity in order to be reborn into a world enriched with divine secrets and mystical knowledge. As Marvin Meyer, historian and editor of *The Ancient Mysteries* (1987), has observed, 'Plants and animals participated in a cycle of death and life, and so also did human beings. Death came to all the divine forces of Nature – Kore, Dionysos, Adonis, Attis, Osiris, the Mithraic bull – but finally life was victorious. Kore returned from the realm of Hades; Dionysos vivified his devotees; Adonis rose from the dead; Attis gave an intimation of new life; Osiris reigned as king of the underworld; and the bull provided life for the world. Hence, if human beings could assimilate the power that made life triumphant in the world of Nature, they too might live in a more complete way.'[13]

The *Homeric Hymn to Demeter*, which dates from approximately 600 BCE, incorporates within its epic form important elements of the mythic drama of Demeter and Persephone. Here we learn that Aidoneus, or Hades, spied on Persephone as she gathered flowers on the Nysian plain. Ensnaring her with a bloom, Aidoneus snatched her away, installing her as Queen of the Underworld. Demeter was so griefstricken by the loss of her daughter that the world became barren. Zeus, therefore, was forced to intervene, but Persephone had eaten some pomegranate seeds in the Underworld, and so could only return to the Earth for eight months each year, while spending the other four with Aidoneus in the Underworld.

The Mysteries of Eleusis celebrated the sacred aspects of cyclic renewal associated with the grain crop and the seasons, and dealt with themes relating to immortality and spiritual rebirth. Eleusis, where Persephone was said to have been restored to her mother, is located on the Rharian Plain near Athens and it was here that the science of agriculture was first practised.[14] The archaeological remains in the initiation temple suggest that the theatrical performances characteristic of

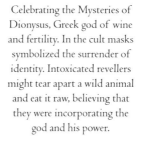

Celebrating the Mysteries of Dionysus, Greek god of wine and fertility. In the cult masks symbolized the surrender of identity. Intoxicated revellers might tear apart a wild animal and eat it raw, believing that they were incorporating the god and his power.

Persephone and her husband Aidoneus (Hades), Lord of the Underworld. From an Attic red-figure cup, *c.* 430 BCE.

Mystery cults were not a central feature of the rites here. We do know, however, that participants consumed a drink that contained barley water and mint, and, according to the ethnomycologist R. Gordon Wasson, the cereal crops in the fields around Eleusis appear to have been contaminated with ergot, a fungal disease. This may well have led to visionary hallucinations of the type associated with LSD, which is itself derived from ergot. According to Wasson, 'what was witnessed here was no play by actors, but *phasmata*, ghostly apparitions, in particular the spirit of Persephone herself'. Wasson draws support for his analysis from the *Homeric Hymn to Demeter*, which describes how participants felt a 'fear and trembling in the limbs, vertigo, nausea and a cold sweat' before the vision appeared in the darkened initiation chamber.[15]

Direct encounters with the gods and goddesses had by now become a central feature of myth and magic, and initiates and magicians alike sought closer contact with the gods, and a means of involving them more directly in their everyday lives. They would also increasingly explore visionary and meditative ways of entering sacred space. Magic involving personal encounters with the gods is known as theurgy, and its offspring is *gnosis*, or sacred knowledge. Gnosis has remained at the very heart of the Western magical tradition from ancient times until the present day.

Chapter Three

Gnosis and Kabbalah

The origins of Gnostic mysticism remain a matter of debate, but there is broad consensus that Gnosticism as a historical movement parallels the rise of early Christianity. Some scholars have seen in Gnosticism residues of pre-Christian Persian dualism, while others believe that it developed in response to the failure of Jewish apocalyptic expectations, and have dated its origins to around 70 CE — coinciding with the fall of the Jerusalem Temple.[1] Others regard Gnosticism as the result of early Christian devotees forsaking religious faith for spiritual inner knowledge when the Messiah failed to return.

Gnostic thought was well established by the second century of the Christian era, with the Syrian Gnostic Basilides acknowledged as an influential intellectual and spiritual force in Alexandria during the reigns of the Roman emperors Hadrian and Antoninus Pius. The Egyptian Gnostic Valentinus (100–180 CE), author of *The Gospel of Truth*, was also active in the mid-second century, and around the year 140 came to Rome from Alexandria as a candidate for election as the Bishop of Rome. Had he been successful, Christianity would have had its first Gnostic pope, and the movement which in due course would become heretical might have established itself as mainstream. The libertine teacher Carpocrates was also active during the reign of Hadrian, and in the third century there was Mani, founder of Manichaeism — a fascinating blend of Christianity and Palestinian Gnostic dualism — whose teachings subsequently spread into Syria, Palestine and North Africa and even as far as central Asia and China.[2] There were also several other major Gnostic sects, such as the Cainites, Sethians, Ophites and Ebionites. Of most interest to us here, however, is the central Gnostic attitude to the nature of good and evil and the quest for *gnosis*, or spiritual knowledge.

The unearthing of a major Gnostic library near the town of Nag Hammadi in upper Egypt in 1945 provided a rich source of material on the Gnostic philosophies. Most Gnostic scholarship had previously been based on other surviving Gnostic commentaries written by such Church Fathers as Irenaeus, Clement and Hippolytus, who were hostile to Gnostic tenets. What was so fascinating about the Nag Hammadi codices — an Ophite-Sethian collection of texts written in Coptic — was that they revealed the syncretistic nature of Gnosticism, which seemed to incorporate elements from Christianity, Judaism, Neoplatonism and the Greek mystery religions as well as material from Egypt and Persia. But essentially Gnosticism was a call for transcendence, seeking a return to the spirit from the pervasive evil of the material world.

James M. Robinson, editor of the 1977 English translation of the Nag Hammadi Library, explains the Gnostic philosophy thus: 'In principle, though not in practice, the world is good. The evil that pervades history is a blight, ultimately alien to the world as such. But increasingly for some the outlook on life darkened; the very origin of the world was attributed to a terrible fault, and evil was given status as the ultimate ruler of the world, not just a usurpation of authority. Hence the only hope seemed to reside in escape.... And for some a mystical inwardness undistracted by external factors came to be the only way to attain the repose, the overview, the merger into the All which is the destiny of one's spark of the divine.'[3]

GNOSTIC COSMOLOGIES

While Gnosticism emphasized the need to experience the supreme reality of the divine, its cosmological solutions soon diverged from those of the early Church Fathers. In some cases Gnosticism differed only slightly from the emerging

The Ancient of Days, William Blake, etching with watercolour, 1794. This All Father, or Demiurge, according to Basilides, was ignorant of his lowliness in the hierarchy. Blake, in fact, was no stranger to Gnostic ideas.

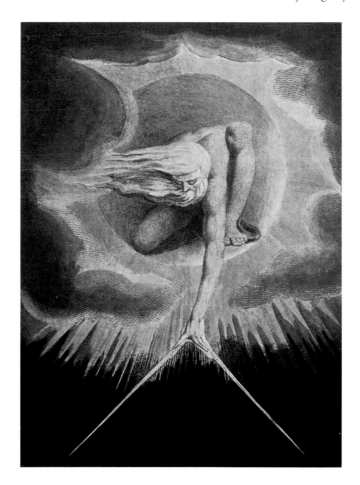

Christian orthodoxy, but in others the differences were more extreme. Several early Christian devotees clearly had Gnostic leanings. Marcion of Sinope, born near the Black Sea at the end of the first century, considered himself a Christian but regarded Jesus as the son of the 'Good God' of the Spirit and not as the son of the Old Testament creator God (or demiurge). Marcion rejected the Old Testament completely, as well as most of the New Testament, but saw Jesus Christ as a saviour figure. The Ebionites were a community of Greek-speaking Jewish Christians who rejected the apostle Paul but followed the gospel according to Matthew. Basilides, Valentinus, Carpocrates and Mani, meanwhile, emerge as major figures whose cosmologies and mystical perspectives provide a conceptual basis for the later Western magical tradition.

Basilides

Basilides conceived of a universe with 365 heavens and proposed a hierarchy of 'divine emanations', a pattern of spiritual creation later associated with the medieval Jewish Kabbalah – an important symbolic framework that has profoundly influenced modern magical thought. In the system of Basilides the supreme reality is that of the 'ungenerated' or 'non-existent' God – sometimes thought of as a seed or egg while nevertheless symbolizing nothingness. This 'non-existent' or non-material God in turn emanated Mind (*nous*), Word (*logos*), Understanding (*phronesis*), Wisdom (*sophia*) and Power (*dynamis*). From Wisdom and Power emerged the archons and angels who formed the first heaven. Each heaven gave rise to another, until there were 365 in all. The year was defined as consisting of 365 days because this mirrored the number of heavens. The angels of the final heaven created the world as we know it. The last of these creator beings was the God of the Jews, and he decreed that his people would be the chosen race on Earth. According to Basilides, however, this All Father, or Demiurge, was an archon who was ignorant of his comparatively lowly position in the heavenly hierarchy, and, as a consequence, chaos reigned in the world. The All Father was obliged to send his son Jesus to work miracles on earth, but, according to Basilides, Christ did not suffer on the cross because his spirit was already liberated. The physical death of Christ was of no consequence. For Basilides, as one Gnostic scholar has written, 'salvation [was] for the soul alone'.[4]

Valentinus

The system of Valentinus similarly regards Creation as a process that unfolds from a state of divine immateriality. The Gnostic tract titled *The Valentinian System of Ptolemaeus* (late second century), written by Valentinus's leading disciple,[5] begins with these words: 'There is a perfect pre-existent Aeon, dwelling in the invisible and

Gustav Doré's engraving – a 19th-century illustration for Dante's *Visions of Paradise*, could serve as a depiction of the Gnostic concept of archons and angels emanating from Wisdom and Power.

unnameable elevations; this is Pre-Beginning and Forefather and Depth. He is uncontainable and invisible, eternal and ungenerated, in quiet and deep solitude for infinite aeons.'[6] As with the system of Basilides, this 'ungenerated' realm of sacred formlessness then begins to emanate subsequent levels of *being*: 'With him is Thought, which is also called Grace and Silence. Once upon a time, Depth thought of emitting from himself a Beginning of all, like a seed, and he deposited this projected emission, as in a womb, in that Silence who is with him. Silence received this seed and became pregnant and bore Mind, which resembled and was equal to him who emitted him. Mind alone comprehends the magnitude of his Father; he is called Only-Begotten and Father and Beginning of All. Along with him, Truth was emitted; this makes the first Four, the root of all: Depth and Silence, then Mind and Truth.'[7]

Here Mind is masculine (Greek: *nous*), but Thought is feminine (*ennoia*) and is the creator Mother who gives rise both to the Primal Man and to God, Creator of Heaven and Earth. She is also identified with Sophia, goddess of wisdom, an important figure in Gnostic thought. In this cosmology Sophia gives rise to a Demiurge who assumes he is the highest god. However, according to Valentinus he is ignorant. He lacks the *gnosis* or spiritual knowledge required for his salvation.

Carpocrates

Carpocrates also challenged the emerging Christian orthodoxy. Not only did he argue that the universe had been created by comparatively lowly powers – as the Church Father Irenaeus put it, 'by angels much inferior to the unbegotten Father' – but he also disputed Christ's divine origins. He believed that Jesus was simply the son of Joseph – a man of the earth – although he does credit him with having a secret teaching that he passed on to his disciples in the form of a deeper and more symbolic body of esoteric instruction.

Extending the central Gnostic tenet that the soul was far more important than the body, Carpocrates and his son Epiphanes believed that indulgences of the flesh were completely acceptable. They advocated sexual licence, and believed that human beings should experience every aspect of life to the full in order to transcend the limitations of physical existence. Carpocrates followed Plato in that he regarded the body as a prison of the soul, but his libertine philosophy was a radical departure from Platonic thought, and made him an easy target for the early Church Fathers who were critical of Gnosticism. Indeed, one can see in Carpocrates an expression of hedonistic mysticism – a precursor of many modern occult groups and reminiscent, too, of the more indulgent aspects of the American counter-culture and personal growth movement.

Mani

Mani emerges from the Gnostic movement as a sensitive and complex thinker, and perhaps capable of challenging the eventual dominance of Christian thought. He experienced – like Jesus – profound archetypal visions of the spiritual realm, and came to regard himself as an apostle of God. Manichaeism has provided us with a rich legacy of mystical literature, and, according to religious scholar Kurt Rudolph, it should be considered as a major world religion, alongside Buddhism, Christianity and Islam.[8]

By his own account, recorded by the Arab scholar Al-Biruni, Mani was born in 216 CE in the village of Mardinu in northern Babylonia, but grew up in a community of Mandaeans – members of a Gnostic Palestinian sect. When he was twelve, Mani received a spiritual revelation inspired by the 'King of the Paradise of Light'. From this time he renounced the community of his birth and became a type of spiritual apostle. According to the Manichaean text *Kephalaia*, after his revelation Mani became the 'twin' of the Holy Ghost. He is credited with saying: '…the Living Paraclete came down and spoke to me [for the first time]. He revealed to me the hidden mystery, hidden from the ages and the generations of Man: the mystery of the Deep and the High: the mystery of Light and of Darkness, the mystery of the Contest, the War, and the Great War, these he revealed unto me.'[9]

A Chinese portrait thought to be of Mani and his followers, Khocho (Turfan).

As with Muhammad – whose revelations similarly came through angelic visions – Mani was appointed as a 'messenger', or prophet, of God. After converting his father and other members of his family, Mani set out to preach his doctrine – journeying to the Persian provinces of Turan and Makran as well as visiting northwestern India. Later he returned to Babylonia. Mani seems to have been strongly impressed by Buddhism during his visit to India, but his religion is primarily a Gnostic synthesis of Christianity and Persian belief. As in classic Gnosticism, Mani distinguishes between God and Matter but this becomes tinged with Persian dualism and the eternal conflict between Ohrmazd/Ahura Mazda (symbolizing good) and Ahriman/Ahra Mainyu (evil). In Manichaeism good is inherently superior to evil, and eventually triumphs.

During Mani's time, a form of Zoroastrianism prevailed in which Ohrmazd and Ahriman were said to have been begotten by a divine primordial being called Zervan, who was androgynous. Zervanism influenced Mithraism – the mystery religion which became popular in ancient Rome – and Zervan is also thought

to have a connection with the cosmic entity Abraxas, who features in the cosmology of Basilides as the great archon who rules 365 heavens. Mani rejected the Zervanite concept that the forces of good and evil were like 'brothers' within the same pantheon of archetypal beings. Instead he described a cosmology in which the highest spiritual reality was that of 'God the Father of the blessed light'. He embodies within his sacred form the divine principles of light, force and wisdom. God the Father 'calls' the Mother of Life into being, and she in turn 'calls' the Primeval Man – who is her son. These three constitute the Manichaean trinity.

Primeval Man battles with the forces of evil and darkness, and finally prevails. In one Manichaean legend, he is defeated by the Prince of Darkness and loses his armour, and in another his five sons are devoured by demons. Eventually Primeval Man returns in glory to the welcoming embrace of his Mother in paradise. As Gnostic scholar Geo Widengren emphasizes in his 1965 study of Mani, Primeval Man symbolizes the Redeemer who is himself in need of redemption, and this becomes a central Gnostic myth.[10] Primeval Man has to overcome the formidable obstacles within the darkness in order to retrieve his true 'self' or 'soul'. His return to his celestial home represents the liberation of the soul and its return to the world of light.

This is very much a message of *gnosis*, of the return of the 'divine spark' to the realm of Spirit whence it came. It is a theme of 'eternal return' which we find also in the Hermetic tradition, in the medieval Kabbalah and in the esoteric tradition

of Western high magic. And it is found similarly in the teachings of Plotinus, the third-century Neoplatonist philosopher who earned widespread recognition during the Renaissance.

Plotinus

A pagan follower of Plato, Plotinus (204–270 CE) was a Hellenized Egyptian who spent most of his life in Rome. His writings (six books known collectively as the *Enneads*) influenced several early Christian theologians, and his criticism of Gnosticism aligns him with the Church Fathers Irenaeus, Hippolytus and Clement. Plotinus rejected the Gnostic idea that human beings are born into a hostile world created by an evil Demiurge-Creator. He was also opposed to the invocation of the gods through sacred incantations, although he accepted that the stars had a symbolic, esoteric meaning and were divine. Plotinus was essentially optimistic, whereas the Gnostics felt a sense of deep alienation from the world around them. His mystical cosmology is similar to that of the Gnostics, however, and his concepts of spiritual reality seem much closer to Gnostic principles than to mainstream Christian thought.

Like the Gnostics, Plotinus considers the supreme spiritual reality to be a state of undifferentiated unity – this is the world of the One. When the human soul returns finally to its spiritual home, it is absorbed within the One, for this is the source of all being. The world is an emanation from the One, but this act of creation does not give rise to something 'other', for there is no dualism in this

Frontispiece to Ficino's
Life and Works of Plotinus,
Florence, late 15th century.

process. The first emanation is Intelligence (*nous*) and the second is Soul. Soul in turn emanates matter, which is darkest because it is furthest from the spiritual sun. An advocate of spiritual visualization, Plotinus instructed his followers to 'shut their eyes and wake to another way of seeing'. The soul acknowledges the presence of light and increasingly becomes one with it, removing the duality of good and evil until awareness of the One alone remains.

According to Plotinus the mystical ascent to the Godhead is accompanied by different stages of perfection, and as with the Gnostics this is essentially an act of transcendence, '…a liberation from all earthly bonds, a life that takes no pleasure in earthly things, a flight of the alone to the Alone.'[11]

THE MEDIEVAL KABBALAH

The medieval Kabbalah continues the emanationist cosmology developed by the Gnostics. Indeed, the renowned Kabbalistic scholar, Gershom Scholem (1897–1982), who was Professor of Jewish Mysticism at the Hebrew University in Jerusalem has referred to the esoteric tradition of the Kabbalah as a form of Jewish Gnosticism.[12]

Traditionally the Kabbalah is regarded as a mystical commentary on the Pentateuch – the written Torah, or 'five books of Moses'. The word 'Kabbalah' itself means 'that which has been received' and refers to an oral mystical tradition. Scholars believe that, at first, the secret mystical teachings were conveyed orally from master to disciple and restricted to small circles of devotees. And the Kabbalah

Melchizedek – King of Righteousness and priest of the Most High God – initiated Abraham into the sacred wisdom teachings relating to man, the universe and the nature of God. This tradition became the Kabbalah. Altar plaque by Nicolas de Verdun, Klosterneuburg, Austria, 12th century CE.

The sacred letters of the Jewish alphabet – the building blocks of Creation.

clearly has much earlier antecedents than its medieval context would suggest. Commentator on Jewish spiritual traditions, Daniel C. Matt, believes that the Kabbalah emerged within Judaism as a response to the need for direct contact with the divine, and that this is already evident in one of the earliest Jewish texts, the Book of Exodus. 'When Moses encounters God at the burning bush he is overwhelmed: "afraid to look at God", he hides his face. Soon God reveals the divine name, "I am that I am," intimating what eventually becomes a mystical refrain: God cannot be defined.'[13]

Even though the Kabbalah did not exist in written form until the Middle Ages, it is thought that the *Sefer Yetzirah*, or *Book of Creation*, was actually composed in Palestine between the third and sixth centuries CE. Here we learn how God created the world by means of the 22 letters of the Hebrew alphabet and the 10 *sefirot* – a term that appears for the first time in Hebrew literature.[14] The 10 *sefirot*, or *sephiroth*, of the Tree of Life were to emerge as the central symbolic motif of the Kabbalah.

Another early Kabbalistic text, *Sefer ha-Bahir*, emerged in Provence, where there was a Jewish community, between 1150 and 1200 CE. Interest in the Kabbalah subsequently spread across the Pyrenees into Catalonia and then to Castile. Then, around the year 1280, a Spanish Jewish mystic named Moses de León (1238–1305) began circulating booklets among his fellow Kabbalists. These texts were written in Aramaic, and de León claimed that he had transcribed them from an ancient book of wisdom composed in the circle of Rabbi Shim'on bar Yohai, a famous disciple of Rabbi Akiva, who lived and taught in Israel in the second century. These booklets gradually formed the text known as *Ha-Zohar ha-Qadosh*, usually referred to as the *Zohar* (*The Book of Splendour*). Although Moses de León may have drawn on early material received through the secret oral tradition, it is now thought that he himself was probably the author of the *Zohar*.

According to the *Zohar*, God first taught the Kabbalah to a select group of angels. After the creation of the Garden of Eden, these angels shared the secret teachings with Adam. They were then passed to Noah, and subsequently to Abraham, who took them to Egypt. Moses was initiated into the Kabbalah in Egypt, the land of his birth, and King David and King Solomon were also initiated. No one, however, dared write them down until Rabbi Shim'on bar Yohai.

Now regarded as the central text of the Kabbalistic tradition, the *Zohar* has clear spiritual links with the earlier schools of Gnosticism and Neoplatonism. In all three movements we find the concept of sacred emanations from the Godhead, the idea of the pre-existence of the soul and its descent into matter, and allusions to the sacred names of God. In all three we find references to archetypal powers that have shaped creation – Archons, Angels, Demiurges and various patriarchal deities – and there are references also to the female aspect of the Divine – Sophia or the

Angelic writing and Hebrew equivalents in the Kabbalistic *Book of the Angel Raziel*, a famous magical text. Published in Amsterdam, 1701.

In the Kabbalistic tradition Adam Kadmon, the archetypal human being, represents the Body of God. This prayer, 13th or 14th century CE, has been written in the shape of Adam Kadmon to facilitate intimacy with the Divine.

Mother of the World — from whose womb all forms emerge. The Manichaean Primeval Man has a Kabbalistic counterpart in the form of Adam Kadmon (Qadmon), who represents the archetypal human form and who also symbolizes the Body of God. And in all three traditions we find an interest in the cyclic journey of the soul through a succession of existences as it ventures steadily towards Union with the Source of All Being.

THE KABBALISTIC TREE OF LIFE

In the Kabbalah all aspects of manifested form, including the sacred archetypes of the Godhead, have their origin in *Ain Soph Aur* — the limitless light — a realm entirely beyond form and conception which 'has neither qualities nor attributes'. In Kabbalistic cosmology the emanations from this profound Mystery, which constitute the spheres upon the Tree of Life, or *Otz Chiim*, reveal different aspects of the sacred universe — but are part of a divine totality. *Ain Soph Aur*, writes Gershom Scholem, 'manifests…to the Kabbalist under ten different aspects, which in turn comprise an endless variety of shades and gradations'.[15] Since these emanations reflect a unity and the human form is created 'in the image of God', the spheres of emanation on the Tree of Life are also spiritual centres within the body of Adam Kadmon. Mystical self-knowledge becomes a journey of regaining undifferentiated One-ness with the Divine.

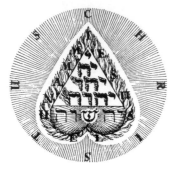

The Tetragrammaton – the sacred name of God, JHVH, usually translated as Yahweh – within an inverted heart. From Jacob Boehme, *Libri apologetici*, 1764 edition.

In the *Zohar* we read: 'In the Beginning, when the will of the King began to take effect, he engraved signs into the divine aura. A dark flame sprang forth from the innermost recess of the mystery of the Infinite, *En-Sof* [*Ain Soph*] like a fog which forms out of the formless, enclosed in the ring of this aura, neither white nor black, neither red nor green, and of no colour whatever. But when this flame began to assume size and extension it produced radiant colours. For in the innermost centre of the flame a well sprang forth from which flames poured upon everything below, hidden in the mysterious secrets of *En-Sof*. The well broke through, and yet did not entirely break through, the ethereal aura which surrounded it. It was entirely unrecognizable until [on] the impact of its breakthrough a hidden supernal point shone forth. Beyond this point nothing may be known or understood, and therefore it is called *Reshith*, that is "Beginning", the first word of Creation.' [16]

According to the Kabbalah, all aspects of Creation flow from the unfolding of God's Will, as it emanates from Him, and thus reveals itself in different stages. The mystical universe is then sustained by the utterance of the Holy Names and the ten emanations represented upon the Tree of Life. These *sephiroth* are none other than 'the creative names which God called into the world, the names which He gave to Himself'.[17] The ten *sephiroth* are as follows (alternative spellings are given in parentheses):

The Ten Spheres on the Tree Of Life

Kether (Keter) — Crown, or the first point of Creation (God's Will)
Chokmah (Hochmah) — Wisdom (the Father)
Binah — Understanding (the Mother)
Chesed (Hesed) — Love
Geburah (Gevurah) — Power
Tiphareth (Tiferet) — Beauty, or Harmony (the Son)
Netzach (Netzah) — Victory, Endurance or Eternity
Hod — Splendour, or Glory
Yesod — Foundation
Malkuth (Malkut) — Sovereignty, or the World (the Daughter)

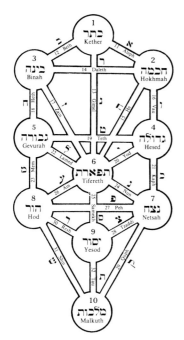

The Kabbalistic Tree of Life with its ten *sephiroth*, or sacred emanations. This diagram shows the Hebrew letters ascribed to the interconnecting paths upon the Tree.

Gershom Scholem writes that the 'Primordial Point' was thought of by most Kabbalists not as Kether, the Crown – normally considered the first emanation upon the Tree of Life – but as the Great Father, Chokmah, or Wisdom. In Kabbalist cosmology the energy of the Great Father unites with that of Binah, the Great Mother (Understanding), and from her womb all archetypal forms come forth. The seven subsequent emanations beneath the trinity of Kether, Chokmah and Binah constitute the seven days of Creation.

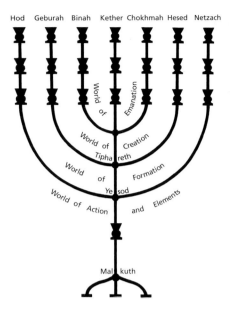

Hod   Geburah   Binah   Kether   Chokhmah   Hesed   Netzach

World of Emanation

World of Creation

Tiphareth

World of Formation

Yesod

World of Action   and   *Elements*

Malkuth

Diagram showing the symbolic links between the Kabbalah and the menorah, the gold candelabrum of Jewish worship. The menorah is also an aid to meditation on the Jewish esoteric tradition.

The Four Worlds

The Kabbalists conceived of 'four worlds' representing four distinct stages of creative manifestation. God is present in each of the four worlds and these worlds in turn are a reflection of the Tetragrammaton – the sacred name of JHVH (*Yod, He, Vau, He,* usually translated as Jehovah, or Yahweh, Lord).

Atziluth, the Archetypal World

This is the level of existence closest to the mysterious, unmanifested realm of *Ain Soph Aur,* containing just one *sephirah,* Kether, described as 'the hidden of the hidden. It is the emergence of God's Will, His creative urge. It is the infinite, the initiation of all that can and will be. It is infinity.' [18]

Briah, the World of Creation

This contains two *sephiroth,* Chokmah and Binah, representing the Great Father and the Great Mother, and reflecting the highest expression of the sacred male and female principles. Their union gives rise to the World of Formation.

Yetzirah, the World of Formation

This contains the *sephiroth* Chesed, Geburah, Tiphareth, Netzach, Hod and Yesod. Yesod literally provides the 'foundation' for all that has preceded it in the process of sacred emanation from the highest realms.

Assiah, the Physical World

This is the final materialization of God's Will in the sphere of Malkuth is represented by the Daughter – Shekinah – spoken of variously as 'the Bride of the Divine Son in Tiphareth', 'the Bride of Kether' and the 'Daughter of Binah'. Shekinah is the personification of the Divine Feminine on Earth.

Each *sephirah* is also said to contain an entire Tree of Life. The 'Malkuth' of the first *sephirah* emanates the 'Kether' of the following *sephirah* , and so on, through the ten emanations. There is thus a sense of sacred emergence implicit in the very structure of the Tree of Life, and each sphere on the Tree is a mirror of the Divine.

GNOSTICISM AND THE KABBALAH

The major difference between Gnosticism and the Kabbalah is that in the former there is a dualistic distinction between Divinity and Matter, whereas the Kabbalah is based on a concept of sacred Unity. Judaism is strongly monotheistic, and nothing exists beyond God.

In Chapter 8 we will consider in more detail how the symbolism of the Kabbalistic Tree of Life has assumed a central place in modern magical consciousness, and how its original monotheistic structure has been extended to encompass all the pantheons of gods and goddesses that feed the occult imagination.

Mezuzah ivory prayer case depicting the 'four worlds' of creative manifestation from the Godhead. Italian, 16th century.

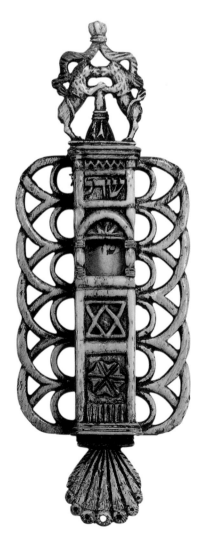

Chapter Four

Medieval Magic and the Witch Trials

In Europe throughout the Middle Ages and the Renaissance magical practice ranged from low sorcery and bewitchment through to transformative, spiritually based 'high magic'. The late Middle Ages was also a time when magic was becoming rudimentary science, and many early scientists were regarded by their peers as magicians.

Christianity was the established religion in western Europe by the end of the eleventh century. Feudalism was the established social order, and Christianity reflected this sense of hierarchy. In the medieval Ideal Universe, God transcended all, and beneath Him were the hierarchy of angels, common humanity and the animal, plant and mineral kingdoms. As St Thomas Aquinas made clear in his *Summa Theologia* (written 1265–73), while every component of the Divine Plan retained its proper place in accordance with Right Reason, Order would prevail. At the same time, growing international commerce and the Crusades brought a certain restlessness to medieval Europe, and the Church gradually became more secular. Some people began to consider their personal salvation more in terms of their relationship with Christ and the Virgin Mary than with the established Church. As the Christian authorities saw their Ideal Universe increasingly threatened by heretics and dissenters, their insistence on strict orthodoxy grew accordingly, and they came to regard heretics and witches as one and the same.

WITCHCRAFT AND HERESY

Long before Christianity became the established religion in western Europe the Catholic bishops were anxious to secure uniformity of Christian doctrine and belief. As early as 382, a law of Theodosius I made heresy punishable by death. This became a powerful tool against lingering Gnostic sects and the followers of Mani, who would re-emerge in a new guise as Bogomils in the Balkans in the tenth century, and as Cathars in southern France in the late twelfth and thirteenth centuries.

A trial for heresy was conducted by King Robert II at Orléans in 1022. A group of Reformist clergymen were charged with holding secret sex orgies at night, chanting the names of demons and burning the children conceived at these gatherings. They were also charged with desecrating Christian sacraments in the presence

In the ongoing struggle between Christianity and heresy, St Dominic disputes with heretics, enumerating the arguments on his fingers. Fresco by Andrea da Firenze, Florence, early 14th century.

of the Devil and receiving money from him. Though they were clearly not witches, the heretics admitted to having angelic visions and felt that they were transported from place to place by a supernatural agency – the earliest known reference to demonic or 'angelic' transportation associated with heresy charges, and a phenomenon that would also be described in later witchcraft trials. Needless to say, the heretics of Orléans were consigned to the flames.

The first permanent tribunal to deal with heresy was established in Toulouse by Pope Gregory IX in 1230. Administered by Dominican friars, the Inquisition, or Holy Office, was intended to end the injustices alleged to have arisen from the confused nature of earlier legislation on heresy. Instead of removing such injustices, however, the Inquisition began to extend them. Soon its principal task was to identify and remove any sign of heresy before it had a chance to take root and spread. In 1231 Pope Gregory IX directed that all convicted heretics would be burnt to death.

During the Middle Ages, malevolent magic was referred to as *maleficium*, which could mean any kind of crime or evil act. At the same time, Church officials assumed that all magic drew upon the help of demons, and that, as a consequence, all forms of magic were innately evil. Officers of the Inquisition used the quotation from Exodus 22:18 which is translated in the King James version as 'Thou shalt not suffer a witch to live' as a justification for their persecutions.

In due course the Inquisition would deal with many different sorts of witchcraft. These included child murder and cannibalism; shapeshifting – or the capacity to change shape magically; the ability to ride through the night sky to gatherings known as witches' sabbats; paying homage to the Devil, invoking demons and engaging in sex orgies, and acts involving the desecration of Christian sacraments. In some parts of Europe charges would also be brought against worshippers of Diana and other pagan fertility deities – a reference to the lingering folk and shamanic underbelly of some forms of witchcraft.

THE CATHARS

Belief in Satan was fuelled in the twelfth century by another group of heretics – the Cathars. The Cathars were Gnostic Christians: they believed that a Spirit of Evil had imprisoned the human soul 'in a cage of flesh' and that the God of the Old Testament was therefore the Devil. They also believed that all the principal figures in the Old Testament, and John the Baptist in the New Testament, were demons. As a pure spirit, Christ had come to the world to show his followers how to overcome the limitations of the physical world. In their view, the Catholic Church had been established by the Devil to deter believers from true spiritual salvation.

In this anti-Cathar propaganda of *c.* 1230, the Cathars in blue gowns corrupt the faithful. They are depicted as immoral, even though they believed bodily lust sprang from the Devil.

As with the Manichaeans and other Gnostic groups, Cathar dualism reflected an innate conflict between matter and spirit. The Cathars did not believe that a holy Christ could assume a flesh-bound form, and they also rejected the notion that any physical objects could have any connection with the spiritual dimension. They therefore rejected all Catholic sacraments and aids to worship, including baptismal water, the use of bread and wine in the Eucharist and the cross.

Catharism distinguished between a pure elite (the *perfecti* or *boni homines*) and the ordinary believers (*credenti*). The *perfecti* were initiated by receiving the sacrament known as the *consolamentum* (the consolation) through the laying-on of hands. The Cathars referred to this as 'heretication'. The *perfecti* had to accept a number of disciplines, including an austere way of life, strict dietary rules and permanent celibacy. Only a few therefore received the *consolamentum* while still involved in active life, and the *credenti* received it only when death was near.[1]

Because of its anti-Catholic position, Catharism has been seen as greatly encouraging the development of demonology and witchcraft, especially between 1140

Witches flying through the sky at night – a woodcut from Ulrich Molitor, *Tractatus von den Bosen Weibern*, late 15th century.

and 1230.[2] This is a surprising correlation because the Cathars hated the Devil as much as conventional Christians. Nevertheless, the fact remains that it was in those areas where Catharism was strongest – Lombardy, the Rhineland and southern France – that witchcraft would become most widespread. The Cathar heresy was regarded by the Church as a threat as great as Islam, and in 1208 Pope Innocent III proclaimed a Crusade against the Albigensians (the city of Albi in south-west France was a Cathar stronghold). By 1230 they had been conquered.

Catharism persisted in pockets after the Crusade but was then weakened by the Inquisition. The same charges of heresy made by the Inquisition against the Cathars would later be made against the witches – namely, desecration of the Christian cross and sacraments, cannibalism, secret gatherings at night, and engaging in sexual orgies.

SORCERERS

The Inquisition was initially set up to deal with heresy, but around 1326 Pope John XXII authorized it to proceed against sorcerers as well, since, in his view, they had 'made a pact with hell'. By excommunicating all sorcerers, the pope automatically defined them as heretics. In Bernard Gui's influential Inquisitors' manual, written around 1320, he proposed that the Inquisition also investigate women 'who ride out at night'. A treatise written around the same time by an English Franciscan provides fascinating details of the visionary realm experienced by such women: 'But I ask, what is to be said of those wretched and superstitious persons who say that by night they see most fair queens and other queens and maidens tripping with the lady Diana and leading the dances with the goddess of the pagans who in our vulgar tongue are called *Elves*, and believe that the latter transform men and women into other shapes and conduct them to *Elvelond*, where now, as they say, dwell those mighty champions, Onewone and Wade, all of which are only phantoms displayed by an evil spirit? For, when the Devil has subjected the mind of anyone to such monstrous beliefs, he sometimes transforms himself now into the form of an angel, now of a man, now of a woman, now on foot, now as knights in tournaments and jousts, now, as has been said, in dances and other sports. As the result of all these things a wretch of this kind deludes his mind.'[3]

WITCHCRAFT IN THE FIFTEENTH CENTURY

The fifteenth century witnessed a flood of literature on witchcraft and witchcraft trials. After 1427 tracts against witchcraft increased, and then in 1486 the notorious *Malleus Maleficarum* (*The Hammer of Witchcraft*) by the Inquisitors Henricus Institoris (also known as Heinrich Kramer) and Jakob Sprenger was published in Germany. It would later appear in France, Italy and England.

A witch, riding on a goat to the Sabbath. Etching by Albrecht Dürer, 1501/2.

The *osculum obscenum*, — heretics kiss the Devil. Here the Waldensians are identified with witches. Frontispiece for the French translation of *Tractatus Contra Sectum Valdensium* by Johannes Tinctor, 15th century.

A highly influential work, the *Malleus Maleficarum* helped define witchcraft in a way that would persist for centuries to come. It said that witchcraft was the most evil of all crimes and the most abominable of all heresies: it was characterized by the renunciation of the Christian faith, the sacrifice of unbaptized infants to Satan, the devotion of body and soul to evil and sexual relationships with incubi. Witches became servants of the Devil by making a pact with him and by engaging in ritual copulation with him. They were also able to shapeshift, and were carried through the air with the help of demons.

During this period the Inquisition began to dominate witchcraft trials. In a series of bulls, Pope Eugenius IV (1431–47) ordered the Inquisition to act against all magicians, accusing them of praying to demons, desecrating the Cross and making pacts with the Devil. Pope Eugenius' successor Nicholas V (1447–55) made it clear that it was acceptable for the Inquisition to prosecute sorcerers, even when their connection with heresy was dubious, and then, in 1484, at the request of the authors of the *Malleus Maleficarum*, Pope Innocent VIII (1484–95) published a famous bull entitled *Summis desiderantes affectibus*. This confirmed complete papal support for the actions of the Inquisition against witchcraft and 'opened the door for the bloodbaths of the following century'.[4]

Appalling allegations against witches remained a hallmark of witch trials for years to come. In a notorious treatise in 1460, Johannes Tinctoris charged witches of creating an ointment by combining the flesh of toads with the blood of murdered children, the bones of exhumed corpses and menstrual blood, and then 'mixing well'. The witches' practice of kissing the Devil – the *osculum obscenum* – was said to involve kissing his buttocks, anus or genitals. The Devil often appeared in the form of a goat whose posterior was 'fetid, cold and either revoltingly soft or repellently hard'. It was said that the Devil also marked his devotees by touching them with his finger or toe. The mark was pale and red and about the size of a pea and could be found on the arm, shoulder or under body hair – especially around the genitals. Withered fingers or other deformities were also sometimes considered evidence of the Devil's mark.

The German Jesuit bishop Peter Binsfeld (*c.* 1540–1603) listed seven major devils in his work *Treatise on Confessions by Evildoers and Witches* (1589), correlating them with the 'seven deadly sins'. Binsfeld's book was quoted throughout Germany for over a hundred years by both Catholics and Protestants, and exerted tremendous influence in promoting the witchcraft delusion.

Lucifer	Pride
Mammon	Avarice
Asmodeus	Lechery
Satan	Anger
Beelzebub	Gluttony
Leviathan	Envy
Belphegor	Sloth[5]

Medieval devils embodied the 'seven deadly sins'. Illustrations below and opposite by Jakob Knoff from *Weingartenspiel*, Zurich, 1539.

In his *Admirable History of a Penitant Woman* (1612), the celebrated Grand Inquisitor and exorcist, Father Sebastien Michaëlis, identified a number of major devils who, he claimed, were specific antagonists for the three major divisions of angels – Seraphim, Cherubim and Thrones (a hierarchical system devised in the fourth century) – and he listed the Christian saints who were their opponents. This information was allegedly provided to Michaëlis by Balberith, one of the devils that possessed Sister Madeleine in Aix-en-Provence.

Witches were frequently accused of having spirit-familiars, such as dogs, toads and cats, that accompanied their owners and provided magical powers. Painted drawings from *A Discourse on Witchcraft*, 1621.

THE CLIMAX OF THE WITCH CRAZE 1560–1660

The height of the European witchcraft craze occurred between 1560 and 1660, and there can be little doubt that increasing tensions between Catholics and Protestants, and the ensuing wars were a major cause of the social upheavals that helped fuel a belief in witchcraft. The Protestant Reformation of the sixteenth century sought a return to the apostolic age, but brought little tolerance for witches in its wake. Even Luther argued that witches should be burnt as heretics for having made a pact with the Devil. Around 1580 witches were blamed for bad weather and plagues of mice and locusts. When ordinary townsfolk were fearful and anxious, witches became the scapegoats.

In all countries except England (and later in the American colonies) where they were hanged, witches were executed by burning. In Italy and Spain they were burnt alive. In Scotland, Germany and France it was customary first to strangle the witch, by garrotting or hanging, before lighting the pyre, always provided that the witch did not recant the confession made under torture. For the unco-operative, the fire was laid with green wood to prolong the dying, and such cruel practices were condoned by the French lawyer Jean Bodin, whose *Demonomanie* (1580) was a standard authority: 'Whatever punishment one can order against witches by roasting and cooking them over a slow fire is not really very much, and not as bad as the torment which Satan has made for them in this world, to say nothing of the eternal agonies which are prepared for them in hell, for the fire here cannot last more than an hour or so until the witches have died.'[6]

The seventeenth century was as violent as the sixteenth. The century of religious strife that culminated in the Thirty Years' War of 1618–48 ravaged Germany and touched most of Europe. The persecutions were especially fierce in Cologne from 1625 to 1636 and in Bamberg from 1623 to 1633 where Bishop Johann Georg II burnt at least 600 witches. Witchcraft hysteria also extended to a number of convents, including Loudun and Aix-en-Provence in France.

The events in Aix-en-Provence in 1611 focus on two members of the small, exclusive Ursuline convent. Sister Madeleine de Demandolx de la Palud, who had entered the convent aged twelve, became depressed, and was sent home to Marseilles. The kindness shown to her by an older family friend, Father Louis Gaufridi, so alarmed the head of the Ursuline convent in Marseilles that she took Madeleine into her convent as a novice. Madeleine then confessed that she had been intimate with Gaufridi, and was transferred back to Aix.

Madeleine developed shaking fits and severe cramps, and had visions of devils. The hysteria spread to the five other nuns, one of whom – Louise Capeau – tried to rival Madeleine with the intensity of her visions. The Grand Inquisitor, Sebastien Michaëlis, now became involved and arranged for the two young women to go to the Royal Convent of St Maximin to be treated by an exorcist. The demonic visions continued, Louise claiming to be possessed by three devils, and accusing Madeleine of being in league with Beelzebub, Balberith, Asmodeus, Ashtaroth and several thousand other evil spirits.

Later Father Gaufridi was called in to attempt an exorcism. Madeleine mocked him with demonic insults, and, when she continued to have visions, neighed like a horse and told fantastic tales of sodomy and witch sabbats, Gaufridi was interrogated by the Inquisition in more depth. In April 1611, he was found guilty of magic, sorcery and fornication, and was sentenced to death and publicly burnt. The following day, Madeleine seemed free of demonic possession. Louise, however, continued to have visions of witches and devils, and similar outbreaks of hysteria were reported at St Claire's convent in Aix, and at St Bridget's in Lille. In 1642, Madeleine was again accused of witchcraft. She was cleared, but another accusation ten years later resulted in the discovery of witch's marks on her body. She spent the rest of her life imprisoned.

In 1633 nuns at the Ursuline convent at Loudun conspired to discredit a priest, Urbain Grandier, after he had fathered an illegitimate child and taken a mistress. To support their claim that Grandier had 'bewitched' them, the nuns exhibited exaggerated erotic behaviour, gasping fits and convulsions. The Mother Superior Jeanne des Anges named Grandier and an assortment of devils, including Asmodeus, Ashtaroth and Zabulon, as the cause of 'spirit possession' at the convent. An investigating commission was set up by Cardinal Richelieu, then Grandier was sent for trial. A highly suspect document, purporting to be a pact signed in blood by Grandier and various demons, was brought as evidence – this

The public burning of Father Urbain Grandier, accused of signing a pact with a group of demons, Loudun, 1634.

The alleged pact between Father Urbain Grandier and the infernal powers, countersigned by Lucifer, Beelzebub, Satan, Elimi, Leviathan, Ashtaroth and Balberith. Loudun, 1634.

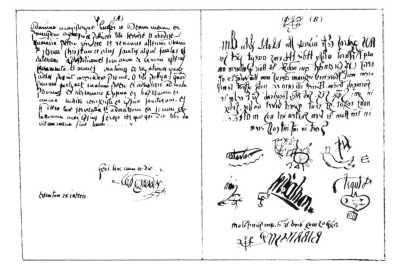

had a highly damaging effect, and in a travesty of justice Grandier was found guilty of practising magic and condemned to be burnt alive for his 'crimes'.

The events at Loudun and Aix-en-Provence provide telling insights into the injustices associated with witchcraft hysteria. The cumulative effect of almost three hundred years of accusations took an extraordinary toll. The persecutions in Europe led to around 200,000 executions, at least half of them in Germany, and with at least twice as many women as men accused of witchcraft.[7]

ENGLAND AND SCOTLAND

On the continent of Europe, charges of witchcraft were often intermingled with charges of heresy. English and Scottish accusations had more to do with low magic and sorcery – with curses directed against young children and farm animals, and spells to cause harm or disease. Witches were also frequently accused of nurturing witch-familiars. There were tests for proving witchcraft, including 'swimming' a witch, who was bound hand and foot and thrown into deep water: if she sank it was proof that God's water had accepted her and she was hauled ashore, often drowning in the process; if she floated she was guilty. Another technique was 'pricking' – the witch was pricked all over in order to detect the 'Devil's mark', said to be insensitive to pain.

During the reign of Queen Elizabeth I (1558–1603) concern with witchcraft was more muted. The astrologer, Dr John Dee, had considerable influence at court, and had been asked to calculate an auspicious date for the Queen's coronation. Nevertheless, in 1563 a statute was issued by Elizabeth ordering the death penalty for witches and sorcerers. Under this law it was a felony to invoke evil spirits for any purpose, irrespective of whether any harm resulted. Charged under civil rather than ecclesiastical law, convicted individuals would be hanged rather than burnt to death. In England around 1,000 witches were hanged during the period. The first major trial under the statute took place at Chelmsford in Essex in 1566.

The practice of 'swimming' an accused witch, If she sank, she was innocent but could drown; if she floated, she was guilty. 16th-century woodcut.

During the sixteenth and seventeenth centuries the assizes in Chelmsford held four major witchcraft trials. In the first three women were charged: Elizabeth Francis, Agnes Waterhouse and Agnes' daughter Joan Waterhouse, all from the village of Hatfield Peverell. It was alleged that their white-spotted cat Sathan was a witch's familiar, was capable of speech and was possessed by the Devil. Francis confessed to having been instructed in witchcraft by her grandmother, Mother Eve, who taught her to renounce God and give her blood to the Devil. She also confessed to bewitching William Auger's baby,

Witches hanging
from the gallows in 1589 at
Chelmsford, Essex, one of the
regions most closely associated
with the witch-craze in
England.

which 'became decrepit'. Francis was sentenced to a year in prison. Agnes Water-house testified that she had bewitched a person named William Fyness who subsequently died, and had willed her cat to destroy her neighbour's cattle and geese. Joan Waterhouse, meanwhile, was charged with bewitching a twelve-year old girl named Agnes Brown, who subsequently became 'decrepit' in her right arm and leg. Joan was acquitted, but her mother was found guilty of 'bewitching to death' and was hanged on 29 July 1566 – the first woman to be put to death in England for witchcraft.

In the second and third trials at Chelmsford in 1579, four women were charged with witchcraft – one of whom was Elizabeth Francis. The charges included two cases of bewitchment causing human death and a charge of bewitching a gelding and a cow, both of which perished. Three of the four witches, including Francis, were hanged.

The fourth major trial at Chelmsford, in 1645, was instigated by the notorious 'witchfinder' and Puritan, Matthew Hopkins, who made his living by travelling through the countryside, encouraging witchcraft hysteria and then exacting payment from local communities for each successful witch-conviction. Hopkins became one of the most feared men in the eastern counties, and, as Wallace Notestein has observed, 'sent to the gallows more witches than all the other witch hunters hung in the 160 years during which this persecution flourished in England'.[8] Hopkins believed King James VI of Scotland who claimed in his

The fourth major trial
at Chelmsford, in 1645, was
instigated by the notorious
'witchfinder' and Puritan,
Matthew Hopkins.
Frontispiece from *Discoverie
of Witches*, 1647.

In the trial of the North Berwick witches, the accused were brought before King James VI of Scotland (later also James I of England). Woodcut from *Newes in Scotland*, 1591.

Daemonologie (1597) that the most important evidence of a witch was that she kept 'familiars' and suckled them with a 'witch mark' on her body. It is not known how many people were charged by Hopkins at Chelmsford, but the jail calendar and pamphlets published after the trials listed 38 men and women, of whom Hopkins claimed 29 were condemned.[9]

James VI (who was also James I of England from 1603) had become a learned proponent of the witch craze after a trial of 1590–92 had convinced him that he had been a victim of witchcraft. The trial of the so-called North Berwick witches is one of the best known witch trials in Scottish history. Gillis Duncan, who worked for David Seaton in the town of Tranent, was suddenly possessed of miraculous healing powers, and would creep out of her master's house at night. Seaton suspected that her powers had been bestowed by the Devil, and had her tortured. When she failed to confess to being a witch, a search of her body revealed a 'Devil's mark' on her throat. She then confessed to being in league with the Devil. Duncan was imprisoned and encouraged to betray others. She named several men and women, including a well known 'wise woman', Agnes Sampson; respectable citizens John Fian, Euphemia Maclean and Barbara Napier. Sampson was brought before King James and a council of nobles, but refused to confess to witchcraft. She was then severely tortured and a Devil's mark found on her genitals. Sampson subsequently confessed to the fifty-three charges against her, most of which involved diagnosing and treating diseases through witchcraft.

According to *Newes from Scotland, Declaring the Damnable Life of Dr Fian, a Notable Sorcerer* (1591) Sampson confessed to attending a sabbat with around two hundred witches on All Hallows' Eve (31 October), where she and her fellow witches had kissed the Devil's buttocks after 'making merrie and drinking'. She also described how she had once hung a black toad by its heels and caught the poison that dripped from its mouth in an oyster shell for a charm of bewitchment. She confessed personally to the king how she and a coven of witches had tried to drown him at sea in 1589, raising a storm as he was sailing from Oslo to Scotland with his bride, Princess Anne of Denmark. The vessel was unharmed, although the storm sank another boat. James was apparently convinced when Sampson repeated a private conversation he had had with Anne on their wedding night.

Finally Sampson described another witches' sabbat in the North Berwick church, attended by over a hundred men and women. The witches paid homage to the Devil and after turning widdershins, or counter-clockwise, several times outside the church, Fian then blew open the church doors with his breath. Surrounded by the light of black candles, the Devil mounted the pulpit, preached a

The Wonders of the Invisible World.

OBSERVATIONS

As well *Historical* as *Theological*, upon the NATURE, the NUMBER, and the OPERATIONS of the

DEVILS.

Accompany'd with,

I. Some Accounts of the Grievous Molestations, by DÆMONS and WITCHCRAFTS, which have lately annoy'd the Countrey; and the Trials of some eminent *Malefactors* Executed upon occasion thereof: with several Remarkable *Curiosities* therein occurring.

II. Some Councils, Directing a due Improvement of the terrible things, lately done, by the Unusual & Amazing Range of EVIL SPIRITS, in Our Neighbourhood: & the methods to prevent the *Wrongs* which those *Evil Angels* may intend against all sorts of people among us - especially in Accusations of the Innocent.

III. Some Conjectures upon the great EVENTS, likely to befall, the WORLD in General, and NEW ENGLAND in Particular; as also upon the Advances of the TIME, when we shall see BETTER DAYES.

IV. A short Narrative of a late Outrage committed by a knot of WITCHES in *Swedeland*, very much Resembling, and so far Explaining, *That* under which our parts of *America* have laboured!

V. THE DEVIL DISCOVERED: In a Brief Discourse upon those TEMPTATIONS, which are the more Ordinary *Devices* of the Wicked One.

By Cotton Mather.

Boston Printed by *Benj. Harris* for *Sam. Phillips*. 1693.

Titlepage from one of Cotton Mather's witch-hunt pamphlets, describing the Salem trials. Boston, Massachusetts, 1693.

sermon and exhorted the members of his assembly to 'not spare to do evil; to eat, drink and be merriye, for he should raise them all up gloriously at the last day.' The coven members then went out to the cemetery where the Devil showed them how to dismember corpses for magical charms.

In all, around seventy people were accused of witchcraft or treason during the North Berwick trials. Many were imprisoned, and Sampson, Fian and Maclean were among those executed for practising witchcraft and necromancy.

THE AMERICAN COLONIES

Witchcraft would not become a major concern in the American colonies until the mid-seventeenth century. The first witch-hanging took place in Connecticut in 1647 and there were hangings in Providence, Rhode Island, in 1662.[10] The best documented trials for witchcraft in the American colonies, however, are those of Salem in 1692.

In Salem Village, now Danvers, Massachusetts, Betty Parris, aged nine, and her eleven-year-old cousin Abigail Williams began experimenting with divination with other girls. They were trying to tell their fortunes and discover the professions of their future husbands, and they had made a primitive crystal ball by floating an egg white in a glass of water. But first Betty Parris and then others became terrified, and began to exhibit nervous symptoms. Betty's father, the Reverend Samuel Parris, called in Dr William Griggs who could not find any physical cause for the symptoms, and suggested that perhaps the girls were the victims of bewitchment. Soon they began to experience convulsions.

Three women were then accused of causing the mysterious symptoms: Sarah Good, Sarah Osborne and a West Indian slave named Tituba. Good and Osborne denied the charges, but Tituba confessed to having had contact with the Devil and having ridden through the air on a pole to 'witch meetings'. She also claimed that there was a coven of witches in Massachusetts headed by a tall white-haired man dressed in black who had forced her to sign his Devil's book in blood.

As the hysteria developed, first in Salem Village and then in Salem Town, it was further claimed that the witches attending the Devil's meetings ate black communion bread, suckled animal spirit-familiars by using their witches' teats, and performed various acts of *maleficia* which they directed against their enemies.

No trials could be held in the former Puritan colony of Massachusetts Bay for six months because the colony's charter of self-rule had been revoked by the English courts. In 1692, however, a new governor, Sir William Phips, arrived in Massachusetts from England with a new charter and authorized the witchcraft trials. Between 10 June and 22 September 1692 nineteen people – including Sarah Good – were hanged, one was pressed to death and more than a hundred were

Ergot infection of cereal crops causes epileptic symptoms and hallucinations (ergot 'cockspurs' on rye, below), and may have been responsible for the many outbreaks of 'dancing sickness' (see Brueghel's 16th-century drawing above), and the Salem witchcraft hysteria.

jailed, among them the son of the colony's former governor. Sarah Good denied the charges to the end, saying to one of her accusers, Reverend Noyes: 'I am no more a witch than you are a wizard and if you take away my life, God will give you blood to drink.' Intriguingly, Noyes died in 1717 of an internal haemorrhage, choking on his own blood.[11]

Research by several scholars, among them Linnda R. Caporael, suggests that ergot in the community's bread caused the witchcraft hysteria. Ergot, a naturally occurring fungus on cereal crops, can cause very powerful hallucinations. In a Puritan community like Salem, gripped by fear of the Devil, ergot ingestion would have dramatic consequences, fuelling hysteria and paranoia that could send many innocent victims to their deaths.[12]

MAGIC, COSMOLOGY AND EARLY SCIENCE

If medieval witchcraft had much to do with heresy and dissent, it is also apparent that medieval magic had much to do with early forms of science. In the twelfth century there were men like Duns Scotus and Ockham who wished to investigate the world of natural phenomena, even if this seemed to conflict with St Thomas Aquinas's concept of a single indivisible system dependent on God. As British historian Andrew McCall has observed, this led to a split in medieval consciousness because early scientific investigators then had to declare 'that there were in fact two sorts of knowledge: on the one hand the purely physical or, as we might say, the scientific, and on the other the theological or Divine. It was this distinction between the physical nature of a thing and its divine nature, as it filtered through to all levels of society and came to be applied to every aspect of life, that gave rise in the later Middle Ages to the prevailing mental attitude of double-think.... To medieval people, the theoretical or Divine nature of the world was just as real as the practical – if not, since the world below was but the imperfect reflection of the Divine World, even more so.'[13]

In the late Middle Ages through to the early Renaissance, certain 'magical' individuals stand out as pioneering investigators, as philosophers and as observers of natural phenomena, seeking to transcend the constrictions of religious orthodoxy while also acknowledging the awesome and mysterious nature of the Universe. They would be branded heretics and magicians in some quarters, but, as Henry M. Pachter has written in his study of Paracelsus, thinkers like this were really engaging in pursuits that would eventually give rise to science: 'Medieval magic...anticipated modern technology. Experiments with the hidden forces of Nature were designed to bring forth the science we know. Paracelsus and his disciples...had quite a lucid and rational idea of what distinguishes superstition from science: "Natural magic is the use of true, natural causes to produce rare and unusual effects by methods neither superstitious nor diabolical...."'[14] Albertus Magnus, Cornelius Agrippa, Paracelsus and Dr John Dee display a different approach to the magical arts – an approach that would in due course help facilitate the transition from magic to science.

ALBERTUS MAGNUS

Albertus Magnus (1206–80), Count of Bollstadt, was born in the town of Lauingen in Swabia. He was highly regarded by his contemporaries as a philosopher, alchemist and theologian. Although he claimed inspiration from the Virgin Mary, became Bishop of Ratisbon and was a mentor to St Thomas Aquinas, many suspected him of communicating with the Devil. He was more a philosopher than a magician, however, for he was essentially an observer of natural phenomena. A keen field-botanist, he visited mines and mineral outcrops, and was fascinated by the 'marvellous virtues' of plants and stones – this study would come to be known as 'natural magic'. Albertus believed that engraved gems had magical powers, and regarded astrology as the basis of all forms of divination. However, this was for the proto-scientific reason that, just as Aristotle had decreed, celestial bodies were seen to govern all things on earth. Albertus similarly considered alchemy as a 'true art' and championed the idea that gold could be produced artificially. According to popular tradition, he owned a precious stone that could produce marvels: 'When

Albertus Magnus – a man of magic and early science who was also a mentor to St Thomas Aquinas. From a fresco by Tommaso da Modena, Treviso *c.* 1350.

William II, Count of Holland, dined with him in Cologne, Albertus had the table set in the garden of the convent in spite of the fact that it was midwinter. When the guests arrived they found a snow-decked table. But as soon as they sat down, the snow disappeared and the garden was filled with fragrant flowers. Birds flew about as if it were summer, and the trees were in bloom.'[15]

Albertus Magnus was both a man of magic and a man of science. He was regarded by his peers as one who truly understood the fundamentally mysterious nature of the world around him. It was therefore entirely credible that *The Book of Secrets* was attributed to him – it was a work on the 'virtues of herbs, stones and certain beasts', and widely known in the Middle Ages. Although the text contains personal references to Albertus Magnus, and some of the material on precious stones is taken from one of his works, it is more likely that the text was by one of his followers. It nevertheless demonstrates the fascination of the time with the secret or 'marvellous' properties associated with herbs, precious stones, animal and bird species, and specific parts of the human body. It was translated into several languages including Spanish, French, Italian, Dutch and English (the English translation appearing *c.* 1550), and its popularity continued until Elizabethan and early Stuart times.

As Michael Best and Frank Brightman have noted: 'The Elizabethans did not

A double-page spread from a printed edition of Albertus Magnus' *Naturalia*, linking the planets with plants, such as Saturn with the lily.

compartmentalize their knowledge; as the philosophical concepts of the four basic qualities and elements formed the basis of all pursuits in natural science – in alchemy, in the herbals and bestiaries, in medical science, astrology, and psychology – so the various areas of human knowledge were felt to be parts of a harmonious whole rather than separate, possibly conflicting disciplines. Each study in its microcosm reflected the macrocosm of an ordered universe; even magic and witchcraft could be made to fit the over-all pattern.'[16]

The Book of Secrets tells us: 'There be seven herbs that have great virtues, after the mind of Alexander the Emperor, and they have these virtues of the influence of the planets…*Daffodillus* (Saturn); *Polygonum* (Sun); *Chynostates* (Moon); *Arnoglossus* or Plantain (Mars); *Pentaphyllon* or Cinquefoil (Mercury); *Jusquiamus*, or Henbane (Jupiter) and *Verbena* or Vervain (Venus).' It describes the 'virtues' of Vervain thus: 'The root of this herb put upon the neck healeth the swine pox, impostumes behind the ears, and botches of the neck, and such as cannot keep their water. It healeth also cuts, and swelling of the tewel, or fundament…and the haemorrhoids. If the juice of it be drunken with honey and water sodden, it dissolveth those things which are in the lungs or lights. And it maketh a good breath.'[17]

The commentaries on various stones and wild beasts are similarly illuminating: 'Take the stone which is called *Adamas*, in English speech a Diamond, and it is of shining colour, and very hard, in so much that it cannot be broken, but by the blood of a Goat, and it groweth in Arabia, or in Cyprus. And if it be bounden to the left side, it is good against enemies, madness, wild beasts, venomous beasts, and cruel men, and against chiding and brawling, and against venom, and invasion of fantasies.'[18] 'The virtue of a Merula [a genus of birds that includes the thrush] is marvellous. For if the feathers of the right wing of it, with a red leaf, be hanged up in the middle of an house which was never occupied, no man shall be able to sleep in that house, until it be put away.'[19] 'If any man bear a Dog's heart on his left side, all the Dogs shall hold their peace, and not bark at him. If any man will bind the right eye of a Wolf on his right sleeve neither men nor Dogs may hurt him.'[20]

AGRIPPA

Cornelius Agrippa (1486–1535) was born of noble parentage in Cologne. He is sometimes portrayed as an archetypal black magician, and was said to possess a magic mirror in which he could divine future events. It was also rumoured that he dabbled in necromancy, believing he could conjure the spirits of the dead, and that the black dog which accompanied him was his demonic familiar. Agrippa, however, is more accurately regarded as a Christian Kabbalist. His famous work, *De Occulta Philosophia*, is now regarded as one of the key works of Renaissance Kabbalistic magic.

Cornelius Agrippa, the famous Christian Kabbalist unjustly accused of necromancy and black magic.

An attendant to Maximilian I, Agrippa studied Albertus Magnus' work in Cologne and then seems to have become a member of various secret societies. After he had written the first version of *De Occulta Philosophia* in Germany *c.* 1509–10, he came to London for Biblical studies — here he was in contact with the British humanist John Colet, then Dean of St Paul's, who was interested in both the Pauline epistles and the Kabbalah. A year later he went to Italy, where he studied the Hermetic tradition and the Kabbalah.

He published *De Occulta Philosophia* and an earlier work, *De Vanitate Scientiarum*, in Antwerp in 1533, thereby adding substantially to his fame as a metaphysician. In *De Vanitate Scientiarum*, Agrippa says that intellectual learning is of no account, and he then goes on to describe both natural magic and mathematical magic. He discusses 'bad magic', which involves demons, and 'good magic' which calls on angels by means of the Kabbalah. Agrippa's basic message is nevertheless conventional in a Christian sense: only Christ can teach moral philosophy, and there is no key to knowledge other than through the Word of God.

In *De Occulta Philosophia*, Agrippa divides the universe into the elemental world, the celestial world and the intellectual world, each receiving influences from the one above it. The virtue of the Creator descends via the archangels to the intellectual world, is then transmitted to the stars in the celestial world, and finally filters down into the physical world where it permeates the elements — from which all things are created.

De Occulta Philosophia is divided into three books. The first is about natural magic, or magic in the elemental world; the second is about the magic of the stars and how to utilize it; and the third is about ceremonial magic, that is to say, magic involving angelic spirits. Knowledge of all three worlds involves a familiarity with the Hebrew alphabet, specific ritual formulae and the sacred names of God.

According to Renaissance scholar Frances Yates, Agrippa regarded himself very much as a Christian Kabbalist. 'He makes sure that only good and holy angelic influences are invoked, and that the star-demons are made harmless through their help. Agrippa's occult philosophy is intended to be a very white magic. In fact it is really a religion, claiming access to the highest powers, and Christian since it accepts the name of Jesus as the chief of the wonder-working Names.'[21]

PARACELSUS

Paracelsus (1493–1541) was one of the most illustrious of the medieval metaphysicians. He was born Theophrastus Bombastus von Hohenheim in Einsiedeln, near Zurich in Switzerland, and spent his childhood in Villach in the Austrian province of Carinthia. He is thought to have pursued medical studies under the direction of his physician father, and to have received his doctorate from the

Paracelsus, physician, alchemist and astrologer, who proclaimed, 'Medicine is founded upon Nature.'

medical school at the University of Ferrara in northern Italy, around 1515. He then travelled to Rome, Naples, Spain, Portugal, Paris, London, Moscow, Constantinople and Greece, and accepted a position as city physician and Professor of Medicine at Basle in 1526. He only stayed in Basle for eleven months, however, and was an itinerant physician for the rest of his life, living in many different places in Austria and Germany.

Paracelsus was highly regarded as a physician, specializing in bronchial illnesses and developing the first comprehensive treatment for syphilis, but he also denounced earlier medical pioneers like Avicenna, Galen and Rhasis for being pedantic and too theoretical. Paracelsus believed that medicine was based on four distinct foundations: a sound philosophical approach; astronomy (by which he really meant medical astrology); alchemy; and the moral purity of the physician himself. He wrote extensively on the connections between medicine and astrology and was interested in the possible links between weather and illness.

Paracelsus emphasized the Hermetic doctrine of the macrocosm and microcosm, believing that each human being was a mirror of the universe, and he also developed the so-called 'doctrine of signatures' which he had inherited from Albertus Magnus. This concept is based on the principle that every part of the human organism (the microcosm) corresponds to a part of the macrocosm, or spiritual universe, and the connection is then established through some similarity in colour or form – which is its essential 'signature'.

Paracelsus regarded disease as a form of imbalance, and maintained that a healthy person combined the three alchemical constituents of sulphur (male), mercury (female), and salt (neutral) in perfect harmony. He also subscribed to the idea that each of the elements were governed by elemental spirits, calling the spirits of fire *acthnici*, the spirits of air *nenufareni*, the spirits of water *melosinae* and the spirits of earth *pigmaci*. Basically, he believed what many holistic practitioners and naturopaths continue to believe today: 'Medicine is founded upon Nature, Nature herself is medicine, and in her only shall men seek it. And Nature is the teacher of the physician, for she is older than he.'[22]

Paracelsus also studied with Johannes Trithemius, Abbot of Sponheim, who had instructed Cornelius Agrippa in the magical traditions.[23] In the *Archidoxes of Magic* he writes: 'Some will think that I write Witchcraft, or some such like things, which are far absent from me. For this I certainly affirm, that I write nothing here which is supernatural and which is not wrought and effected by the power of Nature and Celestial influences.'[24] Nevertheless, he did believe that sacred names, magical motifs and astrological symbols could be inscribed on magical talismans and then hung around the patient's neck at the appropriate astrological time as part of an effective medical cure. By way of explanation, Paracelsus wrote: 'Characters,

Letters and Signes have several virtues and operations, wherewith also the nature of Metals, the condition of Heaven, and the influence of the Planets, with their operations, and the significations and proprieties of Characters, Signes and Letters, and the observation of the times, do concur and agree together. Who can object that these Signs and Seals have not their virtue and operations?'

In the final analysis, like Cornelius Agrippa, Paracelsus considered his magical and medical knowledge compatible with the teachings of the Christian tradition: '…all this is to be done by the help and assistance of the Father of all Medicines, our Lord Jesus Christ, our only Saviour.'[25]

DR DEE

Dr John Dee (1527–1608) was highly regarded during his lifetime as a classical scholar, philosopher, mathematician and astrologer. He was also fascinated by navigation and astronomy. He was the son of a servant at the court of Henry VIII. Initially attracted to the study of mathematics, he studied at St John's, Cambridge, and then at the University of Louvain. His patron was the Duchess of Northumberland, wife of the Chancellor of Cambridge University, and he became a popular lecturer. Lord Robert Dudley, on the instructions of Queen Elizabeth I, commissioned him to calculate an astrologically auspicious date for her coronation.

Following a meeting with a magician named Jerome Cardan in England in 1552, Dee became interested in the conjuration of spirits, but his most serious exploration of the magical realms began when he met Edward Kelley, who claimed to communicate with angels in his spirit-vision. In order to invoke these angels, Dee and Kelley made use of a crystal ball and wax tablets, or almadels, engraved with magical symbols and the sacred names of God. The tablet for a given invocation was laid between four candles and the angels summoned as Kelley stared into the crystal.

In 1582 Kelley began to receive messages in a new angelic language called 'Enochian'. Dee wrote in his diary: 'Now the fire shot oute of E. K., his eyes, into the stone agayne. And by and by he understode nothing of all, neyther could read any thing, nor remember what he had sayde.' On occasions Kelley seemed to become possessed by spirits, some of which – according to Dee – were visible: '…at his side

Dr John Dee's black obsidian mirror, used to glimpse spirits, with its leather case. The Spanish conqueror Hernando Cortés had obtained it in Mexico, where an attribute of the Aztec god Tezcatlipoca was an obsidian mirror in which he could see all things.

Portrait of the celebrated Elizabethan scholar Dr John Dee, *c.* 1585, when he was 67. For a time he became fascinated by the conjuration of spirits.

appeared three of fowr spirituall creatures like laboring men, having spades in their hands and theyr haires hanging about theyr eares'. The spirits wished to know why they had been summoned, and Dee bade them depart. They desisted, nipping Kelley on the arm. Dee wrote: 'Still they cam gaping or gryning at him. Then I axed him where they were, and he poynted to the place, and in the name of Jesus commaunded those Baggagis to avoyde, and smitt a cross stroke at them, and presently they avoyded.'[26] Although Dee's visionary explorations with Edward Kelley may seem to reveal a lack of discernment, they also gave rise to the Enochian system of magic which has since been incorporated into modern Western magic.

As a mathematician and philosopher Dee was regarded during the Elizabethan period as the English counterpart to the great German and Danish astronomers Kepler and Tycho Brahe, and he was considered a first-rate intellect. His approach to astrology in his view followed principles of systematic observation. He first cast horoscopes as early as the 1550s, and he described astrology as '…an art mathematical, which reasonably demonstrateth the operations and effects of the natural beams of light, and secret influences of the stars and planets, in every element and elemental body at all times in any horizon assigned.'[27] Within the frameworks of his time, Dee's approach was fundamentally scientific. Prospero, the magician in Shakespeare's *The Tempest*, may be partly based on John Dee.

Chapter Five
The Hermetic Tradition and Alchemy

During the fifteenth and sixteenth centuries a body of mystical thought now referred to as the Hermetica or the Hermetic tradition enjoyed widespread intellectual influence in Europe. Hermetic philosophy has its roots in Hellenism and enters Western esoteric thought as an essentially Gnostic revival. During the Renaissance, Florence became the focus of the Hermetic tradition, for it was here, in the Medici court, that this metaphysical perspective received significant endorsement.

THE HERMETIC REVIVAL IN EUROPE

In 1460 a monk named Leonardo da Pistoia brought to Florence the Greek manuscripts that were later known collectively as the *Corpus Hermeticum*, or *Hermetica*. These texts, found in Macedonia, were presented to Cosimo de' Medici, a noted collector of Greek manuscripts. Two years later Cosimo asked his young court scholar, Marsilio Ficino, to translate them into Latin. This was completed in 1463, and Cosimo was able to read the translation before his death the following year. Ficino's texts are now in the Medici Library in Florence.

The Hermetic material was essentially a body of Greek mystical and philosophical writings which drew on Platonism and Stoicism, and perhaps also Mithraism, and then developed within a Gnostic-Egyptian context. Most scholars agree that the texts date from the latter half of the second century CE through to the end of the third century. In these writings the central figure, Hermes Trismegistus (Thrice Greatest Hermes) is presented as a wise spiritual teacher – a Gnostic master who in a sense is a composite of Hermes and Thoth. The *Corpus Hermeticum* takes the form of a series of philosophical exchanges between Hermes Trismegistus and his followers.

The best known text, the *Poimandres*, or *Pymander*, which is attributed to Hermes Trismegistus – *Poimandres* translates as 'Shepherd of Man' – describes Creation in the form of a dream. The Master falls asleep and is visited by Poimandres, who explains how knowledge of God may be attained. Marsilio Ficino felt that much of the text was divinely inspired: 'They called Trismegistus thrice great because he was pre-eminent as the greatest philosopher, the greatest priest, and the greatest king. As Plato writes, it was a custom among the Egyptians to choose priests from

Hermes Trismegistus (Thrice Greatest Hermes) with Isis and Moses. Detail from a Pinturrichio fresco in the Borgia Apartment of the Vatican in Rome, 1492–95.

among the philosophers, and kings from the company of priests.…. Being thus the first among philosophers, he progressed from natural philosophy and mathematics to the contemplation of the gods and was first to discourse most learnedly concerning the majesty of God, the orders of daemons, and the transmigration of souls. He is therefore called the first inventor of theology.'[1]

Although it is now acknowledged that the Hermetic texts date from the Christian era, Ficino seems to have believed that Hermes Trismegistus was a contemporary of Moses, and at times implies that Hermes and Moses may have been one and the same. Ficino also accepted that Moses had been entrusted with the secret teachings of the Kabbalah on Mount Sinai – so, like Thoth-Hermes, he was a custodian of the ancient wisdom.

For Ficino the Hermetic texts – in particular the *Asclepius* and the *Pymander of Hermes Trismegistus* – offered profound inspirational instruction. As he writes in his Introduction: 'Mercury [ie. Hermes Trismegistus] knows how to instruct…in divine matters. He cannot teach divine things who has not learned them; and we cannot discover by human skill what is above Nature. The work is therefore to be accomplished by a divine light, so that we may look upon the sun by the sun's light.

Medal showing the
head of Ficino's patron,
Cosimo de' Medici:
Florentine School, *c.* 1460.

Medal showing the head of
Marsilio Ficino. Attributed to
Niccolò Fiorentino, *c.* 1495.

Medal showing the head
of Giovanni Pico, Count
of Mirandola. Niccolò
Fiorentino, *c.* 1495.

For, in truth, the light of the divine mind is never poured into a soul unless the soul turns itself completely toward the mind of God, as the moon turns toward the sun.' [2]

Ficino saw no contradiction in blending Neoplatonism with orthodox Catholic theology, for Hermes had already been endorsed by such Christian figures as St Augustine and the fifth-century Christian poet Lactantius. In this new syncretic cosmology the Christian concept of God the Father, enthroned and surrounded by choirs of angels, mirrored Plato's idea of an uncorrupted archetypal domain. Humanity, meanwhile, lived in a kind of shadow world that was but a pale reflection of its heavenly spiritual counterpart. In the Hermetic philosophy this idea was conveyed through the mystical axiom, 'As above, so below'.

As described in Chapter 3, Plotinus believed that the mystical realm could only be apprehended through *nous* – a blend of higher intellect and intuitive power – but innate to the Neoplatonic (and Gnostic) attitude was a belief that human beings can transcend the world of appearances through spiritual will. The Hermetic devotees of the Renaissance similarly conceived of a universe in which human beings could earn their place in the celestial realms and become one with God. As Tobias Churton notes in *The Gnostics* (1987), during the Renaissance it was possible to blend Neoplatonic and Christian perspectives: 'The wish was to return to the One, the source from which the power derived enabling the philosopher-magician to work the "miracle of creation". Christ had opened the way, the "veil of the temple" had been rent and the true followers of Christ could ascend. "Hermes", he of ancient wisdom, mediator between spirit and matter, with winged feet and winged mind, was both prophet and symbol of this possibility.' [3]

In the Hermetic model of the universe God had made the world, the world had given rise to perceptions of time, and time gave rise to the idea of 'becoming'. Eternity was the domain of God but the temporal world moved within eternity. In this way, and in a holistic sense, one could proclaim that 'All is One'. According to the Hermetic perspective, however, this single universe was divided into three worlds, or emanations. The lowest sphere was the world of Nature, which received divine influences from the more sanctified realms above. At the next level were the stars, as well as spirits and 'guardians'. Higher still was the super-celestial world of *nous* – the world of angelic spirits, or archons, who had a superior knowledge of reality because they were closer to the One – the Godhead or divine source of creation, who lay beyond the three worlds. Transcendence – achieving oneness with God – entailed liberating oneself from the constrictions of temporal life and entering the realm of pure and divine Thought.

A dominant theme of the Hermetic texts is that Hermes Trismegistus embodies the wisdom teachings because he understands the essential Oneness of the

Hermetic motif showing the sacred union of Sun, Moon and Mercury.

universe. Those who hoped to learn from Hermes Trismegistus — figures like Asclepius with whom he entered into dialogue — saw this as a wisdom that had to be earned, and discrimination was required to distinguish the deceptive nature of physical appearances from the true world of sacred reality. There is a clear suggestion here, too, of a secret tradition. Hermes saw the totality of things. Having seen, he understood, he had the power to reveal and show. What he knew, he wrote down. What he wrote, he mostly hid away, keeping silence rather than speaking out, so that every new generation had to seek out these things.[4]

Ficino's work with the *Corpus Hermeticum* was continued by Giovanni Pico, Count of Mirandola, who similarly held to an emanationist view of the world. Pico combined Ficino's Hermetic Neoplatonism with an extensive knowledge of the Kabbalah, Christianity and 'high magic' (*mageia*). He also brought to the court of Cosimo's successor, Lorenzo de' Medici, an extensive knowledge of astrology, geometry, medicine and astronomy. In his nine hundred theses — a work known collectively as *Oratio*, or *The Oration* — Pico explored what he called 'the dignity of man' and maintained that one could come to know God as a 'friend', rather than as a 'fact'. 'Philosophy seeks the truth,' he wrote, 'theology finds it, religion possesses it.... We may more easily love God than comprehend Him or speak of Him.'

Like Ficino, Pico conceived of a universe emanating from the Godhead. At the highest level, Mind is devoted to the contemplation of the divine Being, and below this realm is the celestial world and lower still the domain in which we live. Pico's conception, however, was not simply that of the devotional mystic. According to Pico, man is unique in his capacity to transcend his worldly context: 'Exalted to the lofty height, we shall measure there from all things that are and shall be and have been in indivisible eternity; and, admiring their original beauty, full of divine power, we shall no longer be ourselves but shall become He Himself Who made us.... For he who knows himself in himself knows all things, as Zoroaster first wrote. When we are finally lighted in this knowledge, we shall in bliss be addressing the true Apollo on intimate terms.... And, restored to health, Gabriel "the strength of God", shall abide in us, leading us through the miracles of Nature and showing us on every side the merit and the might of God.'[5]

This was Pico's idea of *mageia* — high magic that could provide humanity with access to the inner workings of Nature and the cosmos. In this magical conception of the universe, Nature is pervaded by spirit. Matter cannot enter spirit, but spirit can enter matter. To this end *mageia* can be employed 'in calling forth into the light, as if from their hiding places, the powers scattered and sown in the world by the loving-kindness of God.' The role of the sacred magician — the practitioner of high magic — is to raise earth (matter) to the level of heaven (spirit). As Tobias Churton observes, this is essentially a Gnostic undertaking: 'The method, or secret of working, lies within the gnosis or knowledge of Man as he is and can be – he knows he has access to the divine world. In a process of contemplation or alchemy he rises through an inner imagination of ascending principles until he feels he is full of "light". In such a condition the *magus* sets to work. That work might be artistic, turning paint into vision, stone into form; mechanical, turning wood and brass into machinery; religious, turning ill thoughts and bitterness into love and brotherhood; landscaping, building, singing, travelling, loving, cooking, writing, capitalizing – the possibilities are endless. In a holy mind the world may be transformed.'[6]

Hermes Trismegistus says in the *Asclepius*, in a text which was also quoted by Pico: '…he takes in the nature of a god as if he were himself a god…. He is united to the gods because he has the divinity pertaining to gods…. He takes the earth as his own, he blends himself with the elements by the speed of thought, by the sharpness of spirit he descends to the depths of the sea. Everything is accessible to him; heaven is not too high for him, for he measures it as if he were in his grasp by his ingenuity. What sight the spirit shows to him, no mist of the air can obscure; the earth is never so dense as to impede his work; the immensity of the sea's depths do not trouble his plunging view. He is at the same time everything as he is everywhere.'[7]

Similarly we read in the *Corpus Hermeticum (Libellus XIII)*: 'I see myself to be the All. I am in heaven and in earth, in water and in air; I am in beasts and plants; I am a babe in the womb, and one that is not yet conceived, and one that has been born; I am present everywhere.' Here, it seems to me, we have a quintessential statement about the spiritual nature of the magical quest. High magic embraces the entire cosmos and proposes an archetypal process of mythic renewal. The quest is to be 'reborn' from the limited and restricted world of material form into the realm of Spirit. This is certainly implicit in Platonic and Neoplatonic concepts of the world and has also shaped the Gnostic-Hermetic tradition, as we have seen. I also believe that this core idea permeates several modern magical belief systems.

But there is the potential here, too, for a magical fundamentalism – a narcissistic attraction to the idea that we are all gods in the making. The ploys of human egotism combined with the pursuit of power – a less attractive aspect of the magical revival – mean that this idea could lead to unintended consequences.

I want to focus now, however, on the mystical aspects of the Hermetic tradition and the *holistic* view of consciousness that underlies it – especially the idea that, in the most complete sense, everything is an aspect of the Body of God. Far from pursuing grandiose notions that we have acquired the status of gods, we acknowledge instead that, as fellow human beings, we all participate in the sacred dynamism – or life force – of the universe. Indeed, from the Hermetic viewpoint this is what binds us together. The Gnostic quest – the journey of high magic – is essentially a return to the source of our being, a journey culminating in the realization of Divine Unity which transcends the limitations of form and material appearances. Exponents of the Western magical tradition, John and Caitlin Matthews, have written: 'Again and again this message is affirmed: there is a god within which gives life to the body and inspiration of all that we do: events in the sphere of incarnation reflect those in the heavenly sphere. It is this emphasis on unity rather than disharmony which marks out the Hermetic mysteries: unity of all things, of God with man, of higher and lower, of divine with mundane. It finds its clearest expression in the famous injunction, "As above, so below," so often quoted and so little understood by occultists throughout the ages.'[8]

THE SPIRITUAL DIMENSIONS OF ALCHEMY

Just as Gnosticism, Neoplatonism and the Hermetic tradition are concerned with the liberation of the human spirit, so, too, can alchemical transmutation be regarded as a metaphor of spiritual renewal. Many scholars, including Titus

A page from the 'Thebes papyrus', *c.* 300 CE, which includes recipes for changing the colour of a metal so that it then resembles gold or silver.

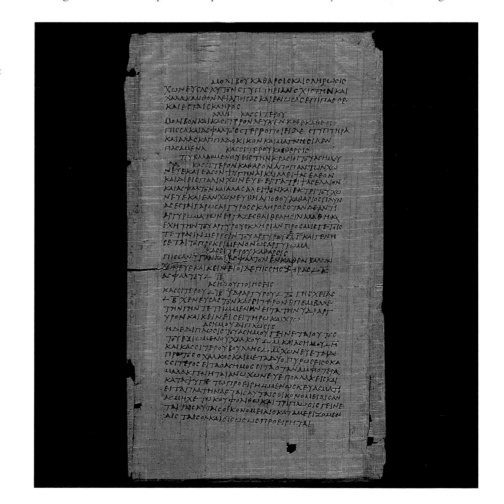

Burckhardt, Kurt Seligmann, Carl Jung, Mircea Eliade and Robert Segal, have considered it in this light, and it is in this capacity that alchemical symbolism has profoundly influenced the Western magical tradition.

Western alchemy dates from the beginning of the second century CE, and flourished in Hellenistic Egypt where there was a high level of proficiency in metalworking, especially in relation to silver and copper alloys that resembled gold. Two papyri found in a gravesite in Thebes – the so-called Leiden and Stockholm papyri which date from around 300 CE – include recipes for transforming the colour of a metal so that it would resemble gold or silver. This was perhaps a precursor of the metaphysical concept of the transmutation of base metals into gold.

The word 'alchemy' itself is thought to derive from an Egyptian word, *chem* or *qem*, meaning 'black' – a reference to the black alluvial soils bordering the Nile. The fourth-century alchemical writer Zosimos of Panopolis (Akhmim) in Egypt maintained that a person named Chemes had given rise to the quest for gold and had written a book of supernaturally inspired instruction called *Chema*, but proof of Chemes' historical existence has not been established.

We know, however, that the Greek word *chyma*, meaning to fuse or cast metals, established itself in Arabic as *al kimia* – from which the term 'alchemy' is derived. It is interesting to note that a knowledge of alchemy passed from the Greeks and Egyptians to the Arabs, by whom it was subsequently transmitted back to Europe. The Arabs translated many ancient alchemical works from the Greek, and a many of them have come down to us today only through their Arabic versions.

As a pagan practice, the study of alchemy thrived in Alexandria in buildings adjacent to the famous Temple of Serapis, but this temple, together with many works of art, was destroyed in 391 on the orders of the Christian archbishop of Alexandria, Theophilus. As a result of this, the persecuted scholars withdrew to Athens where Proclus, the Thracian Neoplatonist, was teaching, and in this way a more comprehensive knowledge of Egyptian alchemy was introduced to mainland Greece.

Although pagan traditions were finally suppressed by Emperor Justinian in 529, interest in alchemy was rekindled in the seventh century when Stephanos of Alexandria dedicated his *Nine Lessons in Chemia* to the Byzantine Emperor Heraclitus, and again in the eleventh century when Psellus revived Platonism. According to Kurt Seligmann (*The History of Magic*, 1948), the writings of Stephanos inspired a number of medieval alchemical poets, and these writers also extolled the virtues of the Hermetic philosophy.[9] Not surprisingly, there are strong philosophical and mystical connections between alchemy, Neoplatonism and the Hermetic tradition.

Like their Neoplatonic and Hermetic counterparts, the medieval alchemists believed in the unity of the cosmos and maintained that there was a clear correspondence between the physical and spiritual realms – with comparable laws operating in each domain. As the sixteenth-century Moravian alchemist Michael Sendivogius writes in *The New Chemical Light*: '…the Sages have been taught of God that this natural world is only an image and material copy of a heavenly and spiritual pattern; that the very existence of this world is based upon the reality of its celestial archetype; and that God has created it in imitation of the spiritual and invisible universe, in order that men might be the better enabled to comprehend His heavenly teaching and the wonders of His absolute and ineffable power and wisdom. Thus the Sage sees heaven reflected in Nature as in a mirror; and he pursues this Art, not for the sake of gold or silver, but for the love of the knowledge which it reveals; he jealously conceals it from the sinner and the scornful, lest the mysteries of heaven should be laid bare to the vulgar gaze.'[10]

The alchemists adopted the Hermetic concept that the universe and humanity reflect each other – and this is the essential meaning behind the idea of the macrocosm and microcosm, and the dictum, 'As above, so below.' It was assumed by the alchemists that whatever existed in the universe must also, to some degree, be latent or present in every human being. A Syriac Hermetic text makes this point very eloquently: 'What is the adage of the philosophers? Know thyself! This refers to the intellectual and cognitive mirror. And what is this mirror if not the Divine and original Intellect? When a man looks at himself and sees himself in this, he turns away from everything that bears the name of gods or demons, and, by uniting himself with the Holy Spirit, becomes a perfect man. He sees God within himself.'[11]

In medieval alchemical thought, each individual consisted of spirit, soul and body, and to this extent contained the very essence of the universe. Alchemy affirmed, as the Hermetic texts had similarly conveyed, that the Universal Mind is indivisible and unites all things in the material universe. The various metals – a specific alchemical concern – were similarly one in essence, and had sprung from the same seed in the womb of Nature. Indeed, as Eric Holmyard points out in *Alchemy* (1957), it was assumed by the medieval European alchemists that because the world was permeated by a universal spirit, this meant that 'every object in the universe possessed some sort of life. Metals grew, as did minerals, and were even attributed sex. A fertilized seed of gold could develop into a nugget, the smoky exhalation was masculine and the vaporous one feminine, and mercury was a womb in which embryonic metals could be gestated.'[12]

The alchemists, however, did not regard all metals as equally mature or 'perfect'. Gold symbolized the highest development in Nature and came to personify

tismam in ablucon pictorn / ut fides et ipsa tes
tant̄ ᶜ Qui habet aures audiendi audi
at / quid dicat spiritus doctrine / filijs disciplme
de spiritu septiformis virtute / quo omnis implet̄ scrip
tura / quod ipsi insinuant hijs verbis / Distilla
septies / et separari ab humid̄ corrumpente /

De domo thauriña quam sapiā fidauit
·C· 10· suñ petram
Sapiencia edificauit sibi domu / qui ꝗs
introierit saluabit̄ / et pascua inueiet
teste ipa In ebriabn ab uber̄. Domus
tue / ꝗ̄ melior e dies una in atrijs eius / sup
milia / O ꝗ̄ beata qui hitant in domo hac / In
ea namꝗ qui petit accipit / et qui queret inue
nit / et pulsanti aperitur / Nam sapia stat ad

ix

Hic iuram patet / ad ipm patet / omnibꝰ hijs figuris

The Arab alchemist Zadith consulting the table of Hermes, from *Aurora Consurgens*, late 14th century.

human renewal and spiritual regeneration. A 'golden' human being was resplendent with spiritual beauty and had triumphed over temptations and the lurking power of evil. The basest metal, lead, represented the sinful and unrepentant individual who was readily overcome by the forces of darkness.

ALCHEMY AND THE ELEMENTS

The four elements – earth, water, fire and air – were first mentioned by the Greek philosopher Empedocles, who lived around 450 BCE, and the concept was further developed by Aristotle (384–22 BCE). According to Aristotle, the basis of the material world was primitive matter which remained in a state of potential existence until it was impressed by what he called 'form'. By 'form' he did not mean shape but, rather, those particular qualities that gave an object its specific properties. Aristotle believed that, in its simplest manifestation, form gave rise to the four elements – fire, air, water and earth – and that these elements could be distinguished by their respective 'qualities'. The four primary qualities were the fluid (or moist), the dry, the hot, and the cold – and each element possessed two of these qualities. Obviously 'hot and cold' and 'fluid and dry' could not be coupled, so the pairs were configured as follows:

hot and dry: **fire**
hot and fluid (or moist): **air**
cold and fluid: **water**
cold and dry: **earth**

In each element one quality would predominate: earth was associated with dryness; water with cold; air with fluidity; fire with heat. According to Aristotle, these elements could also change from one into another, but only *form* could change; prime matter was constant and unchanging. It was this concept that provided the impetus for European alchemy and the quest for the transmutation of metals. For if lead and gold both consisted of fire, air, water and earth, then surely by changing the proportions of the constituent elements, lead could be transformed into gold? Gold was superior to lead because, by its very nature, it contained the perfect balance of all four elements.

The medieval alchemists mirrored Aristotle's theory of form in proposing that all aspects of matter were a reflection of God, and that the four elements – earth, fire, air and water – proceeded from the *quinta essentia*, or 'quintessence', the fifth essence which is the Spirit that fills the universe with life. Sometimes this symbolic division was represented by a cross within a circle, the four quadrants representing the four elements and the central point the *quinta essentia*. On other occasions the

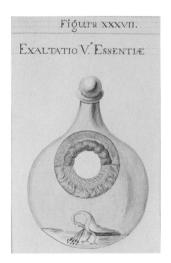

Figura XXXVII.

EXALTATIO V. ESSENTIÆ

Alchemical image depicting the derivation of the Quintessence from the four elements, represented by the ring. From *Sapienta Veterum Philosophorum*, 18th century.

elements were designated by triangles – a triangle pointing upwards representing fire, because fire 'rises' – and a triangle pointing downwards representing water. An upturned triangle with a line through it symbolized air, and its downward-facing counterpart, earth.

The alchemists also associated certain metals with the astrological planets:

Sun – gold
Moon – silver
Mercury – quicksilver
Venus – copper
Mars – iron
Jupiter – tin
Saturn – lead

Gold was known to resist the action of fire, and damage from corrosive liquids (with the exception of *aqua regia*), while lead was readily affected by other chemical agents. Meanwhile the Philosopher's Stone – said to be capable of producing alchemical transmutation – was associated by some Christian alchemists with the figure of Jesus himself. Here alchemical transmutation was considered both as a physical process and a spiritual redemption, the imagery of base and precious metals providing a metaphor for personal transformation.

The Philosopher's Stone was often referred to by alchemists as a powder or wax that could also be rendered in liquid form. Sometimes known as the Elixir, or Tincture, the Philosopher's Stone was credited with prolonging human life indefinitely, and was also said to be able to turn a base metal into gold. In the medieval mind it was assumed that all minerals were alive and grew like plants in the soil. This meant that the technique of transmuting base metals into gold was nothing other than a way of hastening a natural process of development. The key task of the alchemist, then, was to activate a process that would transform a first substance, or *prima materia*, into the Philosopher's Stone. To this extent the alchemist was like an artist who, through his various individual operations, sought to bring Nature to a state of perfection.[13]

The alchemical process consisted of taking the primal material and subjecting it to chemical treatment like heat and distillation, until it finally arrived at a state of balance or perfection. This involved freeing the 'body', 'soul' and 'spirit' of the material – represented in alchemy as salt, mercury and sulphur respectively – and then reconciling these constituents in a new harmony. Alchemists used complex astrological calculations to select propitious times for their work, and would often distil a particular liquid many times. For the medieval alchemists the Philosopher's Stone was an embodiment of perfection and spiritual renewal. In the anonymous

The Mercurial demon – an alchemical illustration from Giovanni Battista Nazari's *Della Transmutatione Metallica*, Brescia, 1589.

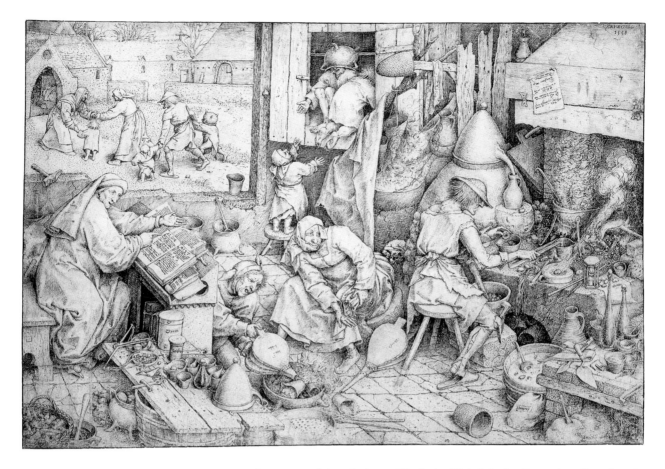

The Alchemist, satirical drawing by Pieter Brueghel the Elder, 1558.

seventeenth-century alchemical text *The Sophic Hydrolith*, the Stone is referred to in these terms: '…the most ancient, secret or unknown, natural incomprehensible, heavenly, blessed sacred Stone of the Sages…the perfect essence of all the elements, the indestructible body which no element can injure, the quintessence; the double and living mercury which has in itself the heavenly spirit – the cure for all unsound and imperfect metals – the everlasting light – the panacea for all diseases – the glorious Phoenix [the mythical bird consumed in the sun's flame but reborn from the ashes] – the most precious of all treasures – the chief good of Nature.' [14]

ALCHEMY AND SPIRITUAL RENEWAL

According to the alchemists, in its original state of pure receptivity, the soul is fundamentally one with the *materia prima* of the whole world. This reflects the Hermetic principle that the macrocosm and microcosm correspond, and enables us to see how alchemy becomes a form of spiritual development. Cherry Gilchrist describes this in *The Elements of Alchemy* (1991): 'The Primal Material that the alchemical seeker takes to work on at the spiritual level is himself. He is made in the image of God and contains the seeds of soul and spirit within him. These are, to some extent, imprisoned in the body; in order to release them that they may

Cerberus was the three-headed dog who prevented the living from entering Hades. In this 15th-century manuscript, he devours the alchemical 'Work' eight times over, symbolizing the many transformations of alchemy.

grow to perfection he must summon up the will and intention to start the work and make the initial effort to dissolve this apparent unity. The body is not rejected as such, but it must be encouraged to loosen its hold upon the inner being so that the process of transformation can begin.'[15]

Clearly, on one level medieval alchemy was a physical attempt to produce gold from base metals, and some practitioners – who can rightly be considered the precursors of scientists – understood it on this level. But for others alchemy was a symbolic expression of the potential for human renewal. Just as the alchemists believed that amorphous *materia* could be burnt, dissolved and purified, and then subsequently 'coagulated' into the form of gold – a literal symbol of wholeness – this process could also be applied to the mystical quest for Oneness with God. As the cultural historian Titus Burckhardt has observed: 'The form of the soul thus "born again" is nevertheless distinguishable from the all-embracing Spirit, as it still belongs to conditioned existence. But at the same time it is transparent to the undifferentiated Light of the Spirit.... We are all like waves within the same sea. The highest meaning of alchemy is the knowledge that all is contained in all.'[16]

Transcending the duality of alchemical opposites – the King and Queen in sacred union. From Arnold of Villanova, *Rosarium Philosophorum*, 16th century.

All is metaphor in alchemy. This detail from a 15th-century manuscript shows Venus, the cold, white, female lunar element – the Rosa Alba produced at the end of the second work – from which flowers its male opposite – hot, solar, red sulphur.

Chapter Six

Astrology and the Tarot

Astrology and the medieval Tarot are perhaps the most important divinatory systems in the development of the Western esoteric tradition. They are much more than simple systems of divination, however – they lead into the very heart of cosmology, drawing on concepts connected to the roles and aspirations of human beings in a metaphysical universe. The enduring appeal of these cosmological systems relates directly to the eternal quest for spiritual insight.

THE BIRTH OF ASTROLOGY

Astrology's root is the Greek *astron*, 'a star' and astrology is among the most ancient of all cultural pursuits. Human beings have always seen significance in the magical lights in the night sky. The stars were often personified as deities, and their ceaseless activities were reflected in the constantly changing nature of the heavens. Whatever happened on Earth was thought to be related to these stellar powers. As ancient astrologers and astronomers in the Middle East, Central America and the Orient acquired more knowledge of the planets, they began to formulate predictions based on their movements. For this reason, astrology has always been closely linked with cyclical doctrines relating to individual destinies and major events.

Astrologers have always distinguished between the fixed stars that follow the apparent movement of the heavens, and mobile stars or planets with their own cyclical movements. But in ancient times, the reasons for these differences were far from clear, and different cultures (among them the Babylonians and ancient Egyptians) developed their own approaches to measuring the portents in the night sky.

The essential premise underlying all ancient astrology was that Heaven and Earth were interconnected. The world was regarded as a living organism, and, as the stars radiated their various energies towards the Earth, they affected every human being. Because different parts of the human organism were believed, in turn, to relate to different stellar dispositions, it seemed evident that the stars were able to exert quite specific influences on individual and collective human destinies.

ASTROLOGY IN MESOPOTAMIA

In the ancient cultures that flourished between the rivers the Tigris and the Euphrates, Babylonia in the south of Mesopotamia and Assyria in the north, the priestly classes included soothsayers who practised divination – interpreting omens and dreams – and who cultivated a knowledge of portents based on astronomical observation. This gradually developed into what we now call astrology.

Tablets depicting astrological motifs and dating from around 700 BCE were unearthed in the ruins of Nineveh in Assyria. Now known as the mul.APIN series – from a term meaning 'Plough Star' – the tablets were part of the library of King Assurbanipal, and are thought to be copies of Babylonian texts dated around 1300 BCE. The tablets list the rising of 18 stars and constellations in the zodiacal belt, within a schematic year of 12 months, and it is thought that this combination of a schematic year, along with the later introduction of the fixed stars Aldebaran and Antares, probably gave rise to the Babylonian zodiac.[1] The mul.APIN tablets show the close link between astronomical observation and the interpretation of omens. One inscription reads: 'Mercury is visible. When Mercury is visible in the month of Kislimu, there are robbers in the land. If a halo encircles the Moon, and Jupiter is found within it, the king of Akkad will be besieged – animals will perish in the countryside.... I have written to the king, my master [that] an eclipse will take place. It has in fact taken place: it is a sign of peace.'[2]

Assyrian astrologers practising their divinatory art during the reigns of Esarhaddon (681–68 BCE) and Assurbanipal (668–26 BCE) established themselves in studios attached to the temple of Ea, the god of oracles and the inventor of writing. Esarhaddon and Assurbanipal, like King Sargon I before them, asked their astrologers to nominate propitious times for beginning such major projects as the construction of sanctuaries for the gods. An inscription on one of the tablets of Assurbanipal reads: 'The month Addaru will have thirty days. During the night of the 13th to 14th, I observed [the sky] carefully. I got up seven times but there was no eclipse. I will send a report to the king.' Unforeseen celestial occurrences were regarded as unfavourable, whereas regular and predictable celestial events were considered favourable for important new undertakings.

The mul.APIN tablets coincide with a period of highly accurate astronomical observation in Babylonia relating to the stars. The Babylonians worked out the duration of day and night, and the rising and setting of the Moon, and with this knowledge finally created a calendar that was sufficiently reliable to predict eclipses. In fact, the basic constituents of the Babylonian calendar are still used today – including the concept of months, weeks, days and hours.

Babylonian tablet, c. 870 BCE, showing Shamash, the sun god, seated beneath a canopy. Above his head are symbols of the Moon, Sun and the goddess Ishtar, representing the star Venus.

Attempts at creating a fixed zodiac were made difficult by the fact that as the Earth rotates the Vernal Point[3] moves backwards through the constellations – a phenomenon known as the Precession of the Equinoxes. While the earliest formulated Babylonian zodiac appears to be a lunar zodiac featuring 18 constellations, the first recorded use in Babylonian astrology of a system of 12 fixed-star zodiacal constellations has been dated to the first half of the fifth century BCE.[4]

EGYPTIAN ASTROLOGY

Ancient Egypt also had an astrological tradition of its own – and this was widely acknowledged during the Graeco-Roman period. The Christian writer Eusebius (260–340 CE) mentions in his book *Evangelical Preparation* that 'it was the Egyptians and the Chaldeans [that is, the Babylonians/Assyrians] who first invented astrology…when the Egyptians picture the world they describe an aerial, burning circle, and place in its middle the image of a serpent in the shape of a sweep-net…. With the circle they designate the world and, with the outstretched serpent, a benevolent spirit.'

When the tomb of Ramses II was excavated, it was found to contain symbols showing the rising and setting of stars, and there is evidence that as early as 1300 BCE the Egyptians recognized the four fixed signs of the zodiac – Aquarius, Leo, Taurus and Scorpio. A tomb of Seti I contained jars protected by four deities – Mestha, associated with Aquarius in the modern zodiac, Hapi with Leo, Tuamutef with Taurus, and Qebhsennuf with Scorpio.[5]

The association of different moments of time with presiding deities seems also to have come from ancient Egypt. An important element is the concept of the decan, a 10° 6.5arc of the zodiac. In the zodiac as we know it today the 12 astrological 'signs' are still divided into 36 equal arcs. Great importance was attached to the influence of these arcs, and Stobaeus, in an essay to his son, writes that the decans '…exert their influence from bodies on high. How could they not act on us as well, on each in particular and all men together? Thus, my child, among all the catastrophes of universal scope due to forces emanating from them, we may cite as examples – mark well my words – the changes of kings, the uprisings of cities, famines, pestilences, flux and reflux of the sea, earthquakes. Nothing of all that, my child, occurs without the influence of decans.'[6]

The modern zodiac is derived from Babylonian, Egyptian and Assyrian astronomy. The Ram, the symbol of Aries, is of Egyptian origin, as is Leo the Lion, whereas Taurus the Bull and Cancer the Crab are Babylonian. The earliest Babylonian zodiac included 10 of the 12 signs in the modern zodiac as well as the Pleiades, Hyades, Orion, Perseus, Auriga, Praesepe and motifs representing southern and northern fish. These are described in the mul.APIN tablets as 'constellations

Detail from the ceiling of the tomb of Seti I, c. 1300 BCE, showing astrological symbols. The Egyptians recognized the four fixed signs of the zodiac: Aquarius, Leo, Taurus and Scorpio.

which stand in the path of the Moon, and into the region of which the moons pass monthly, and which they touch.'[7] During the Roman era, Egyptian astrology was subjected to Graeco-Roman influence, and Egyptian deities were then associated with their Graeco-Roman counterparts. Apis the bull was associated with Taurus, Horus and Harpocrates with Gemini, Isis with Virgo, Nephthys with Pisces, and so on.

GRAECO-ROMAN ASTROLOGY

Graeco-Roman astrology draws substantially on Babylonian thought. Alexander the Great conquered Chaldea during his march to the Indus, and in so doing greatly assisted the path of esoteric knowledge from East to West. Greek astrology, however, pre-dates Alexander. Democritus, around 420 BCE, popularized the idea that the planets influence humanity as they travel through the astrological signs, and from the fifth century BCE to the birth of Christ, astrology maintained strong appeal among a broad cross-section of Greek society. Hippocrates, the famous physician and 'father of medicine', taught astrology to his students so they could distinguish the 'critical days' in an illness.

One of the earliest figures who actively promoted the study of astrology in ancient Greece was a Babylonian priest of Marduk named Berosus, who settled on the Greek island of Cos around 260 BCE and founded a school of astrology. Berosus believed that the god Marduk had created the Sun, Moon, stars and planets, and he became a very influential figure within the prevailing intellectual

ARIES ♈

TAURUS ♉

GEMINI ♊

CANCER ♋

LEO ♌

VIRGO ♍

LIBRA ♎

SCORPIO ♏

SAGITTARIUS ♐

CAPRICORN ♑

AQUARIUS ♒

PISCES ♓

Astrological signs of
the zodiac.

Augustus was the first
Roman emperor to issue
coins showing his birth sign
(Capricornus), *c.* 20 BCE.

Jupiter, the Roman
counterpart of Zeus,
(opposite) seated in the centre
of the zodiac. Villa Albani,
Rome, 2nd century CE.

culture of the times. Berosus used as his textbook a treatise titled *The Eye of Bel*, which existed in tablet form in the library of Assurbanipal, and he believed that the world was governed, during the ages, by a series of what he called the 'Great Years'. By this he meant that the unfolding of human history would be characterized by its 'seasons'. For example, when all the planets were 'united' in the sign of Capricorn, the Earth would experience a Deluge, whereas under Cancer it would experience a conflagration. Each of these cycles were approximately 432,000 years in duration. The duration of the 'Great Year' was traditionally fixed at 25,920 years. Berosus clearly believed that astrology revealed a universal pattern of cosmic cycles.

As early as the fourth century BCE the Greeks had begun to associate the principal gods and goddesses in their pantheon with the planets, naming them after deities like Cronos, Zeus, Ares, Aphrodite and Hermes, and ascribing to them characteristics and attributes. Later the Romans would impose their own pantheon, naming the same planets Saturn, Jupiter, Mars, Venus and Mercury respectively. The constellations of the Graeco-Roman zodiac are mentioned by Aratus of Soli in his poem *Diosemeia*, written around 270 BCE, and they are the same as those in the modern zodiac.[8]

Greek astrologers also made quite specific connections between the stars and earthly functions. For example, they placed the constellation of the Serpent (near the North Star) in correspondence with medical cures – because the serpent was sacred to Asclepius, the patron of medicine, who was worshipped at Epidaurus. According to Serge Hutin in *Astrology* (1972), it is due to the dominion achieved by the Romans over the whole of the Mediterranean basin that Greek astrology was to acquire the influence maintained in the West right to the present day.[9]

There were also influential Roman thinkers, however, who were hostile to astrology. Lucretius denounced it in *De Natura Rerum* (first century BCE), advocating free-will rather than fatalism, while Cicero spoke out against horoscopes in *De Divinatione* (45 BCE). The poet Juvenal was critical not only of naive believers swarming to soothsayers, but also of Greek magic and Egyptian superstitions in general (*Satire XV, c.* 125 BCE). Nevertheless, no lesser figure than Julius Caesar believed strongly in the value of astrological predictions, and the emperors Augustus, Tiberius and Nero all had their own personal astrologers. Augustus even published his own horoscope and ordered a silver coin to be struck, bearing his birth sign – Capricornus.

The most famous astrological treatise composed during the Roman era is a four-volume work known as the *Tetrabiblos*, written by the Greek Claudius Ptolemaeus (Ptolemy) in 140 CE. Ptolemy was born in the Nile Delta and taught in Alexandria. Renowned as a mathematician, geographer and astronomer, he is

perhaps best known for his *Geographia*, which remained a standard text until the Renaissance, and *Almagest*, which presented a system of astronomy influential until the time of Copernicus. However the *Tetrabiblos* (sometimes known by its Latin title, *Quadripartium*) was also highly influential, and would enjoy a popularity among astrologers for a thousand years or more.

In the *Tetrabiblos* Ptolemy summarized the workings of the Sun, Moon and planets and also the fixed stars, describing how astrology could be used to delineate the destinies of individuals as well as cities and countries. The idea of charting a horoscope for the exact moment of conception, and also for calculating the influence of good or bad 'aspects', as well as astrological 'transits' and 'directions', all have their origins in Ptolemy's systematic approach to astrology. Ptolemy says in his book that the 'fixed' signs (Taurus, Leo, Scorpio and Aquarius), if prominent in the horoscope, 'make the mind just, uncompromising, constant, firm of purpose, prudent, patient, industrious [and] strict,' while those strongly aspected by 'mutable' signs (Gemini, Virgo, Sagittarius and Pisces) have minds that are 'variable, versatile, not easily understood, volatile and unsteady [and] inclined to duplicity'. Ptolemy also recognized the issues raised by the Precession of the Equinoxes, arguing that it is the 30° section of the ecliptic within which planets may be placed that is important, not the specific location of a constellation in the heavens at any given time.

Ptolemy's system was based on seven planets, including the Sun and Moon. The sequence of planets in descending order from the sphere of the fixed stars was as follows: Saturn, Jupiter, Mars, Sun, Venus, Mercury, Moon. Earth was at the centre of the concentric spheres, encased within a series of elemental spheres with Fire on the outer, followed by Air, Water, and then Earth itself. In later models of the Ptolemaic system the positions of Venus and Mercury were transposed. Ptolemy's model was used in medieval astrology until it was gradually deposed by the more accurate heliocentric system proposed by Copernicus, in his treatise published in 1543.[10]

Zodiac from a Byzantine manuscript of Ptolemy's *Tetrabiblos*, 820 CE. Although Earth should take pride of place in the zodiac, the sun god is shown riding his chariot in the centre.

Although Christianity has never been willing to embrace astrology – suspecting its pagan origins and a cosmological dynamic in competition with the will of God – the same cannot be said of Islam. While it is true that the Qur'an speaks out against cults of the sun and moon and links them to idolatry, Arab astrologers derived much of their thinking from the Sabaeans of Yemen who venerated the fixed stars and planets, and also worshipped a plurality of gods and spirits transposed into their culture from Graeco-Roman counterparts. The Islamic sense of spiritual destiny was clearly compatible with the planetary determinism of astrology, and most Muslims saw nothing intrinsically wrong with astrology from a religious point of view. The Qur'an proclaims: 'He it is Who hath set for you the stars that ye may guide your course by them amid the darkness of the land and sea.'

Islamic astronomy and astrology derive primarily from Greek, Indian and Persian sources, and were strongly influenced by the regions under Muslim rule. At the height of Saracen power these included the Middle and Near East, substantial parts of northern Africa, parts of western India, as well as Spain, Sicily and the south of France.

The earliest Arab astrologers claimed a lineage dating back beyond Muhammad to Hermes.[11] Under the Caliphs, the city of Baghdad – itself built on a site close to ancient Babylon – saw a blossoming of interest in astrology. Haroun al-Raschid, a contemporary of Charlemagne,

An Islamic depiction of astrological relationships. Here the Moon and Jupiter meet in Sagittarius. Manuscript of the work of ninth-century astrologer Abu Mash'ar ar Balkhi, Cairo, c. 1259 CE.

became known as a protector of astrology, and built an observatory in Baghdad which was used by astronomers and astrologers alike – for they were considered one and the same. One of the most famous Islamic astrologers from this period – Albumasar, also known as Abu Mash'ar ar Balkhi (d. 886 CE) – produced a book entitled *The Flowers of Astrology* which was translated into Latin and was among the first books published in Germany by Gutenberg.

Arab astrologers wishing to improve on the calculations of Ptolemy drew heart from the Qur'an which urged Muslims to achieve maximum precision in their knowledge of solar and lunar cycles. The famous doctor Rhazes (al-Razi, *c.* 864–925 CE) produced treatises on alchemy and astrology, and also wrote an extended commentary on Ptolemy's *Tetrabiblos*. Other notable Islamic astrologers included Abu Ali Mohammed ibn al-Hasan ibn al-Haythan (d. 1038), who had such a vast knowledge of astrology and astronomy that he was dubbed 'the second Ptolemy', and Ibn Abu Ridschal, who developed his career as an astrologer at the palace of the Sultan al-Mamur (1016–62) and wrote an eight-volume work entitled the *Judgments of the Spheres*.

As with the Greeks and Romans, however, there were leading Islamic thinkers who were opposed to astrology. The influential doctor, alchemist and philosopher Ibn-Sina, known in the West as Avicenna (980–1037 CE), rejected the idea of astrological determinism, and the famous Spanish-born Muslim doctor Ibn-Rushd, better known as Averroës (1126–98 CE), attacked the practice of drawing up horoscopes. Nevertheless, the Islamic fascination with astrology proved remarkably resilient, and a knowledge of ancient forms of astrology gradually began to penetrate into the West through Latin translations of Arab authors. It was via this route that a considerable amount of Greek astrological and metaphysical knowledge was preserved in the Byzantine Empire. In some instances, personal connections also proved crucial. For example, the Byzantine scholar and philosopher Gemistos Pletho – who visited Italy in 1438 – became a bridge between medieval Byzantine Hellenism and the beginning of the Italian Renaissance. Pletho was well versed in astrology, and was also a strong advocate of Platonic thought and the study of Greek philosophical texts. He attributed souls to the stars and proposed a worldview based on universal harmony in which physical matter and cosmic intelligence were interconnected.[12] Pletho attracted the attention of Cosimo de' Medici, and subsequently became a friend of the influential Hermeticist, Marsilio Ficino. As a result of his connection with Pletho, Ficino began to translate Platonic and Neoplatonic texts into Latin, enabling mystical philosophers like Plotinus, Porphyry and Iamblichus to become much better known. It soon became evident that Greek metaphysical thought would find a new home in the intellectual and cultural centres of Renaissance Europe.

ASTROLOGY IN THE RENAISSANCE

Although the Renaissance was a time of great scientific and technical discoveries, these did not come at the expense of astrology. In fact, interest in it grew considerably during the fifteenth and sixteenth centuries. The methods used were similar to those of the Arab, Greek and Roman astrologers, and birth horoscopes were of central interest. We are accustomed in modern times to circular horoscopes – a form introduced in the late nineteenth century by the astrologer-scientist Choisnard – but Renaissance horoscopes were in the form of a square within a square, creating internal triangles for the allocations of the twelve signs of the zodiac. These triangles were filled with the planets and constellations in the sky at the time of the birth.

Even though astrology drew on the geocentric model of Ptolemy, the discovery that the earth and the other planets revolve around the sun did not lead to a collapse in the belief of astrological determinism. Even Copernicus himself did not deny his belief in planetary influences. And as the distinguished scholar Frances Yates points out in her influential book *Giordano Bruno and the Hermetic Tradition* (1964), Giordano Bruno also included astrological determinism within his philosophical speculations on the universe, exalting the unity of the sky and the movement of the stars '...which sing the excellence and glory of God.'

The great astronomer Tycho Brahe (1546–1601) was a dedicated astrologer as well. While employed as a mathematics lecturer at the University of Copenhagen, he drew up astrological birth charts for members of the Danish royal family, making his own astronomical observations in order to construct them. He was also fascinated by the prospect of foreseeing major cataclysms, and was especially drawn to the study of conjunctions of Jupiter and Saturn. Although their conjunction in Scorpio in 1488 had not led to disaster, Brahe was intrigued to discover that a conjunction in Leo (near the star nebuli of Cancer) coincided with an epidemic of the plague.

The German astronomer Johannes Kepler kept his own 'horoscope book'. After taking up a position as a teacher of mathematics in Graz in 1594, he produced four annual astrological almanacs to help supplement his salary. In the introduction to his work *Tertius Interveniens,* Kepler makes the point that, while one should always seek to discard superstition, there is much to be gained from understanding valid astrological principles: '...nothing exists nor happens in the visible sky that is not sensed in some hidden manner by the faculties of Earth and Nature, [so that] these faculties of the spirit here on earth are as much affected as the sky itself...the sky...does not endow a man with his habits, history, happiness, children, riches or a wife, but it moulds his condition.'[13]

For Brahe and Kepler the appeal of astrology lay in the fact that it seemed to provide insights into the dynamics of the natural world, and it would appear that Martin Luther also subscribed to this view. In a preface to an astrological work by Johannes Lichtenberger, Luther wrote: 'The signs in the sky and on the earth should not be overlooked since they are the work of God and the angels; they arrive as a warning to impious countries and all have justification.'[14]

The Roman Catholic orthodoxy, however, remained strongly opposed to all forms of divination, as the Papal Bulls of 1586, *Constitutio Coeli et Terra* and *Constitutio Inscrutabilis,* make clear. Nevertheless, contradictions continued to flourish. When the Florentine astrologer Cosme Ruggieri was taken before the Roman

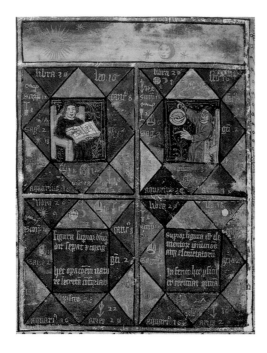

Inquisition, he was released after his brilliant explanation that the practice of astrology was based on natural laws and had nothing to do with magic or the evocation of spirits. The crucial point in his defence was to distinguish astrology from the occult and magical arts with which it was so frequently associated.

Ruggieri was fortunate because it is undoubtedly true that he was one of a small group of astrologers favoured by the Queen of France who was deeply fascinated by the occult sciences. Cathérine des Médicis, the Florentine wife of Henry II of France, became Regent of France following his death in 1559. She introduced astrology to the Valois court and surrounded herself with magicians and astrologers, including Michel de Nostredame (later known as Nostradamus, and appointed a royal councillor and the King's physician), Luc Gauric and Ruggieri himself. In Paris Ruggieri lived in the Hôtel de Soissons, owned by Cathérine des Médicis. The observatory tower erected behind the Halle aux Blés is all that now remains. It was from this observatory that Cathérine was said to observe the portents of the heavens with Nostradamus and later Ruggieri.

Michel de Nostredame
(Nostradamus) performs a
magical ritual for the Queen of
France, Cathérine des Médicis.
French School, pen and ink
and wash on paper, 1559.

As above, so below –
Zodiacal Man (opposite) as
the microcosmic reflection of
the heavens. From *Les Très Riches
Heures du Duc de Berry*, French,
early 15th century.

We know from court records that in 1392 King Charles VI of France made a payment to a painter named Jacquemin Gringonneur for three packs of cards described as 'gilded and coloured, and ornamented with various devices, supplied to the King for his amusement'.[15] It is not clear, however, whether these were early Tarot cards or simply playing cards. The Bibliothèque Nationale in Paris has in its collection seventeen cards, sixteen of them identifiable as Tarot cards. Originally thought to have been those created for Charles VI by Gringonneur, they are now acknowledged as Venetian in origin, and date from *c.* 1470. The Gringonneur cards themselves have not been found, and it is possible that Tarot cards did not exist as early as 1392.[16]

Tarot cards, some scholars believe, were invented between 1410 and 1425 in northern Italy, and most of the decks that survive from fifteenth-century Italy reflect the fashion of the nobility of Milan and Ferrara of that period.[17] But the earliest specific references to Tarot cards were in 1442 and come from the d'Este court of Ferrara. Interest in the Tarot spread from Italy to France and Switzerland.

The modern Tarot deck is descended from the Piedmontese Tarot and the Tarot of Marseilles, both of which were widely known in northern Italy and France by the beginning of the sixteenth century. These packs consisted of 78 cards divided into 22 cards of the Major Arcana and 56 cards of the Minor Arcana. The Minor Arcana consists of four basic suits – swords, wands, cups and pentacles – and parallel the four suits in the modern card deck.

Irrespective of their historical origin, there can be little doubt that the Tarot cards conceal a hidden symbolic language and are based on authentic esoteric themes. This, however, has also led to many fanciful explanations of the Tarot's actual origins and purpose. Even today, many enthusiasts continue to claim that the Tarot cards originated in ancient Egypt and belong to a mystical wisdom tradition dating back thousands of years. This was first proposed by French theologian Antoine Court de Gebelin, author of one of the earliest works on the Tarot, *Le Monde Primitif* (nine volumes), published in Paris between 1775 and 1784. De Gebelin claimed that the Major Arcana of the Tarot came from an ancient Egyptian book, *The Book of Thoth*, which had been saved from the ruins of burning Egyptian temples, and that the symbolic wisdom of the Tarot had subsequently been introduced to Europe by wandering gypsies, themselves of Egyptian origin.[18] De Gebelin also believed that the word 'Tarot' meant 'Royal Way' and was derived from *tar* (road) and *ro* (king, or royal).[19] One of de Gebelin's followers, a wig-maker named Alliette, reversed his name to Etteilla and published a book on the Tarot in 1783 in which he claimed that the Tarot had been created by 17 Magi, 171 years

A woodcut showing cards being used for gambling. A suit corresponding to hearts is visible on the table. German, *c.* 1470.

after the Deluge. He further claimed that one of these Magi – Athotis – was descended from Mercury and Noah. Alliette went on to create a deck of cards accompanied by a book titled *Manière de tirer: Le Grand Etteilla où tarots Egyptiens.*

De Gebelin and Etteilla are not alone in emphasizing an Egyptian connection for the Tarot. The famous ceremonial magician Aleister Crowley, who created a visionary Tarot deck in the 1940s with Lady Frieda Harris, continued the tradition by naming his deck *The Book of Thoth*, and as recently as 1989 an Egyptian Tarot deck purporting to emanate from the 'Inner Temple of Isis' was published in the United States.[20]

That the Tarot has become central to the Western magical tradition is due largely to the influence of the nineteenth-century French occultist Eliphas Lévi (1810–75). It was he who first suggested combining the Major Arcana of the Tarot with the Kabbalistic symbol of the Tree of Life. Lévi believed that the Tarot cards incorporated a sacred occult alphabet – an alphabet attributed by the Jews to Enoch, by the ancient Egyptians to Hermes Trismegistus, and by the Greeks to Cadmus, who founded the city of Thebes. Lévi linked the 22 paths that connect the 10 spheres of the Kabbalistic Tree of Life with the 22 letters of the Hebrew alphabet and in turn with the 22 cards of the Major Arcana. In his book *Dogme et Rituel de la Haute Magie* – published in English as *Transcendental Magic* – Lévi provides details of the 'source' of the esoteric Tarot, while also acknowledging the contribution of De Gebelin and Etteilla: 'When the Sovereign Priesthood ceased in Israel, when all the oracles of the world became silent in presence of the Word which became Man, and speaking by the mouth of the most popular and gentle of sages, when the Ark was lost, the sanctuary profaned, and the Temple destroyed, the mysteries of the Ephod and Theraphim, no longer recorded on gold and precious stones, were written or rather figured by certain wise kabbalists first on ivory,

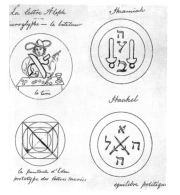

By the end of the 15th century, the Tarot of Marseilles deck (a selection shown here) had become very popular in France. These cards were made by B. P. Grimaud and are still a popular Tarot deck.

parchment, on gilt and silvered leather, and afterwards on simple cards, which were always objects of suspicion to the Official Church as containing a dangerous key to its mysteries. From these have originated those tarots whose antiquity was revealed to the learned Court de Gebelin through the sciences of hieroglyphics and of numbers, and which afterwards severely exercised the doubtful perspicacity and tenacious investigations of Etteilla.'[21]

Lévi's concept of merging the Kabbalistic Tree of Life with the Major Arcana of the Tarot was developed by the French physician Gérard Encausse (1865–1916). In 1889 under the name of Papus he published an influential work entitled *The Tarot of the Bohemians* which was illustrated with images from the Tarot of Marseilles. These images were modified to incorporate letters of the Hebrew alphabet, reinforcing the idea that the Tarot and the Jewish mystical tradition were symbolically interconnected. The idea of mapping the Major of Arcana of the Tarot as a network of symbolic pathways upon the Tree of Life was then taken up by the ceremonial magicians of the Hermetic Order of the Golden Dawn, whose philosophy and practices are described in Chapter 8. Chief among them was Arthur Edward Waite who, with Pamela Colman Smith, created the famous Rider-Waite Tarot deck, which remains one of the most popular Tarot decks today.

The Devil from
the Rider-Waite deck
created by A. E. Waite and
Pamela Colman Smith in
the early 20th century.

MAGICAL APPLICATIONS OF THE TAROT

When the 22 Tarot cards of the Major Arcana are mapped as mythic pathways linking the 10 different spheres of the Kabbalistic Tree of Life — in a sequence from the lowest sphere through to the highest — they follow a specific configuration:

Tarot Paths on the Tree of Life

The World	Malkuth-Yesod
Judgement	Malkuth-Hod
The Moon	Malkuth-Netzach
The Sun	Yesod-Hod
The Star	Yesod-Netzach
The Tower	Hod-Netzach
The Devil	Hod-Tiphareth
Death	Netzach-Tiphareth
Temperance	Yesod-Tiphareth
The Hermit	Tiphareth-Chesed
Justice	Tiphareth-Geburah
The Hanged Man	Hod-Geburah
The Wheel of Fortune	Netzach-Chesed
Strength	Geburah-Chesed
The Chariot	Geburah-Binah
The Lovers	Tiphareth-Binah
The Hierophant	Chesed-Chokmah
The Emperor	Tiphareth-Chokmah
The Empress	Binah-Chokmah
The High Priestess	Tiphareth-Kether
The Magus	Binah-Kether
The Fool	Chokmah-Kether

The Major Arcana of the Tarot have magical significance because they represent a series of sacred archetypal images. Some of these 'mythic' cards are specifically male, and include the Magus, the Emperor, the Charioteer and the High Priest. Others are specifically female, and include the High Priestess, the Empress, Justice and the Moon. There are also cards that are symbolically 'neutral' — that is to say, neither male nor female — like Death and the Wheel of Fortune.

According to magical practitioners who follow the Levi-Papus-Waite alignment of the Tarot with the Tree of Life, the cards of the Major Arcana represent symbolic paths leading to a mysterious transcendent reality — a spiritual journey through the maze-way of the soul. The following summary of the 22 cards of the Major Arcana extends from the lowest sphere of the Tree of Life through to the highest. It provides an overview of the essentially mythic nature of the Major Arcana as used by modern magical practitioners, and extends the associated imagery of the Tarot well beyond its medieval Italian origins.

The World represents the 'descent' into the 'underworld' of the magical mind, represented by the descent of Persephone into the land of the dead, but here death is regarded as the other side of life. Persephone symbolizes the wheat grain, which grows, matures and then dies in an eternal cycle, yielding potentially unending harvests. She has special significance because she takes her place both among the living and the dead.

Judgment is also associated with the theme of rebirth. Human figures rise in triumph from the 'grave' of ignorance, gesturing with their arms to form the word LVX — 'light'.

The Moon mirrors the symbolism of the 'lunar' sphere, Yesod on the Tree of Life. Two dogs bark at the sky, one domesticated and the other untamed. The dog is sacred to the lunar goddess Hecate, who is also associated with Persephone in her deathlike aspect. This card depicts the ebb and flow of the tides and is symbolic of spiritual evolution — a lobster emerges from the sea to reinforce this effect.

The Sun reflects the light of Tiphareth located at the heart of the Tree of Life. Naked twins dance in a magical ring beneath the Sun. They represent innocence, and also, as a boy and a girl, the synthesis of opposites — a common theme in the Tarot. They are ruled by the Sun, representing unity, vitality and the path of enlightenment, but here they are separated from the cosmic mountain by a wall. In an occult sense, the children are still inexperienced in their mystical quest, and barriers still exist.

The Star is associated with intuition, meditation and the hidden qualities of Nature, represented by Netzach. The beautiful naked White Isis — a lunar deity — kneels by a pool pouring water from flasks held in each hand. One flask is made of gold (the Sun) and the other of silver (the Moon). From a golden star in the sky, the goddess transmits precious life-energy to the world below.

The Tower reaches to the highest sphere of Kether — symbolically it embraces the entire mystical universe. Lightning strikes the upper turrets, causing

Knight of Swords

0

The Fool

XVI

The Tower

Three cards from the Thoth deck created by Aleister Crowley and Lady Frieda Harris in the 1940s.

them to crumble, and figures are shown falling to their death. This is a reminder that humility is required on the inner journey, and that the influx of divine energy from the higher realms of the Tree will devastate unless the 'magical personality' is well balanced and has a solid foundation. The Tower is ruled by Mars, who ruthlessly destroys ignorance and vain conceptions.

The Devil depicts a 'demonic' man and woman bound by chains to a pedestal upon which sits a gloating, torch-bearing Devil. Capricorn the Goat here represents darkness and bestiality. Upon his brow is an inverted pentagram indicating that his spiritual aspirations are directed more towards earth than towards the higher consciousness, and reflects the plight of all unenlightened human beings. Nevertheless, the light of Tiphareth lies beyond.

Death indicates humanity's shortcomings, and the limited nature of the ego-bound personality. But death is also the herald of new life, and new light appears on the horizon. The scythe is associated with Kronos – the ancient Greek creator-god who transcended time – and on the Tree of Life the path of Death leads into Tiphareth, the sphere of spiritual rebirth.

Temperance represents the line of direct mystical ascent to a state of spiritual illumination. The archangel of Fire, Michael, stands astride a river of light, pouring the waters of Life from a Sun-vessel into a Moon-vessel. This constitutes a tempering, or union of opposites. Michael has one foot on earth and the other in water, and he is also shown reconciling a white eagle (representing the Moon) and a red lion (representing the Sun). Above him arches a rainbow symbolizing God's covenant with humanity, and new light dawns over a distant mountain.

The Hermit connects Tiphareth and Chesed, and is ruled by Mercury who in turn connects with Chokmah and Thoth – the 'Great Father' archetypes of the Kabbalah and the Egyptian mysteries. The Hermit climbs up the magic mountain, but his final goal is firmly in his mind, and the lamp he holds illumines his pathway.

Justice would be considered a path of *karma* in Eastern mysticism, where the individual encounters the consequences of his or her actions. It demands balance, adjustment and total impartiality. Ruled by Venus, holding scales and the sword of justice, this path leads to the sphere of her lover Mars. On this path the magician begins to discover the nature of the true inner self by overcoming the illusory aspects of outer appearances.

The Hanged Man like Justice leads to Geburah, the sphere of action. The Hanged Man swings by his foot, symbolizing sacrifice, but also looks like a reflection in water, the element ascribed to this path. The head of the Hanged Man is shining like a beacon, and seems to be reflecting inspirational light through to lower levels of the Tree of Life. The waters themselves flow from Binah, the Great Mother, who personifies the 'Ocean of Being'.

The Wheel of Fortune symbolizes the forces of fate and destiny. In Kabbalistic magic, words composed of similar letters are said to have related symbolic meanings, and TARO or ROTA – the word inscribed upon the Wheel of Fortune – reads ATOR in reverse. According to one interpretation, this is a variant spelling of the White Goddess, Hathor, showing her influence on this path. The path itself leads to Chesed and therefore comes under the jurisdiction of Jupiter. Chesed lies in the region of pure archetypes – a realm of sacred being just below the Trinity on the Tree of Life.

Strength is positioned horizontally across the Tree of Life and occupies a position equivalent to but higher than The Tower, which separates the ego-based personality from the true spiritual self. Strength represents the gulf between individuality and universality. A woman prises open the jaws of a lion – the triumph of spiritual intuition over brute strength and symbolizing mastery over any vestiges of the 'animal soul'.

The Chariot represents motion and provides a possible symbolic connection with the *Merkabah* (chariot) tradition in Kabbalistic mysticism which focused on the visionary journey of the soul from one heavenly palace to another. Here the chariot carries the king to the furthest reaches of his realm, while on the opposite side of the Tree, in Chesed, the ruler of the universe views his kingdom from the stationary vantage point of his heavenly throne. On this path the king is a mediator, indicated by the central symbolism of the card, which shows the king bearing the sacred vessel of the Holy Grail.

The Lovers depicts the Twins naked in the innocence of Eden regained, the Holy Guardian Angel above them, bestowing grace. In Greek mythology Zeus allowed the half-brothers Castor and Polydeuces (Pollux), one mortal and the other immortal, a common destiny, placing them in the sky as the constellation Gemini. The path of The Lovers flows upwards from Tiphareth (Harmony) and shows the happy and enduring union of opposites.

The Hierophant refers to the merciful qualities of the Great Father (Chokmah-Chesed) enhanced by the love and grace of Venus, who rules this card which embodies the enduring bond of wisdom and mercy. The inspiration of the Spirit – which emanates from the highest spheres of the Tree of Life – is manifest in this card as an archetypal expression of enlightened intuition. Divine authority owes its inspirational origin to this realm of the Tree.

The Emperor faces towards Chokmah, the 'unmanifested' Great Father of the Trinity, and draws upon his spiritual energy for his authority in 'governing' the universe of Creation below. The Emperor embodies the qualities of divine mercy, for, although he is capable of aggression in his Geburah aspect, he extends compassion to all his subjects. The universe itself has come into being through his union with the Empress.

The Empress is warm and beneficent and with child. She is symbolically the Mother of All, since from her womb will flow all the potential forms in the entire cosmos. Mythologically she is Hathor and Demeter, and epitomizes Love and Nature on a universal scale. She sits in a field of wheat among luxuriant trees – with the River of Life flowing from her domain. She is the feminine embodiment of the sacred life-energy that emanates from the highest spheres of the Tree of Life. On this path the magician enters the realm of pure illumination.

The High Priestess is virginal. She has not given birth, that is, made essence into form. She therefore belongs in the highest spheres of the Tree of Life. Those who follow her path undergo a dramatic transformation, for they rise above form itself, returning to a pure and undifferentiated state. This path reaches to the peak of Creation – the first sephirah: Kether, The Crown.

The Magus is linked to Mercury – the cosmic intelligence. This path reflects a masculine purity which equates with the virginity of the High Priestess. The Magus stands above Creation in an archetypal sense. He raises a hand to Kether so that he may draw its energy down, and transmit it to the lower reaches of the Tree of Life.

The Fool is a symbol for 'he who knows nothing', and this can be interpreted esoterically. On this path the magician draws near to the veil of non-existence – No-Thing – that which is unmanifest, or beyond the tangibility of Creation. This is a realm of true Mystery, and of this dimension nothing can meaningfully be said, or attributes ascribed. On the card The Fool is about to plunge into the Abyss of formlessness – embracing the infinite and sacred transcendence of *Ain Soph Aur*, the Limitless Light.

Chapter Seven
Freemasons and Rosicrucians

Allied to the alchemists and hermeticists are two other mystical fraternities – the Rosicrucians and Freemasons. While both have continued to the present day in various permutations – in some instances more as social organizations than as advocates of a mystical tradition – Freemasonry and Rosicrucianism have nevertheless contributed strongly to modern magical consciousness. Both build on mystical metaphors and themes of spiritual transformation that continue to underpin contemporary occult perspectives.

SYMBOLIC ASPECTS OF FREEMASONRY

Modern Freemasonry has eighteenth-century origins. The Masonic Grand Lodge of England was established in London in 1717 when members of four London Lodges met in a tavern in Covent Garden and constituted themselves 'A Grand Lodge pro Tempore [for the time being] in Due Form and...resolved to hold the Annual Assembly and Feast, and then to choose a Grand Master from among themselves, till they should have the Honour of a Noble Brother at their Head.' All forms of Freemasonry today can be traced to this meeting, and since 1721, when the Duke of Montague was appointed to the position, the so-called Grand Master has been a person of noble or royal birth. The present incumbent is the Duke of Kent.

Freemasonry as a tradition, however, extends back much further than the eighteenth century, and derives from the practices of the highly skilled European stonemasons who built magnificent cathedrals and worked on other large-scale constructions during the Middle Ages. These masons formed lodges and recognized 'degrees' in order to maintain their professional skills and standards. An itinerant builder, for example, would be required to answer veiled questions and respond to special signs and passwords in order to establish his credentials as a Master Mason. In due course an elaborate system of masonic rituals developed, sheathed in secrecy and maintained by oaths of fidelity and fraternity.

Despite its secret rituals, it is important to emphasize that Freemasonry is not itself a religion so much as a symbolic response to the Universe. Joseph Fort Newton, a leading authority on Freemasonry, has stressed that it has its spiritual

Building the Tower of Babel – a miniature from a late 15th-century Flemish *Book of Hours*. The mason's 'lodge' – originally a shelter for the stone-cutters – is visible on the left.

omine labia mea a
prics. Et os meu anu

roots in a mystical appreciation of architecture, and that architecture in turn encompasses both physical necessity and spiritual aspiration: 'Of course, the first great impulse of all architecture was need, honest response to the demand for shelter; but this demand included a Home for the Soul, not less than a roof over the head…. The story of the Tower of Babel is more than a myth. Man has ever been trying to build to heaven, embodying his prayer and his dream in brick and stone. Freemasonry is built on the idea of uniting material and spiritual realities.'[1]

Indeed, in terms of spiritual origins, there are resonances of the philosophy of Freemasonry even in the Bible. For example, in Hebrews iii, 4 we read, 'For every house is builded by some man; but the builder of all things is God…whose house we are.' I Peter ii, 5 expresses a similar idea: 'Ye also, as living stones, are built into a spiritual house,' and similarly, in 2 Corinthians v, 1 it is written: 'For we know that when our earthly house of this tabernacle is dissolved, we have a building of God, an house not made with hands, eternal in the heavens.'

According to some sources the medieval stonemasons derived their secret signs and passwords from the builders of the Temple of Solomon. Traditionally Masonic lodges include figures representing the steps that led to Solomon's Temple as well as symbolic motifs derived from ancient Egypt. All lodges have a vaulted ceiling, painted blue and covered with golden stars to represent the heavens. The floor is mosaic, its variegated colours representing the earth covered with flowers after the withdrawal of the waters of the Nile. In the modern lodge two bronze pillars are located in the west, inscribed J and B (representing Jachin and Boaz and, symbolically , the summer and winter solstices), and there are ten other pillars connected to them by an architrave. Masonic initiatory ritual also focuses on the figure of Hiram Abiff, the architect slain during the building of the Temple of Solomon.

THE LEGEND OF HIRAM ABIFF

When Solomon decided to build the Temple in Jerusalem, the king of Tyre sent cedar trees cut from the forests of Lebanon in exchange for corn, wine and oil. He also offered the services of a skilled artisan – Hiram Abiff (*Abiff* is father in Hebrew) – as superintending architect, and also to make the two bronze pillars Jachin and Boaz and metal ornaments.

According to Masonic tradition, 85,000 workmen were employed in building the Temple, which took seven years. Those who laboured diligently were promised the status of Master Mason on completion. Some workers, however, demanded the higher status before completion, and higher wages. When Hiram Abiff refused, three of them killed him in the unfinished Temple, and buried his body on

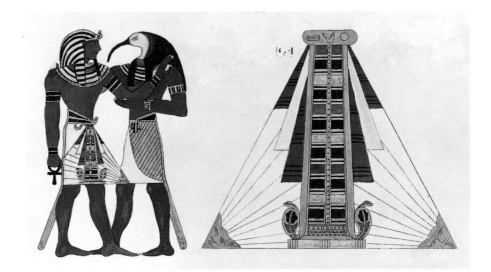

a solitary hill, planting a sprig of acacia over the grave. King Solomon sent out a search party for him, and the body was discovered after fourteen days. In due course the heads of the three murderers were presented to the king.

Hiram Abiff came to embody all the human values that Masons should strive to attain, especially virtue and integrity. For some Masons he is also a counterpart of Osiris – the Egyptian deity who was slain by Set and restored to life by Isis. In a Masonic context he is therefore symbolic of death and spiritual rebirth.[2]

MASONRY AND THE 'ARCHITECT OF THE UNIVERSE'

Despite its symbolic references to the Temple of Solomon and the mythology of ancient Egypt, Freemasonry does not limit its conception of the Divine. Adherents are now asked simply to confess their faith in 'God the Father Almighty, the Architect and Master-builder of the Universe.' Indeed one could readily discern in Freemasonry a pantheistic element, for according to the masonic perspective, 'behind the pageant of Nature, in it and over it, there is a Supreme Mind which initiates, impels and controls all…. In short the first and last thing in the universe is mind, the highest and deepest thing is conscience, and the final reality is the absoluteness of love.'[3]

Although Freemasonry has itself been a secret organization, it has championed the freedom of body, mind and spirit – a sentiment it shares with certain forms of Gnosticism. Here the human soul is seen as 'akin to God' – the edifice on which all of Creation is built. Modern Freemasonry seeks to combine science, logic and faith so that these elements become the basis for living spiritually in the world. Freemasonry is strongly opposed to sectarian differences, and acknowledges that love should provide the basis for tolerance. This acknowledgment of spiritual

God the Divine Architect and Master Builder holding dividers. French miniature, 15th century.

These masonic training boards of 1819 show the First, Second and Third Degrees. The first shows the individual in the metaphysical scheme, and the second the spiral stair to the Temple. Symbolic death on the third allows the individual to transcend human limitations.

Painting of a meeting of a Masonic lodge in Vienna, *c.* 1780. The Master of Ceremonies (centre) is Prince Nicolaus Esterházy and the figure seated on the far right is believed to be Mozart.

diversity has made it a traditional enemy of the Roman Catholic Church in some countries – it is still banned in Spain and Portugal, though not in Italy – but for Newton the essence of Masonry is friendship combined with an attitude of tolerance and understanding. The so-called 'great secret' of Freemasonry is that 'it makes a man aware of that divinity within him, wherefrom his whole life takes its beauty and meaning, and inspires him to follow and obey it.'[4]

Winwood Reade in his *The Veil of Isis* (1861) similarly emphasizes the universality of Freemasonry as a mystical tradition: 'Love is the key-stone which supports the entire edifice of this mystic science. Love one another, teach one another, help one another. That is all our doctrine, all our science, all our law. We have no narrow-minded prejudices; we do not debar from our society this sect or that sect; it is sufficient for us that a man worships God, no matter under what name or in what manner.'[5]

Symbol of the 19th-century
Cabalistic Order of the
Rosy Cross, headed by
Marquis Stanislas de Guaita
(1861–97) and Joséphin
Péladan (1858–1918).

THE ROSICRUCIAN FRATERNITY

The Rosicrucian Fraternity announced its existence with the release of four pamphlets, the first of which was the *Fama Fraternitatis Rosae Crucis* issued in Cassel in 1614, together with a satirical work by the Italian writer Boccalini called *The General Reformation of the World*. In 1615 the anti-Papal *Confessio* appeared, followed by the allegorical *Chemical Marriage of Christian Rosencreutz*. The last is especially important in contemporary occult thought because of its alchemical themes and spiritual rebirth symbolism, and its influence on the nineteenth-century Hermetic Order of the Golden Dawn. Both the *Fama* and the *Confessio* concern the mythical figure Christian Rosencreutz (Rosycross) and the formation of his Order.

The *Fama* begins by declaring that God has now revealed a more profound understanding of Jesus Christ and Nature, and that there are wise men who understand the nature of the Microcosmus. The reader is then introduced to Brother Rosencreutz, 'an illuminated man', who has travelled extensively and received the wisdom of the East. It asserts that in Germany there are many learned magicians, Kabbalists, physicians and philosophers who should collaborate. It explains how the Church can be reformed through this new sacred knowledge, and goes on to explain how the Rosicrucian Fraternity came into existence, initially with four members, and then with a much bigger following, meeting annually in the House of the Holy Spirit.

The text also describes the discovery of Brother Rosencreutz's seven-sided burial vault, illuminated by an inner sun and containing a round altar, covered with a plate of brass on which was engraved: 'I have made this Tomb a compendium of the Universe.' Around the brim were the words 'Jesus is all things to me.' There were geometrical figures on the walls, lamps, magical mirrors and bells, and writings by the alchemist Paracelsus (who is not claimed as a member of the Fraternity). Most significant of all, when the altar was moved aside by the Rosicrucian brethren and the brass plate lifted, they found a 'fair and worthy body, whole and unconsumed. ... In his hand he held the book T...which next to our Bible is our greatest treasure.'

Clearly Christian Rosencreutz had strong spiritual associations with the perfect Christ. It is especially significant that the seventeenth-century Rosicrucian apologist Robert Fludd should have interpreted the story of the vault of Christian Rosencreutz as symbolic of mystical rebirth and the quest for spiritual perfection: 'Some writers have dealt with this mystery in dark sayings and methinks the great Rosarius hath described it shrouded in sacred symbols. For here we see a corpse, buried, wherefrom the soul hath gone and seemeth to soar heavenward. The body duly prepared for burial, or even now decaying; yet we see the soul that belongeth thereto, clothed with greater powers, descending to its body. We see a light, as if it

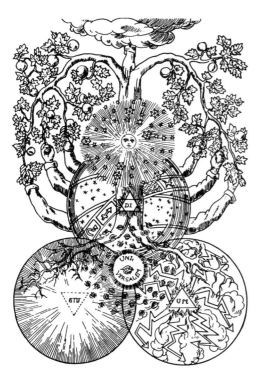

The Tree of Knowledge, an engraving from *Geheime Figuren der Rosenkreuzer*, 1785.

were the Sun, yet winged and exceeding the Sun of our heaven, arising from the tomb. We see displayed with wondrous courage, a picture of the making of the perfect man.'[6]

The discovery of the vault – indicated as the year 1604 – was also proclaimed as the symbolic beginning of a new era of spiritual reformation: 'We know…that there will now be a general reformation, both of divine and human things, according to our desire and the expectations of others.' The followers of Christian Rosencreutz would bring about this spiritual transformation.

The *Fama* was published in German but the first edition of the *Confessio* was in Latin, implying that it was aimed at a more learned audience.[7] The *Confessio* boldly declared that the Pope of Rome was the Antichrist and, like the *Fama*, it urged readers of the tract to co-operate with the Order in bringing about a new spiritual orientation, equivalent to the state of Adam in Paradise. God would allow light and truth to flood the land, and the Pope would be overthrown. It was said that new stars had appeared in the constellations of Serpentarius and Cygnus as omens of what was to come.

Many readers tried to make contact with the Fraternity when these pamphlets appeared, but were met with silence. This intensified interest in the Rosicrucian mystery, especially since the identity of the Brothers remained unknown. According to Renaissance scholar Frances Yates, it now seems certain that the *Monas Hieroglyphica* by Dr John Dee influenced the Rosicrucian writers – his text representing their 'secret philosophy' – and it is also evident that the Lutheran pastor Johann Valentin Andrae (1586–1654) played a central role in issuing the tracts. Andrae is generally regarded as the author of the *Chemical Wedding*, and in Kurt Seligmann's view Rosencreutz and Andrae were 'one and the same person'.[8] It is also possible that the physician Oswald Croll – a follower of Paracelsus – was involved in the movement.[9]

Of all the Rosicrucian documents, *The Chemical Marriage* is undoubtedly the most fascinating. It describes how, just before Easter, Christian Rosencreutz is summoned by a female angelic being to attend a royal wedding. The summons shows a cross with a solar disc and lunar crescent. The next day Christian Rosencreutz wakes early and prepares for his journey. He is wearing four red roses in his hat and carrying with him bread, salt and water. Venturing through a forest he discovers that four different roads lead to the Palace of the King. Only one of these is the Royal Road but whichever he chooses he must hold to, because to turn back will result in his death. Initially he cannot decide which road to take, but, after offering bread to a snow-white dove who is being tormented by a black raven, he finds himself before a large gate inscribed with various 'noble figures' and devices. Christian Rosencreutz is asked for his name and replies that he is a brother of the Rosy Cross. In exchange for water he is given a gold token, and comes to a second gate also inscribed with mystical symbols and which is guarded by a lion. He is allowed through after giving salt. He ventures through a third gate and is just in time for the wedding feast. In the hall he discovers a 'great multitude of guests', including emperors, kings, princes and lords and also poor and 'ignoble' people. After the feast the guests are told that the following day they will be weighed in the Scales of Judgement.

Most of the guests fail this test and are given a potion which dissolves their memory of the event. They are then turned away from the palace. However Christian Rosencreutz and a few others continue. Each member of this group is presented with a Golden Fleece and Medal of Gold surmounted with the Sun and Moon, before being shown various mysteries of the Palace, including the Great Phoenix (a resurrection symbol associated with Christ). The next day the candidates attend another banquet, but after they have replaced their white garments with black ones, a black man appears, beheads the King and Queen and places them in coffins.

Christian Rosencreutz and his colleagues now journey with a guide called the Virgin to a seven-storeyed Tower of the Gods where they prepare material for the Great Work – the supreme achievement of the alchemists. Employing the blood of the Phoenix, they bring the King and Queen back to life, and in turn are proclaimed by the Virgin to be Knights of the Golden Stone.

HIGH MAGIC

In Rosicrucianism, as in the masonic myth of Hiram, the theme of death and spiritual rebirth plays a central role. It is an enduring theme in the Western esoteric tradition, and re-emerges, as we shall see, in the defining initiatory ritual of the Hermetic Order of the Golden Dawn. A point that should be emphasized here, however, is that the Western esoteric tradition has many strands united by a few central themes. We have seen how the mystical universe has been variously interpreted by the Gnostics, Neoplatonists and Hermeticists as *emanationist* – successive levels of being, each emanating in turn from a Divine and transcendent source. Also, that the medieval alchemists and their later counterparts, the Freemasons and Rosicrucians, shared a common interest in spiritual rebirth and the idea of the archetypal perfected human. These elements all seem to be central to the ever-mutating but nevertheless essentially Gnostic idea that has evolved into the magical consciousness of the twentieth-century – becoming in our own time the individual transpersonal quest to incarnate the God and Goddess. High

Poster by Carloz Schwabe, 1892, for the Salon Rose Croix, established in Paris by the Rosicrucian Joséphin Péladan.

magic, or *gnosis*, is essentially about embodying deity — about becoming as gods and goddesses on the path to transcendence.

From the perspective of conventional Western religion, gnosis of this type remains a potent heresy, and it is not hard to see why the mystical and Neopagan traditions should have been so strongly persecuted by the Roman Catholic Inquisition during the Middle Ages. The magical traditions consistently advocate the view that direct contact with the Divine — archetypal sacred consciousness — is not only possible but desirable. This heresy persists to this day, though in less confrontational terms, and it comes as no surprise that both Pope John Paul II and the Roman Catholic Church remain strongly opposed to 'New Age' philosophies, which are regarded as a modern form of Gnosticism and pantheism.

Prior to the 1960s, when classic works on alchemy, magic and Rosicrucianism began to be more widely available, the fragments of the esoteric tradition that have been described here have remained substantially hidden — *occult* in the literal meaning of the word. This inclination towards secrecy seems to be changing, and many groups and individuals are sharing their esoteric knowledge and wisdom more openly. At at the beginning of the twentieth century, however, occultists were still thoroughly *occult*. As in the traditions of Freemasonry and Rosicrucianism, secrets had to be preserved and enlightenment earned gradually — literally, by degrees.

In 1918 Joseph Fort Newton made observations about the 'occult myth' in The *Builders* that are still relevant today: 'God ever shields us from premature idea, said the gracious and wise Emerson; and so does Nature. She holds back her secrets until man is fit to be entrusted with them, lest by rashness he destroy himself. Those who seek find, not because the truth is far off, but because the discipline of the quest makes them ready for the truth and worthy to receive it. By a certain sure instinct the great teachers of our race have regarded the highest truth less as a gift bestowed than as a trophy to be won. Everything must not be told to everybody. Truth is power, and when held by untrue hands it may become a plague.'

Rosicrucian emblem of winged hourglass and scythe, symbolizing the flight of time and the certainty of death, 17th century.

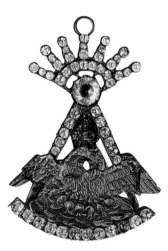

Masonic jewel of the 18th degree Ancient and Accepted Rite, with the pelican, symbol of nurture and sacrifice. German, *c.* 1800.

Newton says that the 'more withdrawn teaching' has become known as the Secret Doctrine or Hidden Wisdom: 'A persistent tradition affirms that throughout the ages, and in every land, behind the system of faith accepted by the masses an inner and deeper doctrine has been held and taught by those able to grasp it...those who have eyes to see have no difficulty in penetrating the varying veils of expression and identifying the underlying truths; thus confirming in the arcana of faith what we found to be true in its earliest forms – the oneness of the human mind and the unity of truth.' [10]

This is the 'occult myth': 'We are told that behind the age-long struggle of man to know the truth there exists a hidden fraternity of initiates, adepts in esoteric lore, known to themselves but not to the world, who have had in their keeping, through the centuries which they permit to be dimly adumbrated in the popular faiths, but which the rest of the race are too obtuse, even yet, to grasp save in an imperfect and limited degree. These hidden sages, it would seem, look upon our eager aspiring humanity much like the patient masters of an idiot school, watching it go on forever seeking without finding, while they sit in seclusion, keeping the keys of the occult.'[11]

Significantly, Newton himself does not subscribe to this view: 'It is,' he says, 'only one more of those fascinating fictions with which mystery-mongers entertain themselves and deceive others.' He acknowledges that there are sages in all lands and times but denies it is a 'continuous fellowship of superior souls holding...secret truths denied to their fellow men.' Nevertheless, Newton does ascribe to the idea of society and culture being shaped by visionaries guided by the grace of God and by 'the divine right of genius'. These people embody what he calls the *Open Secret* of the world. Essentially the truth is always there for those who persist on the spiritual quest and who prove themselves capable of receiving it. 'What kept it hidden,' he says, 'was no arbitrary restriction, but only a lack of insight and fineness of mind to appreciate and assimilate it.'

Newton finally distinguishes between faith and spiritual knowledge in true Gnostic style: 'What then, is the Secret Doctrine but...the kinship of the soul with God.... Now to accept this faith as mere philosophy is one thing, but to realize it as an experience of the innermost heart is another and a deeper thing. *No man knows the Secret Doctrine until it has become the secret of his soul, the reigning reality of his thought, the inspiration of his acts, the form and colour and glory of his life.*'[12]

At the end of the nineteenth century the magical traditions were still undergoing a period of consolidation. The 'secret society' that would later help stimulate the revival of contemporary magical consciousness – and bring 'the occult' out into the open – had only just been born. This was the Hermetic Order of the Golden Dawn.

Chapter Eight

The Hermetic Order of the Golden Dawn

Madame Helena Blavatsky, co-founder of the Theosophical Society. Its London esoteric lodge was a rival to the Golden Dawn.

Rosicrucian scholar Arthur Edward Waite, a key figure in the Golden Dawn. Photograph by F. C. Stoate, 1929.

In 1887 Dr Wynn Westcott, a London-based coroner and Freemason, acquired a manuscript in cipher. It had been discovered among the papers of a deceased member of an esoteric society called the Societas Rosicruciana in Anglia. SRIA's principal focus lay in the exploration of alchemical symbolism and ceremonial ritual, and Westcott was its secretary-general.

By means of an alchemical code, Westcott transcribed the manuscript, which yielded five masonic rituals. Westcott then invited his friend Samuel Liddell Mathers to expand the material as the basis of a 'complete scheme of initiation'.[1] Westcott also claimed to have found among the leaves of the manuscript the name and address of a certain Fraulein Anna Sprengel, said to be an eminent Rosicrucian adept. On her authority, and following a lengthy correspondence, Westcott announced in Masonic and Theosophical circles that he had been instructed to found an English branch of her German occult group, calling it the Hermetic Order of the Golden Dawn.

Research into the history of the Order suggests that both the correspondence and Fraulein Sprengel were fictitious.[2] Westcott seems to have created them in order to compete with the esoteric school that Madame Helena Blavatsky had established within the Theosophical Society after bringing her organization to London in 1884. Blavatsky claimed to be inspired by Mahatmas, or spiritual Masters, living in Tibet, with whom she had psychic rapport, and this impressed devotees seeking mystical 'authority'. Westcott was meeting a need for an authentic occult lineage, and would soon develop the notion of Secret Chiefs to rival Madame Blavatsky's Mahatmas.

Theosophy had attracted a diverse and interesting coterie of mystical seekers, and the Hermetic Order of the Golden Dawn similarly recruited some fascinating and often very talented individuals. These included the distinguished homeopath Dr Edward Berridge; the Scottish Astronomer Royal, William Peck; Arthur Edward Waite, an authority on the Kabbalah, Rosicrucianism and the Holy Grail legends; the distinguished poet William Butler Yeats; eminent physician and pioneer of tropical medicine, Dr R. W. Felkin; lawyer Dr John Brodie-Innes; fantasy novelists Arthur Machen and Algernon Blackwood; and the controversial ritual magician and adventurer Aleister Crowley. Despite its patriarchal connections

Portrait of W. B. Yeats painted by his father, John Butler Yeats, 1900.

The Red Rose and the Cross of Gold. This symbol was worn by adepts of the Golden Dawn and symbolized spiritual rebirth.

with Freemasonry, the Order also attracted several notable women, among them Annie Horniman, later a leading patron of Irish theatre; artist and scholar Moina Bergson, sister of the French philosopher Henri Bergson; Celtic revivalist Maud Gonne; actress Florence Farr; and, in later years, Violet Firth, better known as the magical novelist Dion Fortune.[3]

As a Freemason Westcott liked the concept of a hierarchy and ritual degrees, and he designed the grades of the Hermetic Order of the Golden Dawn to correlate with the *sephiroth*, or levels of mystical consciousness, upon the Kabbalistic Tree of Life. The spiritual journey for the occult devotee was a mystical ascent from the lowest levels of the Tree of Life to the highest – an essentially Gnostic process of transcending Creation and returning to the One Source of All Being.

The five rituals in the cipher manuscript were grades in the SRIA. Four had imposing Latin names – Zelator, Theoricus, Practicus and Philosophus. There was also a Neophyte grade which, in a symbolic sense, was *below* the Tree of Life because here the seeker had not yet embarked on the magical journey. Westcott designated the first grades (from Neophyte to Philosophus) the First Order, then developed a Second Order in which Adeptus Minor, Adeptus Major and Adeptus Exemptus corresponded to the sixth, fifth and fourth spheres.

The fourth sphere of consciousness lies just below the Trinity on the Kabbalistic Tree, and in Jewish cosmology represents the first of the Seven Days of Creation. The three higher *sephiroth*, on the other hand, constitute the Trinity – levels of sacred being untarnished by the so-called 'Fall' of the Spirit into successive levels of manifest reality. The seven lower and three higher *sephiroth* are separated by the Abyss, which symbolically distinguishes the domain of Creation *below* from the sacred purity of the transcendent Godhead *above*.

In the Jewish mystical tradition the levels of mystical reality above the Abyss essentially lie beyond the realm of Creation. Nevertheless, Westcott conceived of a mystical Third Order corresponding to the exalted levels of awareness above the fourth *sephirah*. For Westcott this sacred domain was the home of mystical beings known as Secret Chiefs, whose inspiration guided the vision of the Golden Dawn.

This claim to exclusive access to Secret Chiefs would have enormous significance for the history of the Order. Westcott was appointing himself, and his selected

Maud Gonne,
photographed in 1897.

colleagues, as members of a visionary elite with privileged access to a unique source of Divine Power. Westcott maintained that contact with this transcendental realm above the Abyss would be possible only through 'astral consciousness', a mystical process known as 'rising on the planes', or through the performance of specific esoteric rituals designed to inflame the sacred imagination.

THE RED ROSE AND THE CROSS OF GOLD

In 1888 Westcott established the Isis-Urania Temple of the Hermetic Order of the Golden Dawn in London, inviting Mathers and his Masonic friend Dr William Woodman to join him as Chiefs in the new Temple. By implication they were the Secret Chiefs incarnate. All three assumed the grade of 7° = 4°, which corresponded with the *sephirah* Chesed, the fourth emanation on the Tree of Life, and the sphere symbolically associated with the Ruler of the Universe. They used secret magical names, since members of the Golden Dawn were only allowed to know the magical names of their peers and those on lower grades. Westcott became Non Omnis Moriar, Woodman was Vincit Omnia Veritas and Mathers Deo Duce Comite Ferro.

According to Kabbalistic tradition there is a 'veil' named Paroketh between the sixth and seventh emanations on the Tree of Life, representing the transition between old and new being. The sixth emanation, Tiphareth, represents the visionary state of consciousness where spiritual transformation, or 'rebirth', occurs. Westcott, Mathers and Woodman used different ceremonial names associated with this grade to interact with members of the Order with ritual grades below the Veil of Paroketh, that is, those who had not yet been fully initiated.

The three supreme grades upon the Tree of Life were those of the Third Order 8° = 3° (Magister Templi), 9° = 2° (Magus) and 10° = 1° (Ipsissimus). In appointing themselves as Chiefs, Westcott, Mathers and Woodman clearly considered themselves spiritual leaders who could bring the other Order members through into the Light.

Shortly after Sprengel's 'death' in 1891, Westcott claimed that 'all the knowledge was safe with him'. Indeed, it had probably never resided anywhere else. Following Dr Woodman's death in the same year, however, and Mathers' increasing importance as author of the rituals of the Golden Dawn, Westcott was forced into an administrative role of secondary importance.

In 1892 Mathers claimed to have established a special spiritual connection with the Secret Chiefs that enabled him to write rituals for the so-called Second Order. These encompassed the sixth, fifth and fourth *sephiroth* – Tiphareth/Adeptus Minor (5° = 6°) Geburah/Adeptus Major (6° = 5°) and Chesed/Adeptus Exemptus (7° = 4°), which he and Westcott already held in an honorary capacity.

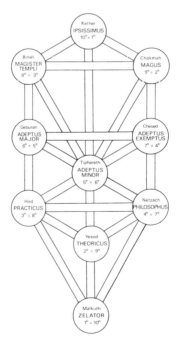

Tree of Life symbol showing the ritual grades associated with each sphere of mystical consciousness.

Golden Dawn magician
Samuel Liddell MacGregor
Mathers in his ceremonial
regalia. Painting by his
wife Moina Bergson
Mathers, c. 1895.

Influential Golden Dawn
patron Annie Horniman.
Portrait by Flora Lion,
c. 1912.

This gave Mathers the spiritual edge as a 'communicant' of the higher ritual grades, which he named the Rosae Rubae et Aurea Crucis (the Red Rose and the Cross of Gold, often abbreviated to RR et AC).

The Golden Dawn temples continued to grow in number. In 1896, in addition to the Temple of Isis-Urania in London, there were Temples of Osiris in Weston-super-Mare, Horus in Bradford, Amen-Ra in Edinburgh and Ahathoor in Paris. In 1892 Mathers moved to Paris with his wife Moina Bergson, and became engaged in translating a lengthy occult manuscript entitled *The Sacred Magic of Abramelin the Mage*, written in the fifteenth century.

A clerk and infantryman by profession, Mathers had certain social pretensions and was now referring to himself as MacGregor Mathers, MacGregor of Glenstrae and Count of Glenstrae. Supported financially by Annie Horniman, a tea heiress and key member of the London Isis-Urania Temple, Mathers was presiding over the Ahathoor Temple while trying to maintain dominance over the English temples across the Channel. Annie Horniman would later question some of the expenses of Mathers' stay in Paris and his reply to her is revealing: 'Prior to the establishment of the Vaults of the Adepts in Britannia (the First of the Golden Dawn in the Outer being therein actively working)…it was found absolutely and

Actress Florence Farr,
whose secret magical name in
the Golden Dawn was *Sapientia
Sapienti Dono Data*, 'Wisdom
is a gift given to the Wise'.
This is how she appeared in
Sicilian Idyll at the Vaudeville
Theatre, 1891.

imperatively necessary that there should be some eminent Member especially chosen to act as the link between the Secret Chiefs and the more external forms of the Order. It was requisite that such Member should be me, who, while having the necessary and peculiar educational basis of critical and profound occult archaeological knowledge…must further pledge himself to obey in everything the commands of the aforesaid Secret Chiefs…body and soul, without question and without argument whether their commands related to Magical Action in the External World; or to Psychic Action in Other Worlds, or Planes, whether Angelic, Spiritual or Demonic, or to the Inner Administration of the Order to which so tremendous a knowledge was to be communicated.'[4]

It is clear that the central doctrine of Secret Chiefs helped maintain Mathers' position as head of the hierarchy – an occult equivalent to the feudal concept of the Divine Right of Kings. Nevertheless, while consolidating his own position, Mathers was unable to supply any detailed information about these spiritual entities: 'I do not even know their earthly names. I know them only by certain secret mottoes. I have *but very rarely* seen them in the physical body; and on such rare occasions *the rendezvous was made astrally by them* at the time and place which had been astrally appointed beforehand. For my part I believe them to be human and living upon this earth but possessing terrible superhuman powers.'[5]

The concept of magical beings whose mystical inspiration emanated from a source beyond the Abyss on the Tree of Life suggested that there were 'living gods' who could be contacted at the highest initiatory grades. And Mathers was not alone in subscribing to this idea. Florence Farr, who conducted an offshoot within the Golden Dawn known as the Sphere Group, believed her coterie to be controlled by a 'certain Egyptian astral form'. And Dr Felkin, who founded the Order of the Stella Matutina (Morning Star) after several members of the London Temple deserted Mathers in 1900, continued to strive for contact with the Secret Chiefs. In May 1902 Felkin wrote to his colleagues: 'We beg to assure you that we are in entire sympathy with the view that if in fact the Order is without the guidance and inspiration of higher intelligences its rationale is gone.' It occurred to certain members of the Stella Matutina, however, that it might be possible, by reverting to the original constitution, to re-establish a link with the Third

Order.[6] Felkin opted instead for certain 'Sun Masters' and then for a mysterious being named Ara Ben Shemesh, whom he described as a 'discarnate Arab [with a] Temple in the Desert where the Sons of Fire live [who] are personal communication with the Divine and are no longer bound in the flesh so that their material life is a matter of will.'

There is also evidence that W. B. Yeats believed in the existence of transcendental guides. In his essay 'Is the Order of the RR & AC to remain a Magical Order?', written in 1901, Yeats refers to 'the stream of lightning awakened in the Order, and the Adepts of the Third Order and of the Higher Degrees of the Second Order summoned to our help.'[7]

THE MAGICAL JOURNEY

The structure of the Hermetic Order of the Golden Dawn provided the core impetus for the twentieth-century magical revival. Those members who had actually entered the Inner Order of the Rosae Rubae et Aurea Crucis, took the following pledge: 'I will from this day forward apply myself to the Great Work which is to purify and exalt my Spiritual nature, that within the Divine aid I may at length attain to be more than human, and thus gradually raise and unite myself to my Higher and Divine Genius and that in this event I will not abuse the Great Power entrusted to me.'[8] Most of the Golden Dawn members, however, remained in the Outer Order, and their spiritual endeavours focused ritually and meditatively on the four *sephiroth* located at the lower levels of the Tree of Life.

The Neophyte degree was the starting point of the whole magical journey, and Francis King has described it as 'unquestionably the most important, since it gave not only a glimpse of the Light to be experienced in the future but a key (albeit in an embryonic and undeveloped form) to the inner and hidden significance of the entire Order.'[9] This view is endorsed by Dr Israel Regardie, a member of the Stella Matutina: 'From the candidate's first reception in the Hall of the Neophytes when the Hierophant adjures him with these words – 'Child of Earth, long hast thou dwelt in darkness. Quit the night and seek the day' – to the transfiguration in the [Second Order] Vault Ceremony, the whole system has as its objective the bringing down of the Light.'[10]

THE GOLDEN DAWN COSMOLOGY

For the Golden Dawn magician, the ultimate mythic attainment was to come forth ritually into the Light – the very essence of spiritual rebirth. The act of ascending the Kabbalistic Tree of Life through sacred ceremonial involved a powerful act of creative imagination – the magician had to feel that he was fully engaging with each sphere of consciousness in turn. Judaism and the Kabbalah, however, are

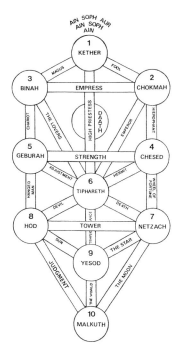

Tree of Life symbol showing Major Arcana Tarot paths connecting the ten spheres of the Tree. These Tarot paths were used in the Golden Dawn for visionary 'pathworkings'.

monotheistic: each *sephirah* is an aspect of the Godhead – not an individual deity in itself – and in the Jewish mystical tradition there is finally only the Unity Consciousness of *Ain Soph Aur.* This presented the Golden Dawn occultists with a paradox, for, while they acknowledged the sacred unity of the Tree of Life in all its emanations, they also believed that they had to focus their creative awareness upon specific archetypal images if they were to ascend to the Light.

The solution to this was to regard the Kabbalistic Tree of Life as a unifying matrix upon which the archetypes of the great Western mythologies could be charted. It then became possible to interrelate the major deities from the pantheons of ancient Egypt, Greece, Rome and Celtic Europe in a cumulative approach to the Western mythological imagination. In due course, other aspects of magical symbolism would also be charted upon the Tree so that precious stones, perfumes, minerals and sacred plants could also be assigned to specific gods and goddesses in a ceremonial context. These were known as 'magical correspondences'.

Guided in this task by MacGregor Mathers, the Golden Dawn cosmology became very elaborate. Mathers was a self-taught scholar with a sound knowledge of French, Latin and Greek, as well as some Coptic and Hebrew. He had translated Knorr von Rosenroth's seventeenth-century Latin text of *Kabbala Denudata* into English – the specialist esoteric publisher George Redway issued *The Kabbalah Unveiled* in 1887 – and one of his major interests was to translate key magical documents that might otherwise have remained in obscurity in museum archives.

MAGICAL CORRESPONDENCES

Mathers' vision for the Golden Dawn was that its magicians should follow the mythic pathways on the Tree of Life, a cosmological metaphor for the hierarchy of energy levels in the manifested universe, and grow in spiritual awareness as they ascended through each level. Several methods were open to them. They could simulate each level imaginatively through ritual, they could meditate upon each sphere of consciousness, or they could 'rise on the inner planes' in a state of magical trance. The essence of Mathers' approach was to list the deities from the different pantheons and correlate them as magical archetypes, extending beyond classical Graeco-Roman and Egyptian mythology to include Scandinavian gods, Western astrology, Buddhist meditations, magical weapons and the letters of the Greek, Arabic and Coptic alphabets.

This work was published in 1909 under the title 777 – not by Mathers himself but by his colleague Aleister Crowley, who appears to have added a number of Oriental listings to Mathers' original table of magical correspondences, as well as including some individual elements of his own.[11]

Magical Correspondences

	Kabbalah	Astrology	Egyptian	Greek
1	Kether	Primum Mobile	Harpocrates	Zeus
2	Chokmah	Fixed Stars	Ptah	Uranus
3	Binah	Saturn	Isis	Demeter
4	Chesed	Jupiter	Amoun	Poseidon
5	Geburah	Mars	Horus	Ares
6	Tiphareth	Sol (Sun)	Ra	Apollo
7	Netzach	Venus	Hathor	Aphrodite
8	Hod	Mercury	Anubis	Hermes
9	Yesod	Luna	Shu	Diana
10	Malkuth	The Elements	Seb	Persephone

The perfumes and precious stones listed below were considered appropriate in rituals corresponding to the invoked god or goddess:

	Precious Stones	Perfumes
1	Diamond	Ambergris
2	Star Ruby, Turquoise	Musk
3	Star Sapphire, Pearl	Myrrh, Civet
4	Amethyst	Cedar
5	Ruby	Tobacco
6	Topaz	Olibanum
7	Emerald	Benzoin, Rose, Sandalwood
8	Opal	Storax
9	Quartz	Jasmine
10	Rock Crystal	Dittany of Crete

As a document, 777 represents the parameters of the modern magical imagination, and its historical significance lies in the fact that it was an early attempt to systematize the various images associated with different levels of spiritual awareness — predating Jung's concept of archetypes and the collective unconscious. From a psychological perspective the magicians of the Golden Dawn regarded the Tree of Life as a complex symbol of the spiritual world within. To simulate the gods and goddesses was to become like them through methods of direct encounter. They therefore had to imagine that they were partaking of the nature of each of the gods in turn, embodying within themselves the very essence of the deity. The rituals were designed to control all the circumstances that might assist

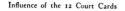

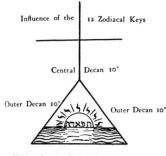

Hidden Sun of Tiphareth operating and rising above the Waters of Space

The Sun of Tiphareth rising, from Israel Regardie, *The Relation Between the Tree of Life and the Tarot: The Golden Dawn*, 1937–40.

them in their journey through the subconscious mind and mythic imagination. They included all the symbols and colours of the god, the utterance of magical names of power, and the burning of perfume appropriate to the deity concerned.

In the Golden Dawn tradition – an approach to archetypal magic that remains influential over a century later – the ritual magician imagines that he has become the deity whose forms he imitates in ritual. It is now the magician himself and not the gods of Creation who utters the sacred names that sustain the universe. The underworld of the subconscious mind is entered through Malkuth at the base of the Tree, and the various pathways culminate in the solar vision of Tiphareth, at the very heart of the Tree of Life.

The most 'direct' route upon the Tree of Life was the vertical path from Malkuth through Yesod to Tiphareth, upon the so-called 'Middle Pillar'. The Golden Dawn grades, however, also encompassed the other *sephiroth* Hod and Netzach on the outer extremities of the Tree, and the process here was to follow the so-called 'zig-zag lightning flash' of sacred manifestation – retracing the path of the Divine Energy of Creation through each of the *sephirah* in turn.

MYTHOLOGICAL LEVELS ON THE TREE OF LIFE

When one considers the Tree of Life as a composite matrix of archetypes, the ten *sephiroth* acquire a richly mythological character.

Malkuth Associated with the earth, crops, the immediate environment and living things, represents the beginning of the inner journey. In Roman mythology the entrance to the underworld was through a cave near Naples, and symbolically Malkuth is the entrance through the earth, the totality of the four elements, leading to what in psychological terms is the subconscious mind. Malkuth in itself represents familiar everyday consciousness.

Yesod Associated with the Moon, and, like Malkuth, a predominantly female sphere, it is the recipient of impulses and fluxes from the higher realms on the Tree of Life and the transmitter of these energies into a more tangible physical form in Malkuth. Consequently it contains an ocean of astral imagery, and is associated with water. It is also the seat of the sexual instinct, corresponding to the area of the genitals when 'mapped' upon the figure of Adam Kadmon, the archetypal human being. It is the sphere of subconscious activity immediately entered through sexual magic, and is the level of awareness activated through basic forms of witchcraft. Modern Wicca is primarily a form of lunar worship.

Hod Associated with the planet Mercury, it represents intellect and rational thinking. It is a lower aspect of the Great Father (Chokmah: Wisdom), for Mercury is the messenger of the gods. As the next stage beyond Yesod, Hod represents the conquest of the animal instincts, albeit at an intellectual rather than an emotional level. Hod symbolizes the structuring principle in the manifested universe, and is considered a levelling and balancing *sephirah* which embodies a sense of order. It is in this capacity that we perceive 'God the Architect' made manifest in a world of myriad forms and structures.

Netzach Associated with the planet Venus, it represents creativity, subjectivity and the emotions. In the same way that Hod (to some extent clinical and rational) lies on the Pillar of Form, the left-hand pillar on the Tree of Life, Netzach resides on the Pillar of Force, the right-hand pillar. Outward-going in its emphasis, with an element of instinctual drive, it is the sphere of love and spiritual passion. A fine balance exists between Hod and Netzach upon the Tree of Life as the process of Creation weaves a web of love-energy between the polarities of Force and Form. These potencies flow through the uniting *sephirah* of the Moon, lower on the Tree, and are channelled through to the earth – where they are perceived as the beauty within living forms.

Tiphareth This is an embodiment of the Sun (masculine), and therefore the opposite of Yesod, embodiment of the Moon (feminine). If Yesod represents the animal instincts, Tiphareth is the mediating stage between humanity and the Godhead on the journey of mystical ascent. It is here that the individual experiences spiritual rebirth. The personality has acquired a sense of true and authentic balance, and its aspirations are now oriented towards higher states of being. Tiphareth is associated with deities of rebirth and resurrection and in a planetary sense with the Sun as a giver of life and light. It is also the sphere of sacrifice, for the old persona is now offered in place of new insight. The individual now begins to function in a spiritual way.

Geburah Associated with Mars, a god of war, it represents severity and justice. The energies of Geburah are absolutely impartial, since there can be no flaw of self-pity or sentiment in a wise ruler. The destructive forces of this sphere are intended as a purging, cleansing force and are positive in their application. Geburah thus embodies a spiritual vision of power operating in the universe to destroy elements after their usefulness has passed. As an aspect of the Ruler, Demiurge, or 'Father of the Gods' below the Abyss, Geburah shows discipline and precision in his destructiveness. His mission in the battlefield of the cosmos is to inculcate a rational economy of form which at a lower level upon the Tree is reflected in Hod.

Chesed Associated with Jupiter, the other face of the destructive Ruler, it represents divine mercy and majesty. Whereas Mars rides in his chariot and is a purging force, Chesed is seated upon his throne viewing his kingdom, the entire universe, and reinforces and consolidates. Through his stabilizing influence, the sacred potencies that originate in the transcendent spheres above the Abyss (at the level of the Trinity) are channelled down the Tree into various forms of being. Within Chesed are all archetypal ideas, for he is mythologically located at the highest level of the Collective Unconscious.

Binah The first of the three levels known collectively as the Trinity where we find the Great Mother in all her mythological aspects. She is the Womb of Forthcoming, the source of all the great images and forms that will enter the manifested universe as archetypes. She is also the supreme Female principle in the process of Creation, and as such is invariably the mother of the god-man or messiah who in turn provides the bridge between humanity and the gods (or God). Binah is thus associated with the Virgin Mary, mother of Christ in Tiphareth, but she is also associated with Rhea and Isis. Because she is the Mother of Creation, she is often the consort or lover of the ruler of the manifested universe – Demeter and Zeus were lovers.

Chokmah The Great Father who provides the seminal spark of life which is potency only, until it enters the womb of the Great Mother. From the union of the Great Father and the Great Mother come forth all the images of Creation. Chokmah is associated with deities who sustain existence itself.

Kether Represents the first spark of Creation that emanates from beyond the veils of non-Existence (*Ain Soph Aur* – the Limitless Light). Kether is located on the Middle Pillar of the Tree of Life and transcends the duality of male and female polarities. Sometimes represented as the Heavenly Androgyne for this reason, Kether represents a level of sublime spiritual transcendence.

THE POWER OF THE SACRED WORD

In the Western esoteric tradition, sound – and more particularly the power of the magical utterance – is of central importance. According to the Kabbalistic *Zohar*, the world was formed by the utterance of the Sacred Name of God, a forty-two letter extension of the Tetragrammation JHVH, *Yod, He, Vau, He*. The Word, or *Logos*, therefore permeates the entire mystical act of Creation. According to the Czech occultist, Franz Bardon, 'the divine names are symbolic designations of divine qualities and powers'.[12] In the Hermetic Order of the Golden Dawn, magical ritual involved the invocation of deities and archetypal beings through the potency of the spoken word, and this relates strongly to the concept of

Aleister Crowley in ritual garb, wearing a Uraeus serpent crown and the Rose and the Cross. His magical implements include a wand, cup, sword, bell, sacred book and a phial of holy oil.

the *magical will*, which distinguishes ceremonial magic from passive forms of mysticism. As an initiate of the Golden Dawn, Aleister Crowley took the magical name Perdurabo – 'I will endure to the end' – and as he himself noted: 'Words should express will; hence the Mystic Name of the Probationer is the expression of his highest Will.'[13]

The Golden Dawn magicians believed that one of their most important goals was to employ the magical will to communicate with the Higher Self – often referred to as the Holy Guardian Angel. This required a level of mystical awareness associated with the most transcendent levels of the Tree of Life. Sometimes this also involved techniques of magical trance and 'rising in the planes', and Dion Fortune, a member of the Alpha and Omega Temple of the Golden Dawn, wrote in her book *Applied Magic* (1962): 'In my own experience of the operation, the utterance to myself of my Magical name led to the picturing of myself in an idealized form, not differing in type, but upon an altogether grander scale, superhuman in fact, but recognizable as myself, as a statue more than life-size may yet be a good likeness. Once perceived, I could re-picture this idealized version of my body and personality at will, but I could not identify myself with it unless I uttered my Magical name. Upon my affirming it as my own, identification was immediate.'[14]

THE SYMBOLS OF RITUAL MAGIC

There are certain magical symbols that were employed by members of the Golden Dawn, and that are also used by the modern magical groups following in the Golden Dawn tradition.

The Magic Temple This represents both the entire Universe and the individual figure of the magician through the relationship between the macrocosm and the microcosm – 'as above, so below'. Upon the walls are banners emblazoned with sacred symbols and colours appropriate to the ritual, and on the floor are certain inscriptions, the most important of which relate to the magic circle. The circle represents the Infinite Godhead – the Alpha and Omega – the state of spiritual awareness and transcendence. By standing in the centre of the circle, the magician is able to identify with the sacred source of Creation, and his magical will is oriented totally towards the spheres of higher spiritual

Engraving by French ceremonial magician Eliphas Lévi, showing a fusion of the magical lamp, wand, sword and dagger, 1896.

aspiration. The circle also symbolizes the process of magical invocation – the act of reaching towards a higher spiritual reality by identifying with a goddess or a god.[15]

The Central Altar This symbolizes the foundation of the ritual. Within the magic circle, it is a double cube of wood – traditionally made of acacia or oak – with 10 exposed faces, corresponding with the 10 *sephiroth* upon the Tree of Life. The lowest is Malkuth – the World. The upper face represents Kether, the Crown. Oil, wand, cup, sword and disc are placed on this altar to channel the imagination of the ritual magician towards transcendence.

The Holy Oil Ideally this is contained in a vessel of rock-crystal. The magician uses it to anoint the Four Points of the Microcosm (Kether, Chesed, Geburah and Malkuth) upon his forehead, left and right shoulders and solar plexus respectively, while reflecting on the sacred task ahead. It consists of the oils of olive, myrrh, cinnamon and galangual, these corresponding in turn to Chokmah (Wisdom), Binah (Understanding), Tiphareth (Harmony/ Spiritual Awakening) and Kether-Malkuth (the Union of Being and Creation upon the Tree of Life).

The Wand This symbolizes the pursuit of Higher Wisdom (Chokmah), achieved through the Will. Symbolically the tip of the wand is said to rest in Kether, the first *sephirah* of the Tree of Life which contains the Union of Opposites and represents the transcendence of duality in all its forms. A multicoloured lotus wand was used – its upper end white, its lower black, and in between twelve bands of colour corresponding to the signs of the zodiac:

Red	Aries	*Lemon-yellow*	Leo	*Blue*	Sagittarius
Red-orange	Taurus	*Yellow-green*	Virgo	*Indigo*	Capricorn
Orange	Gemini	*Emerald*	Libra	*Violet*	Aquarius
Amber	Cancer	*Green-blue*	Scorpio	*Purple*	Pisces

A lotus flower, with three whorls of petals, was placed upon the tip of the wand, the white end used for magical invocation, the black end for 'banishing' malevolent forces. The wand represents the first letter, Yod, of the Tetragrammaton JHVH (Jehovah – the sacred name of God) and also the element Air.[16]

The Cup This is a feminine, receptive symbol, associated with Binah, the Mother of Understanding. The magician believes he must fill his cup of consciousness with an understanding and knowledge of his Higher Self. As a symbol of *containment* rather than of *becoming*, the cup is not used in rituals of invocation, but in ceremonies related to acts of manifestation. The cup represents the element Water.

The Sword This indicates the magician's mastery over evoked and invoked powers. Symbolizing human force, it parallels the wand representing divine power. Suggestive of control and order, the sword is the 'offspring' of Wisdom and Understanding (Chokmah and Binah) and is therefore attributed to Tiphareth, the sphere of harmony. The sword represents the element Fire.

The Disc (Pentacle) This is paired with the cup as a feminine symbol in the same way that the sword is paired with the wand as both masculine. Symbolic of Malkuth, the Heavenly Daughter and goddess of the manifest universe, the disc is said to 'induce awe' in the consciousness of the magician. Malkuth represents the first step upon the mystical journey to the Source of All Being. It is also represents the consciousness of the magician *prior* to spiritual illumination. The disc represents the element Earth.

The Crown (or headband) This is representative of Kether. The ceremonial magician wears it upon his head. Golden in colour, it is a symbol of aspiration towards the Divine.

The Robe This is worn to protect the magician against adverse 'astral' influences. Hooded, and normally black in colour, it symbolizes anonymity and silence, and is the dark vessel into which the light of the spirit will be poured.

The Lamen (or breastplate) This protects the heart (Tiphareth), and is attached to the robe or sewn across the chest. In the same way that Tiphareth is the focal point of all the *sephiroth* because of its central position upon the Tree of Life, the Lamen has inscribed upon it symbols that relate to all aspects of the magical purpose. Considered an 'active' form of the passive disc, the lamen indicates strength.

The Magical Book The magician holds this in his hands. Indicating strength, it contains details of the individual's ritual aims and practice, and represents the unfolding 'history' of the magical will, a symbol of personal power and resolve.

The Bell This is worn on a chain around the neck if employed in the ritual. Representing a state of alertness, it is said to be the bell that sounds 'at the elevation of the Host', a reference to the sublime music of the higher spheres.

The Sacred Lamp 'The light of the pure soul' is positioned above the ritual implements on the altar, it represents the descent of spirit into form, and light into darkness. It stands for all that is eternal and unchanging, and also the first swirlings of the primal energy that gave rise to the Universe ('Let there be Light…').

TRANCE TECHNIQUES

Magicians working in the Golden Dawn tradition have often described the inner journeys of the psyche by referring to such terms as 'astral projection', 'pathworkings' and the 'Body of Light'. They combined bodily relaxation with a state of mental acuity, focusing increasingly on inner psychic processes. This involved concentrating on specific visual symbols as well as activating specific 'energy centres' within the spiritual body – equivalent to the *chakras* of yoga.[17] Usually magical meditation took place in the dark to enable the shifting of attention away from external visual stimuli towards an internal perspective, and to reinforce the sense of the 'alternative reality' provided by the mythological images or visionary landscapes that arose as a result of willed imagination.

Personal accounts of magical trances are recorded in a series of papers known as 'Flying Rolls' by leading members of the Golden Dawn. Frater Sub Spe – Dr John W. Brodie-Innes – a prominent figure in the Amen-Ra temple in Edinburgh, gives a graphic account of the switch in consciousness: 'Gradually the attention is withdrawn from all surrounding sights and sounds, a grey mist seems to swathe everything, on which, as though thrown from a magic lantern on steam, the form of the symbol is projected. The Consciousness then seems to pass through the symbol to realms beyond…the sensation is as if one looked at a series of moving pictures…. When this sensitiveness of brain and power of perception is once established there seems to grow out of it a power of actually going to the scenes so visionary and seeing them as solid, indeed of actually *doing things* and producing effects there.'[18]

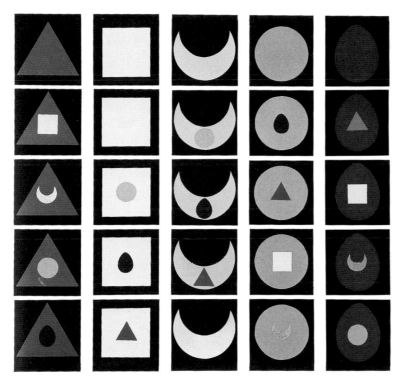

The Tattvas – Hindu symbols of the five elements Earth, Water, Air, Fire and Spirit – in their various combinations.

The Golden Dawn magicians also used the so-called Tattva (or tattwa) symbols of the five elements as an entry point for their magical visions. The Tattvas derive from Hindu mythology and are among the few Eastern components directly incorporated in the Western esoteric tradition. In their basic form they are as follows:

Prithivi: a yellow square, representing the element Earth
Apas: a horizontal silver crescent with upward tips, representing the element Water
Vayu: a blue circle, representing the element Air
Tejas: a red triangle, representing the element Fire
Akasha: a black oval, representing Spirit

The following description of the Tattva visualization technique was written down in 1897 by Moina Mathers – wife of MacGregor Mathers. Here she refers to a composite image combining the Tattva symbols for Earth and Water:

Supposing the symbol you were experimenting with was Prithivi of Apas, that is, the 'earthly aspect of elemental Water', represented by a miniature yellow square mounted on a silver crescent, then fill your mind with the ideas thus symbolized. Place the tattwa card before you. . .and look at the symbol long and steadily until you can perceive it clearly as a thought vision when you shut your eyes. . . . It may help you to perceive it as a large crescent made of blue or silvery water containing a cube of yellow sand. Continue trying to acquire a keen perception of the tattwa until. . .its shape and its qualities shall seem to have become a part of you, and you should then begin to feel as though you were one with. . .Apas, elemental Water, completely bathed in it, and as if all other Elements were non-existent. If this be correctly done, you will find that the thought of any other Element. . .will be distinctly distasteful to you. . . . Continue. . .with the idea well fixed in your mind of calling before you on the card a brain picture of some scene or landscape. This, when it first appears, will probably be vague, but continue to 'make it more real', of whatever nature – deriving from perhaps imagination or memory – you believe it to be. . . .the thought picture may eventually become so clear to you. . .that it will seem as though the picture were trying to precipitate through the symbol. . . . But you can arrive at a great deal by merely receiving the impression of the landscape as a thought. . . .You may modify the earlier stages of the working by so enlarging the symbol astrally i.e. by the use of the visual imagination that a human being can pass through it. When very vivid. . .pass, spring or fly through it. . .till you find yourself in some place or landscape...it would appear well to act exactly as one would in a physical experience of a landscape, realizing each step as one goes. . .but turning first to the right hand and examining that, then turning to the left, then right around, and so on. . .the more practically the experiences are worked, the more chance of success.[19]

It is fascinating to read the reference to 'brain pictures', 'thought visions' and 'thought pictures'. Today these techniques would be called 'creative visualization' or 'magical imaging'. Regardless of terminology, they proved highly effective.

Moina Mathers and her colleagues soon found that they could use their Tattva visualizations to enter quite specific realms of magical awareness.

Flying Roll XI, 1893, describes a vision that Moina Mathers experienced as she sat meditating in her ceremonial robes, contemplating a Tattva card combining *Tejas* and *Akasha* — a black egg within a red triangle (Spirit within Fire). The symbol seemed to grow before her gaze, enabling her to pass into a 'vast triangle of flame'. She then felt herself to be in a harsh sandy desert. Intoning the god-name *Elohim*, she perceived a small pyramid in the distance and, drawing closer, she noticed a small door on each face. She vibrated the magical name *Sephariel*, and a warrior appeared, leading a procession of guards. After a series of tests involving ritual grade signs, the guards knelt before her and she passed inside:

> *...Dazzling light, as in a Temple. An altar in the midst — kneeling figures surround it, there is a dais beyond, and many figures upon it — they seem to be Elementals of a fiery nature.... She sees a pentagram, puts a Leo in it [a Fire sign], thanks the figure who conducts her — wills to pass through the pyramid, finds herself out amid the sand. Wills her return — returns — perceiving her body in robes.*[20]

The beings that Moina Mathers encountered were fire elementals which in the occult hierarchy are considered far beneath the level of gods. On another occasion, however, Moina Mathers was able to conjure beings of a more archetypal nature. Here she used the Tattva combinations Water and Spirit. In this vision she used her knowledge of magical god-names to invoke powerful spiritual guides:

> *A wide expanse of water with many reflections of bright light, and occasionally glimpses of rainbow colours appearing. When divine and other names were pronounced, elementals of the mermaid and merman type [would] appear, but few of the other elemental forms. These water forms were extremely changeable, one moment appearing as solid mermaids and mermen, the next melting into foam. Raising myself by means of the highest symbols I had been taught, and vibrating the names of Water, I rose until the Water vanished, and instead I beheld a mighty world or globe, with its dimensions and divisions of Gods, Angels, elementals and demons — the whole Universe of Water. I called on HCOMA and there appeared standing before me a mighty Archangel, with four wings, robed in glistening white and crowned. In one hand, the right, he held a species of trident, and in the left a Cup filled to the brim with an essence which he poured down below on either side.*[21]

However, not all the Golden Dawn magicians were content with Tattva meditations and visionary encounters. Another member of the Golden Dawn was to produce an entirely new cosmology. This magician was Aleister Crowley.

Chapter Nine
Aleister Crowley: The Beast 666

Of all the magicians associated with the Golden Dawn, Aleister Crowley is the most controversial. He was known as the Great Beast 666 and 'the wickedest man in the world'. He was, nevertheless, a ceremonial magician of considerable style and originality, and his legacy continues to the present day.

Born at Leamington Spa, Warwickshire on 12 October 1875, Crowley was raised in a fundamentalist Plymouth Brethren home. His father was a prosperous brewer who had retired to Leamington to study the Christian scriptures. Crowley came to despise the Plymouth Brethren primarily because of his unfortunate experiences at the special sect school in Cambridge. Much of his subsequent experience of school was also unhappy because of poor health and bullying – but he went up to Trinity College, Cambridge, in 1895, and enjoyed much of his time there

Aleister Crowley photographed during the 1902 expedition to Chogo Ri (K2). He is seated in the middle row, on the right.

The Adeptus I.A. Chab.a.Mac G.
Ac. 1896

= Al Ayn ben Ayt ~ Ananda Metteya =

Aleister Crowley's mentor, Allan Bennett (Frater Iehi Aour), is referred to here as Adeptus I. A. When Bennett later became a Buddhist monk, he was known as Bhikku Ananda Metteya.

reading poetry and classical literature, as well as confirming his reputation as a champion chess player. He later became an enthusiastic mountaineer, joining an expedition in 1902 to scale Chogo Ri (K2) in the Himalayan range, second in height only to Everest.

Crowley's association with the Western esoteric tradition began in London in 1898 with his introduction to George Cecil Jones, a member of the Golden Dawn. By the following year Crowley had also become a close friend of magical initiate Allan Bennett, who for a time rivalled MacGregor Mathers as a leading English occultist. Within the Golden Dawn, Bennett took the magical name Frater Iehi Aour ('Let there be Light'), and he became a mentor to the young Crowley. He taught Crowley applied Kabbalah and the techniques of magical invocation and evocation, and showed him how to create magical talismans.

Crowley quickly grasped the fundamentals of magic. In one of his most influential books — *Magick in Theory and Practice*, privately published in 1929 and frequently reprinted since — Crowley outlined the basic philosophy of magic as he had come to see it: essentially as a process of making man god-like, both in vision and in power. Crowley's magical dicta reveal the particular attraction that magic had for him:

A man who is doing his True Will has the inertia of the Universe to assist him.[1]

Man is ignorant of the nature of his own being and powers. Even his idea of his limitations is based on an experience of the past and every step in his progress extends his empire. There is therefore no reason to assign theoretical limits to what he may be or what he may do.[2]

Man is capable of being and using anything which he perceives, for everything that he perceives is in a certain sense a part of his being. He may thus subjugate the whole Universe of which he is conscious to his individual will.[3]

The Microcosm is an exact image of the Macrocosm; the Great Work is the raising of the whole man in perfect balance to the power of Infinity.[4]

There is a single main definition of the object of all magical Ritual. It is the uniting of the Microcosm with the Macrocosm. The Supreme and Complete Ritual is therefore the Invocation of the Holy Guardian Angel, or, in the language of Mysticism, Union with God.[5]

Crowley was initiated as a Neophyte in the Golden Dawn on 18 November 1898. He soon realized that those with the highest grades, claiming rapport with the Secret Chiefs, wielded great spiritual influence over their followers. Eager to ascend to as high a rank as possible, Crowley took the grade of Zelator and then those of Theoricus and Practicus in the following two months. Initiation into the grade of Philosophus followed in May 1899.

He was the first of the Golden Dawn magicians to attempt the fifteenth-century rituals of Abramelin the Mage, translated from French by MacGregor Mathers. During these rituals, which he performed in a house called Boleskine near Loch Ness in Scotland, Crowley had visions of Christ, and then saw himself crucified. His principal biographer, John Symonds, records: 'He stood within the Divine Light with a crown of twelve stars upon his head; the earth opened for him to enter to its very centre, where he climbed the peak of a high mountain. Many dragons sprang upon him as he approached the Secret Sanctuary, but he overcame all with a word. This was an alchemical vision of his success in the Great Work. Crowley realized that he was born with all the talents required for a great magician.'[6]

Apart from allegedly providing the magician with the services of 316 spirit-advisers, the Abramelin system of magic was also said to grant the practitioner

A bust of W. B. Yeats by Albert Power. Yeats prevented Crowley's bid for supremacy in the Golden Dawn.

communion with the Holy Guardian Angel, an embodiment in visionary form of the higher spiritual self. But there was another potential benefit: Crowley could claim spiritual parity with Mathers in the Golden Dawn. For the time being, however, he was content for Mathers to be his ally on the path to magical power.

In January 1900, under Mathers' supervision in Paris, Crowley entered the Second Order — the Red Rose and the Cross of Gold — being admitted 'to the Glory of Tiphareth', the archetype of spiritual rebirth. He then challenged the authority of W. B. Yeats, who was the leader of the Golden Dawn in England. Yeats was unimpressed, regarding Crowley as an 'unspeakable mad person', and Crowley was unsuccessful in his bid for supremacy. The dispute, however, caused a rift among the Golden Dawn membership because Crowley had been sent by Mathers — and Mathers, in a letter to Annie Horniman, had claimed a spiritual infallibility over the Order as his right.

Having failed to dislodge Yeats, Crowley, apparently acting on impulse, withdrew from the dispute altogether, and in June 1900 left England to travel through Mexico, the United States, Ceylon and India before finally arriving in Cairo.

A REVELATION IN EGYPT

On 17 March 1904, in his apartment in Cairo, Crowley performed a magical ceremony invoking the Egyptian deity Thoth, god of wisdom. Crowley's wife Rose appeared to be in a dazed, mediumistic state, and the following day, when in a similar state, announced that Horus was waiting for her husband. According to his diary, she led him to the nearby Boulak Museum to a statue of Horus (in one of his several forms — this one being Ra-Hoor-Khuit). Crowley was amazed to find that the exhibit was numbered 666, the number of the Great Beast in the *Book of Revelations.* Crowley regarded this as a portent, and returned to his hotel, where he invoked Horus:

> *Strike, strike the master chord !*
> *Draw, draw the Flaming Sword !*
> *Crowning Child and Conquering Lord,*
> *Horus, avenger!*

On 20 March Crowley received a communication through Rose as medium that 'the Equinox of the Gods had come'. He arranged for an assistant curator at the Boulak Museum to make notes on the inscriptions from Stele 666, and Rose, meanwhile, advised her husband that at noon on 8, 9 and 10 April he should

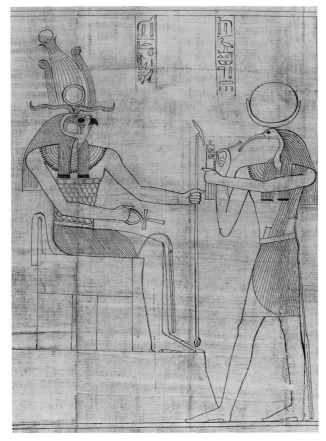

Drawing from the Greenfield papyrus, of falcon-headed Horus, in a crown with plumes and central sun-disc, *c.* 1305–1080 BCE. Ra-Hoor-Kuit is Crowley's rendering of the sun god's name Re-Herakhty, Horus-of-the-Horizon. Crowley's Tarot deck was named after ibis-headed Thoth, the scribe.

spend an hour in the room where the transcriptions had been made, writing down any impressions received. The messages, allegedly dictated by a semi-invisible Egyptian entity named Aiwaz (or Aiwass) – a messenger of Horus – resulted in the document that Crowley later called *Liber Al vel Legis* (*The Book of the Law*).[7] This became a turning point in his magical career. He was instructed to drop the ceremonial magic of the Golden Dawn: 'Behold! the rituals of the old time are black. Let the evil ones be cast away; let the good ones be purged by the prophet!' He was exhorted to pursue the magic of sexual partnership instead: 'Now ye shall know that the chosen priest and apostle of infinite space is the prince-priest The Beast, and in his woman called The Scarlet Woman is all power given. They shall gather my children into their fold: they shall bring the glory of the stars into the hearts of men. For he is ever a sun and she a moon.'

Crowley now increasingly identified with the Horus figure Ra-Hoor-Khuit. He came to realize that Aiwaz equated with Hoor-paar-Kraat (or Harpocrates, the God of Silence) – an entity whose sacred origins lay above the Abyss. He had contacted a Secret Chief without the assistance of MacGregor Mathers.

In Egyptian mythology the deities Nuit (female–the circle–passive) and Hadit (male–the point–active) produced through their union a divine child,

Ra-Hoor-Khuit. According to Crowley this combination of the principles of love and will incarnated the 'magical equation known as the Law of Thelema'.[8] *Thelema* is the Greek word for 'will', and the main dictum in his *Book of the Law* was, 'Do what thou Wilt, Love is the Law, Love under Will.' By this he meant that one should live according to the dictates of one's true Will, or spiritual purpose. Kenneth Grant, the leader of a modern OTO group in Britain and who knew Crowley at the end of his life, wrote: 'According to Crowley the true magical revival occurred in 1904, when an occult current of cosmic magnitude was initiated on the inner planes. Its focus was Aiwaz and it was transmitted through Crowley to the human plane.... The initiation of this occult current created a vortex, the birth-pangs of a New Aeon, technically called an Equinox of the Gods. Such an event recurs at intervals of approximately 2,000 years. Each such revival of magical power establishes a further link in the chain of humanity's evolution, which is but one phase only of the evolution of Consciousness.'[9]

Crowley was the 'divine child' who had been chosen by transcendent forces to bring to humanity a consciousness of the union of Nuit and Hadit. Previously there had been two other Aeons. The first – the Aeon of Isis – was a Matriarchal Age characterized by the worship of lunar deities: 'The Virgin,' said Crowley, 'contains in herself the Principle of Growth.' The second – the Aeon of Osiris – was a Patriarchal Age associated with the Sun: 'the formula of incarnating demi-gods or divine Kings, these must be slain and raised from the dead in one way or another.' Osiris and the resurrected Christ both belonged to this Aeon, and had now been superseded by the Aeon of Horus.

'With my Hawk's head,' Ra-Hoor-Khuit (Horus) proclaims in *The Book of the Law*, 'I peck at the eyes of Jesus as he hangs upon the Cross. I flap my wings in the face of Mohammed and blind him.... With my claws I tear out the flesh of the Indian and the Buddhist, Mongol and Din. Bahlasti! Ompedha! I spit on your crapulous creeds.'

The Age of Horus was based on the union of male and female polarities. This meant that the legendary symbol of the androgyne – a sacred figure in spiritual alchemy – assumed special importance. In *Magick in Theory and Practice*, Crowley writes: 'God is above sex, and so therefore neither man nor woman as such can be said fully to understand, much less to represent, God. It is therefore incumbent on the male magician to cultivate those female virtues in which he is deficient, and this task he must of course accomplish without in any way impairing his virility.'[10]

Since Crowley had received his revelation through a deity designated 666, it was clear to him that he must also be the Great Beast 666 – the Anti-Christ referred to in the *Book of Revelations*. He believed that he was a new magical messiah – the Lord of the New Aeon – whose doctrine would supersede Christianity and all the other

Aleister Crowley,
a self-portrait accompanied
by his phallic signature.

religions that had blocked spiritual freedom, which for him was based in sexuality. In *The Book of the Law*, the lunar principle was 'Babalon', the Scarlet Woman. And the Great Work – the attainment of Absolute Consciousness – would be achieved through the sexual union of the Great Beast with the Whore of Babalon: 'The Beast, as the embodiment of the Logos (which is *Thelema*, Will) symbolically and actually incarnates his Word each time a sacramental act of sexual congress occurs, i.e. each time love is made under Will.'[11]

According to Kenneth Grant in *The Magical Revival* (1972), Crowley maintained that in the Aeon of Horus, 'physical life is recognized as a sacrament. The sexual act of union for Crowley involved possession by the Highest Consciousness (namely Aiwaz).'[12] Crowley would spend much of his life seeking his Divine Whore. Although he never found a suitable and enduring partner, there were many who filled the role temporarily.[13]

Crowley was proposing a very different form of magic from that of the Golden Dawn. Mathers had considered Osiris a supreme symbol of spiritual rebirth, and had included references to this deity in the Tiphareth ritual of the Second Order. Crowley, as the new avatar, could offer his followers transcendental consciousness through the sacrament of sex: 'In sexual congress each coition is a sacrament of peculiar virtue since it effects a transformation of consciousness through annihilation of apparent duality. To be radically effective the transformation must be also an initiation. Because of the sacramental nature of the act, each union must be magically directed...the ritual must be directed to the transfinite and non-individualized consciousness represented by Egyptian Nuit.... The earthly Nuit is Isis, the Scarlet Woman.'[14]

His *Confessions* (first published in 1969) tell us: 'I was told that...a new epoch had begun. I was to formulate a link between the solar-spiritual force and mankind. Various considerations showed me that the Secret Chiefs of the Third Order [of the Argenteum Astrum] had sent a messenger to confer upon me the position which Mathers had forfeited.'[15] Crowley now believed he could speak 'with absolute authority'.[16] *Thelema*, he noted, '...implies not merely a new religion, but a new cosmology, a new philosophy, a new ethics.'[17]

Crowley notes in his *Confessions*: 'I wrote a formal note to Mathers informing him that the Secret Chiefs had appointed me visible head of the Order, and declared a new Magical Formula. I did not expect or receive an answer. I declared war on Mathers accordingly.'[18] Nevertheless, the next three years proved to be a magical hiatus for Aleister Crowley. For some time after the Cairo revelation he did not fully engage with the implications of *The Book of the Law* – perhaps he felt daunted by his cosmic role. The manuscript of *The Book of the Law* was even temporarily mislaid until Crowley rediscovered it in an attic in 1909.

The seal of the
Argenteum Astrum, Crowley's
magical order.

After the extraordinary events in Cairo, Crowley returned to Boleskine with Rose – who would soon give birth to their daughter Nuit Ma Ahathoor Hecate Sappho Jezebel Lilith. Crowley also founded a publishing company called The Society for the Propagation of Religious Truth as an outlet for his erotic poetry.

Soon he was planning a trip to Kangchenjunga, the world's third highest mountain – but this would end in tragedy, with the deaths of several guides in an avalanche. Devastated by this outcome, Crowley wrote to his brother-in-law, Gerald Kelly: 'I say today: to hell with Christianity, Rationalism, Buddhism, all the lumber of the centuries. I bring you a positive and primaeval fact, Magic by name: and with this I will build me a new Heaven and a new Earth. I want none of your faint approval or faint dispraise; I want blasphemy, murder, rape, revolution, anything, bad or good, but strong.'[19]

FROM ABRAMELIN TO ALGERIA – AND BEYOND

Despite the communications from Aiwaz, Crowley was still seeking a full spiritual experience of his Holy Guardian Angel, and, after a period of travel through China and North America in 1905–6, he once again turned his attention to the potent evocations of Abramelin the Mage. His letter to Gerald Kelly had called for 'anything strong', but the initial result of these new ritual workings induced a state of reverie. Crowley started work on a series of mystical tracts he called *The Holy Books*. Written between 1907 and 1911, these were not from dictation like *The Book of the Law* but had come to Crowley almost like automatic writing: 'I can only say that I was not wholly conscious at the time of what I was writing.' *The Holy Books* are among Crowley's most lyrical mystical writings and reveal an aspect in marked contrast to his more assertive and wilful persona:

> *Into my loneliness comes*
> *The sound of a flute in dim groves that haunt the uttermost hills*
> *Even from the brave river they reach to the edge of the wilderness*
> *And I behold Pan...*

1907 was also for Crowley the year he 'went wrong' – a time when he could, perhaps, have 'turned back'.[20] In this year he established his new magical order, the Argenteum Astrum, or Silver Star. Crowley mentions in a letter to John Symonds that at this time he took an oath to devote himself 'wholly to the uplifting of the human race'.[21] Initially the Argenteum Astrum seems to have been quite innocuous, drawing as it did on conventional borrowed sources. Crowley began rewriting Mathers' rituals, employing an amended form of the

Golden Dawn grades as well as including some yogic and Oriental material of his own. He also published the secret rituals of Mathers' Second Order, the Red Rose and Cross of Gold, in his occult journal *The Equinox*. Interestingly, although Crowley had made a commitment to the sex magic proclaimed in *The Book of the Law*, he did not initially include it within the grades of his new magical order. But the A∴ A∴ would nevertheless gradually develop as a vehicle for Crowley's increasingly overt bisexuality, and this would eventually bring Crowley's sex magic into public disrepute.

One of the early members of the A∴ A∴ was Victor Neuburg, a young poet who, like Crowley, had studied at Trinity College, Cambridge. From another A∴ A∴ member, Captain J. F. C. Fuller, Crowley heard that Neuburg had experimented with mediumship. In June 1907 he invited Neuburg to Boleskine, and there he demonstrated a remarkable facility for 'rising in the planes', at one stage having a vision of the archangel Gabriel, clad in white, with green spots on his wings and a Maltese cross on his head.[22] They soon entered into a homosexual magic liaison, tinged with sado-masochism, that would last until 1914.[23]

Following a painful divorce from Rose in 1909, Crowley went with Neuburg to Algeria to explore the magic of the sixteenth-century occultists Dr John Dee and Edward Kelley. This involved conjuring thirty so-called 'Aethyrs' or 'Aires' – magical entities from another dimension of time and space. Deep in the Algerian desert – at such locations as Aumale, Ain El Hajel, Bou-Saada, Benshrur, Tolga and Biskra – Crowley summoned the different Aethyrs in turn. Crowley brought with him a large golden topaz set in a wooden rose-cross decorated with ritual symbols. Choosing a solitary place, he would recite the required conjuration and then use his topaz as a focusing glass to concentrate his attention on the visionary landscape as it unfolded before his gaze. As a result of his Enochian 'calls' he had a number of visionary experiences transcribed by Neuburg as they occurred.

These visions included 'spirit-journeys' to magical mountains and sacred shrines, as well as mystical encounters with archetypal beings, temple guardians and other mythological entities, and are reminiscent of Gnostic and Merkabah apocalypses. Here is an extract from Crowley's conjuration of *Aethyr 24: Nia*: 'An angel comes forward into the stone like a warrior clad in chain-armour. Upon his head are plumes of gray, spread out like the fan of a peacock. About his feet a great army of scorpions and dogs, lions, elephants, and many other wild beasts. He stretches forth his arms to heaven and cries: "In the crackling of the lightning, in the rolling of the thunder, in the clashing of the swords and the hurling of the arrows: be thy name exalted!" Streams of fire come out of the heavens, a pale brilliant blue, like plumes. And they gather themselves and settle upon his lips. His lips are redder than roses, and the blue plumes gather themselves into a blue rose,

Crowley's less than convincing sketch of the demon Choronzon.

and from beneath the petals of the rose come brightly coloured humming-birds, and dew falls from the rose – honey-coloured dew. I stand in the shower of it.'[24]

The most dramatic conjuration was the tenth Aethyr, Zax, which included an encounter with the 'mighty devil' Choronzon. Crowley already knew that the tenth Aethyr was 'accursed' and he marked out a magical circle in the sand-dunes, fortifying it with sacred god-names to protect his friend. He then traced the triangle in which to evoke Choronzon, inscribing its sides with the magical names Anaphaxeton, Anaphaneton and Primeumaton, a protection against Choronzon breaking free. Crowley and Neuburg made a blood sacrifice within each point of the triangle, cutting the throats of three pigeons. Neuburg entered the circle with his ritual sword, dagger and writing equipment, while Crowley entered the triangle. 'This', writes John Symonds, 'is the only recorded instance of a magician's seating himself in the triangle of exorcism instead of remaining within the protection of the magic circle. It was to invite obsession by the demon when he was evoked into the triangle.'[25]

Crowley made the conjuration and began to describe to Neuburg what he saw in the topaz. It did not take long for Choronzon to appear from the outermost Abyss. Here are the opening lines of commentary for the tenth Aethyr from *The Vision and the Voice*: 'There is no being in the outermost Abyss, but constant forms come forth from the nothingness of it. Then the Devil of the Aethyr, that mighty devil Choronzon, crieth aloud, Zazas, Zazas, Nasatanada Zazas. I am the Master of Form, and from me all forms proceed. I am I. I have shut myself up from the spendthrifts, my gold is safe in my treasure-chamber, and I have made every living thing my concubine, and none shall touch them, save only I. And yet I am scorched, even while I shiver in the wind. He hateth me and tormenteth me. He would have stolen me from myself, but I shut myself up and mock at him, even while he plagueth me. From me come leprosy and pox and plague and cancer and cholera and the falling sickness. Ah! I will reach up to the knees of the Most High, and tear his phallus with my teeth, and I will bray his testicles in a mortar, and make poison thereof, to slay the sons of men.'[26]

Neuburg now began hallucinating – seeing within the magic triangle not Crowley but a beautiful Parisian courtesan with whom he had earlier fallen in love. Then, suddenly, Choronzon himself appeared within the triangle: '...the terror of darkness, and the blindness of night, and the deafness of the adder, and the tastelessness of stale and stagnant water, and the black fire of hatred, and the udders of the Cat of slime; not one thing but many things. Yet with all that, his torment is eternal. The sun burns him as he writhes naked upon the sands of hell, and the wind cuts him bitterly to the bone, a harsh dry wind, so that he is sore athirst.'[27]

Choronzon called out to Neuburg for water, but he refused to co-operate. An exchange of taunts now began, with Neuburg summoning the highest god-names he knew as a protection. Choronzon uttered a challenge: 'I feed upon the names of the Most High. I churn them in my jaws, and I void them from my fundament. I fear not the power of the Pentagram, for I am the Master of the Triangle.'

Then the figure in the triangle – Choronzon or Crowley, Neuburg could hardly distinguish between them now – began throwing sand from the triangle, breaking the circumference of the magical circle. 'Choronzon, in the form of a naked savage, leapt from the triangle into the circle, and fell upon Neuburg, throwing him to the ground. "He flung him to the earth," said Crowley, "and tried to tear out his throat with his froth-covered fangs." '[28]

Neuburg was able to ward him off with his magical dagger, and he transformed again into the French courtesan. There was 'an unsuccessful seduction scene' as the bisexual Crowley – or Choronzon – endeavoured to bring the conjuration towards completion. The ritual finally resolved itself without serious injury, but for a novice magician like Neuburg it must have been a terrifying lesson.

Back in England the Argenteum Astrum was growing modestly, building on a core membership that included Captain Fuller and Crowley's old teacher George Cecil Jones. In due course there were around a hundred initiates, among them Neuburg's friend and fellow-poet Pamela Hansford Johnson, Australian violinist Leila Waddell, mathematics lecturer Norman Mudd from Bloemfontein, and the visionary English artist Austin Osman Spare.

In May 1912 Crowley was visited one evening at his London flat by one Theodore Reuss, the head of a German masonic order called the Ordo Templi Orientis (Order of the Temple of the East). He was outraged that Crowley had published a statement that revealed the most prized secret of the Order's ninth degree – the sacrament of magical sex. Reuss pulled down from Crowley's bookshelf a copy of his recently published *The Book of Lies*,[29] a collection of magical commentaries. There, in the section entitled 'The Star Sapphire' were the lines: 'Let the Adept be armed with his Magick Rood and provided with his Mystic Rose.'

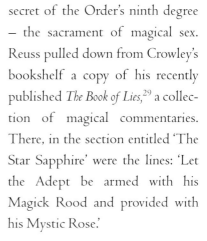

Lord of the New Aeon – the magical messiah for the Age of Horus, *c.* 1910.

The beautiful Australian violinist Leila Waddell, one of Crowley's many lovers, from *The Occult Review*, 1920s. Crowley called her the 'Mother of Heaven', and she became a probationer in the Argenteum Astrum in 1910.

Crowley told Reuss that he had never taken the ninth degree of the OTO, so he could hardly be in a position to reveal its secrets. He had used the Old English word *rood* meaning cross, but Reuss had assumed that he was referring to the phallus. Crowley now engaged Reuss in a discussion about sex magic which lasted for several hours. The outcome was that Crowley was to head a new magical order called the Mysteria Mystica Maxima, effectively an English subsidiary of the OTO.

In due course Crowley visited Berlin where he received instructional documents, was granted the title 'King of Ireland, Iona and all the Britains within the Sanctuary of the Gnosis', and took *Baphomet* as his new magical name. Later Crowley would adapt the ninth degree of the OTO to identify the priest and priestess as Osiris and Isis, 'seeking Nuit and Hadit through the vagina and the penis'.

Crowley also developed a series of homosexual magical rituals with Victor Neuburg featuring invocations to Thoth-Hermes. At one point in these rituals – known collectively as the *Paris Working* – Crowley scourged Neuburg on the buttocks and cut a cross on his chest.[30]

THE ABBEY OF THELEMA

If Crowley's magic was becoming debased and increasingly sadistic, his public notoriety still lay ahead. On 1 March 1920, following a modest inheritance from an aunt, Crowley consulted the *I Ching* – the ancient Taoist oracle – about where he should go to start the Great Work, the Law of Thelema. The oracle seemed to favour Cefalu, a small port in northern Sicily. So on 22 March Crowley set off with a Frenchwoman, Ninette Shumway, and her young son, soon to be joined by Leah Hirsig, who had already become his Scarlet Woman and had borne a daughter, Poupée.

In Cefalu he found a run-down villa to rent. The mighty rock of Cephaloedium lay to the north, and an ancient temple dedicated to Jupiter was also nearby. Crowley referred to the villa as his *Collegium ad Spiritum Sanctum.* The Abbey of Thelema would be a sanctuary where he could explore sex magic in earnest.

The central hall became the temple of Thelemic mysteries, and Crowley painted a magic circle, superimposed with a pentagram, upon the red-tiled floor. In the centre of the circle was a six-sided altar with full occult regalia – bell, lamen, sword and cup – and a copy of *The Book of the Law* with six candles on each side. Crowley's 'throne of the Beast' was in the eastern quarter of the temple, facing the altar, with a throne for the Scarlet Woman in the west. Painted around the inside of the magic circle were Hebrew names of God.

Crowley's paintings soon adorned the walls of the other five rooms. One was of a naked man being sodomized by the Great God Pan while ejaculating over the Whore of Stars; another featured a phallic serpent. Crowley maintained that sexually explicit paintings would help viewers to lose any inhibitions about sex.

Crowley had by now assumed the grade of Magus – the occult equivalent of Gautama Buddha – and was calling himself Mega Therion 666. Leah was known as Alostrael, and Ninette as Sister Cypris, or Beauty. Crowley considered both of them his concubines, although Leah remained his Scarlet Woman.

There was a steady stream of visitors to the Abbey – among them American film actress Jane Wolfe, who was much less glamorous than Crowley anticipated; Cecil Frederick Russell, an American naval hospital attendant whom Crowley had met in New York and who had fallen foul of the authorities for taking cocaine (Crowley enjoyed discussing drug experiences with him); a Lancashire bricklayer, Frank Bennett, who was also a member of Crowley's A∴ A∴ as well as the OTO;

The Ascension of the Ego from Ecstasy to Ecstasy, Austin Osman Spare, 1910. The artist joined the Argenteum Astrum in 1910 after contributing drawings to Crowley's occult journal *The Equinox*, but he later distanced himself from the Beast altogether.

Leah Hirsig, also known as Alostrael, became Crowley's Scarlet Woman and bore him a daughter. She is seen here in front of Crowley's painting of her as a 'dead soul'.

the novelist Mary Butts and her lover, Cecil Maitland; and Ninette's sisters Mimi and Helen. It wasn't long before Mary Butts and Cecil Maitland left for Paris, appalled by what they saw at the Abbey – especially the ritual 'baptism' of a cockerel slain in honour of Ra-Hoor-Khuit, and the spectacle of Crowley's Scarlet Woman endeavouring to copulate with a billy-goat.

Maintaining the Abbey was a drain on meagre resources, and Crowley once again began to run short of money. For a brief period he returned to England, and there met the novelist J. D. Beresford, an adviser to the London publisher William

Raoul Loveday, whose death at Cefalu in 1918 made Crowley even more notorious, leading to newspaper headlines.

Collins. As a consequence Collins signed Crowley up for his first commercial book venture: *Diary of a Drug Fiend.* He also received a contract from Rider to translate *The Key of the Mysteries* by French occultist Eliphas Lévi. So with some advance royalties, he returned to Cefalu.

A new follower was due to arrive, Raoul Loveday, an Oxford history graduate who had studied *The Equinox.* His wife, Betty May, was an artist's model who had at one time posed for the sculptor Jacob Epstein. Loveday was extremely anxious to meet Crowley in person. Betty was not so enthusiastic, but together they arrived in Cefalu in November 1922. Loveday warmed to the 'huddle of high lemon-coloured houses lying between the paws of a titanic rock fashioned roughly like a crouching lion' and he felt a sense 'of exultation as [he] stood there inhaling the sweet morning air.'[31] Betty, on the other hand, was soon complaining about the lack of food and poor sanitation.

Crowley installed Loveday as High Priest of the Abbey of Thelema, feeling that he 'possessed every qualification for becoming a Magician of the first rank. I designated him from the first interview to be my Magical heir.' Crowley gave him the title of *Frater Aud,* meaning 'magical light'. Like all male members of the Thelemic group Raoul had to shave his head, leaving a phallic forelock, and Betty, like the other women at the Abbey, was obliged to dye her hair either red or gold to symbolize the magical energy of Horus.

Only Crowley was allowed to use the pronoun 'I'. His followers had to learn to repress their egos, slashing their bodies with a razor every time they used the word, and Loveday's body was soon covered with cuts. His health declined further after he drank some blood from a silver cup at a ritual sacrifice of the Abbey's cat. On 16 February 1923, in spite of the ministrations of a local doctor, Loveday died. Proclaiming the passing of a worthy follower of Thelema, Crowley and the other members of the Abbey presided at his funeral with appropriate magical rites and readings from *The Book of the Law,* and Loveday was buried in the local cemetery.

Loveday's death precipitated a torrent of bad publicity for the Abbey of Thelema. Betty May returned to England – her fare paid by the British Consul in Palermo – and was interviewed by the *Sunday Express* which on 25 February ran this headline across its front page – 'NEW SINISTER REVELATIONS OF ALEISTER CROWLEY'. Gruesome details appeared in the article, many of them inaccurate, and adverse publicity was building against the Great Beast. Crowley's *Diary of a Drug Fiend* had been released in England just four months earlier, attracting hostile coverage in the *Sunday Express* and other newspapers. Mary Butts had also been interviewed, and spoke of 'profligacy and vice' in the Abbey of Thelema, while *John Bull* dubbed Crowley 'the wickedest man in the world'. In England Crowley's name became synonymous with bestiality and depravity. Worse was to come. Italy

Film maker Kenneth Anger
(right) in 1955 with sexologist
Alfred Kinsey at Crowley's
Abbey of Thelema in Cefalu,
which Anger was restoring
for a film on Crowley.
The pornographic
wallpaintings had been
whitewashed and the magic
circle cemented over when
the abbey had been
exorcised in 1918.

now had a new leader, Benito Mussolini, who disapproved of secret societies.
The Italian authorities had read about the Argenteum Astrum and the OTO in the
London newspapers. Crowley was summoned to the local police station on
23 April 1923 to be told that he had to leave Sicily immediately.

With the end of the Abbey of Thelema, Crowley's magical career was effectively
over. It is true that two years later, in 1925, Crowley was invited by the German
occultist Heinrich Traenker to become the international head of the OTO
(although a substantial minority of German members rejected both Crowley and
The Book of the Law)[32] and that the OTO subsequently took root in Britain and the
United States, albeit with different figures in charge. Crowley also assisted Gerald
Gardner in formulating a practical approach to modern witchcraft — both were
fascinated by sex magic rituals. But by 1930 most of Crowley's most powerful
writings and innovative ideas were behind him — a notable exception being his
work on the Tarot, The Book of Thoth, published in 1944 three years before his death.

Aleister Crowley's systematic approach to transcendent levels of magical and mystical consciousness, his emphasis on a personal commitment to ceremonial techniques and visualization – the hard work of practical magic – and his focus on self-empowerment – these are all among the most enduring aspects of his legacy. In the *Book of the Law*, he wrote, 'Every man and woman is a star', stressing that we have an innate obligation to discover our true spiritual purpose in the cosmos, wherever this may take us.

On the other hand, although Crowley hungered for spiritual illumination, he was also a slave to his need for public recognition. He loved power, was frequently cruel and disdained human weakness. His magical records reveal that he regarded women essentially as sex-objects.[33]

For all his notoriety, however, Aleister Crowley made himself an icon of the modern magical revival. His place in occult history is assured. Kenneth Grant continues Crowley's occult vision in the 'typhonic' tradition of the British OTO, and in the United States Crowley's influence has extended to the Temple of Set.

Crowley also succeeded in mythologizing himself in mainstream culture. He appeared as a character in novels – for example, Oliver Haddo in Somerset Maugham's *The Magician*, Karswell in M. R. James' *Casting the Runes*, and Theron Ware in James Blish's science fiction classic *Black Easter*. His photograph is featured on the cover of the Beatles' legendary *Sergeant Pepper* album, and David Bowie referred to him in 'Quicksand'.

Crowley has also been an inspiration for Led Zeppelin's guitarist Jimmy Page. Page studied Crowley's writings as a schoolboy, purchased Crowley's former home Boleskine in Scotland, and still owns one of the largest collections of Crowleyan books and manuscripts in the world. He composed a soundtrack for Kenneth Anger's Crowleyan film *Lucifer Rising*, before having a dispute with the film director.

Crowley has received strong endorsements in the international counterculture, from figures such as Timothy Leary – who cited him as a key influence in his autobiography *Flashbacks* – and from Robert Anton Wilson, author of *Cosmic Trigger* and the *Illuminatus* trilogy. Cult bands with Crowleyan connections include David Tibet's Current 93 group, the late Graham Bond, and Psychic TV and their association with the Crowleyan cult The Temple Ov Psychick Youth.[34]

Crowley was provocative in defying the status quo, and was a fierce defender of personal freedom and empowerment. Gerald Suster in *The Legacy of the Beast* (1989) wrote that the essence of the Law of Thelema is individualistic libertarianism.[35] Crowley's celebration of the individual has a timeless appeal, despite the infamy he attracted through his own unique approach to ritual magic.

Chapter Ten
Wicca and the Goddess

The current resurgence of witchcraft, or Wicca as it is generally known, is directly related to the rise of feminism as a social movement since the 1960s. In essence, modern witchcraft is a Nature-based religion with the Great Goddess as its principal deity. She can take many forms: the Great Mother or Mother Nature, or, more specifically, Artemis, Astarte, Athene, Demeter, Diana, Aphrodite, Hathor, Isis, Persephone, and many others.

In Wicca ritual the High Priest 'draws down the Moon' into the body of the High Priestess who becomes the incarnation of the Goddess. The High Priestess is the receptacle of wisdom and intuition, symbolized by the cup, and her consort is represented by a dagger known as an athame. Many rituals feature the act of uniting athame and cup as a symbol of sexual union, and there is a comparable relationship in Celtic mythology between the sacred oak tree and Mother Earth. Accordingly the High Priest, or consort, is sometimes known as the Oak King – a reference to the Oak of the Celts – and at other times as Cernunnos, 'The Horned One' – a reference to the Celtic lord of wild animals. In ancient Greece the Great God Pan – the goat-footed and horned god – was a symbol of Nature and the universal life-force, and in witchcraft the Horned God personifies fertility. There is no connection with the Christian horned Devil, although this has been a common error since the time of the witchcraft persecutions of the Middle Ages.

The name 'Wicca' derives from the Old English words *wicca* (masculine) and *wicce* (feminine) meaning 'a practitioner of witchcraft'. W*iccan*, 'witches', occurs in the Laws of King Alfred (*c.* 890 AD) and the verb *wiccian* – 'to bewitch' – was also used in this context. Wicca is sometimes known as the 'Craft of the Wise'.[1]

Wiccan covens vary in size, although the membership is usually thirteen – six men, six women and the High Priestess. When the group exceeds this number, some members leave to form a new coven. Wiccans take special magical names which they use in a ritual context. Contemporary Wicca recognizes three initiations. The first confers witch-status upon the neophyte, the second promotes a first-degree witch to the position of High Priestess or High Priest, and the third celebrates the bonding of the High Priestess and High Priest in the Great Rite – either real or symbolic sexual union.[2] It is also generally the rule that a man must be initiated by a woman and a woman by a man, although a parent may initiate a child

'The Horned One'. In Wicca the horned god is a personification of fertility – there is no connection with the Christian Devil.

of the same sex. Most covens do not admit anyone under the age of twenty-one.

There is also an emphasis in Wicca on the three-fold aspect of the Great Goddess in her role as Maid (youth, enchantment), Mother (maturity, fulfilment) and Crone (old age, wisdom). This personification of the phases of womenhood are represented, for example, by the Celtic triad Brigid-Dana-Morrigan; the Greek goddess in her three aspects Persephone-Demeter-Hecate, or by the three Furies – Alecto (goddess of beginnings), Tisiphone (goddess of continuation), Megaera (goddess of death and rebirth). These three-fold aspects are particularly important in the 'women's mysteries' of feminist Wicca groups.

In Wicca, as in other modern forms of esoteric practice, magic is usually classified as 'black' or 'white' and this has very much to do with intent. Black magic is pursued in order to cause harm to another person, and also to enhance the personal power of the magician in bringing this about. White magic, on the other hand, seeks a beneficial outcome, and is often associated with rites of healing, with eliminating evil or disease, and with the development of spiritual awareness.

ESBATS AND SABBATS

Wiccans honour both the lunar and the solar cycles of Nature. Esbats are the meetings of the coven held at full moon in each of the thirteen lunar months. The late Doreen Valiente (1922–99), a British Wiccan priestess and an authority on

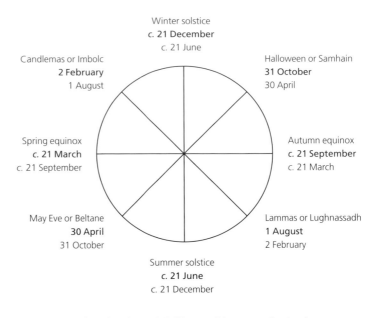

The Wheel of the Year

Winter solstice
c. **21 December**
c. 21 June

Candlemas or Imbolc
2 February
1 August

Halloween or Samhain
31 October
30 April

Spring equinox
c. **21 March**
c. 21 September

Autumn equinox
c. **21 September**
c. 21 March

May Eve or Beltane
30 April
31 October

Lammas or Lughnassadh
1 August
2 February

Summer solstice
c. **21 June**
c. 21 December

Northern hemisphere dates are in **bold type**, and the corresponding dates for the southern hemisphere are given beneath.

contemporary witchcraft, has written that 'the esbat is a smaller and less solemn occasion than the sabbat'.[3] Wiccans believe that at full moon lunar energy creates heightened psychic awareness, and many perform their invocations, love magic and healing ceremonies at esbats. But they are also a time for dancing, drinking and feasting — the word 'esbat' itself is thought to derive from the Old French *s'esbattre*, meaning 'to frolic and amuse oneself'.

The solar cycle is marked by eight sabbats referred to collectively as the Wheel of the Year: these are the two solstices, the two equinoxes and the four points between. Margot Adler, a leading Wiccan and author of *Drawing Down the Moon* (1988), a key work on American Neopaganism, has observed that these meetings renew a sense of living communion with the changes in the seasons and the land.[4] The major sabbats in the Wiccan Wheel of the Year are Candlemas, May Eve, Lammas and Halloween. They take their names — Imbolc, Beltane, Lughnasadh, Samhain — from the language of a branch of the Celtic tribes (Irish, Manx and Scots Gaelic). The lesser sabbats, probably festivals of Anglo-Saxon origin — are at the midsummer and midwinter solstices and the spring and autumn equinoxes.

The Wheel of the Year represents not only the cycle of the seasons but more specifically the cycle of Nature's fertility. This is also reflected in the major Wiccan initiations, which culminate with the sacred marriage of the God and Goddess whose union brings forth new life.

Halloween/Samhain (31 October)

The traditional beginning of the pagan year, Samhain means 'summer's end', and it is a time of grieving as the dying sun passes into the nether world. This is a celebration to honour the dead, and is said to be the time when the thin veil between the everyday and netherworld is most transparent, allowing Wiccans to communicate more readily with the spirits of the departed. It is also a time to reflect on one's own mortality. Mythologically, the dying God sleeps in the underworld awaiting rebirth. The seed of new life gestates within the womb of the Great Mother, the Queen of Darkness.

Candlemas/Imbolc (2 February)

This is 'the quickening of the year, the first stirrings of Spring in the womb of Mother Earth'[5] – Imbolc means 'in the belly', and this is a fertility celebration. The focus is on light and new life, as opposed to the receding darkness of winter. Imbolc is sometimes known as the Feast of Lights. Mythologically, the Goddess has become a Virgin.

May Eve/Beltane (30 April)

This marks the beginning of summer and is another fertility celebration. The name may come from the Celtic deity Bel or Balor – god of light and fire – in ancient times 'bel-fires' on hilltops celebrated the return of life and fertility to the world.[6] Wiccans often celebrate Beltane by dancing round the Maypole and celebrating the love between men and women. Mythologically, Beltane honours the mating of the Sun God with the fertile Earth Goddess. The Goddess is now pregnant.

Lammas/Lughnassadh (1 August)

Lammas is thought to mean 'Loaf Mass', and this is the time when the first corn is harvested, and marks the season of autumn. Lughnassadh was a celebration of Lugh, the Celtic sun god, associated with the waning power of the sun. Wiccans gather at Lammas to celebrate the gifts of abundance from the womb of the Goddess. Mythologically, Lughnassadh represents the God starting to die, but also fulfilment, the reaping of all that has been sown.[7]

Wicca is primarily a religion of the Goddess, but it is clear from the mythic cycle of the Greater Sabbats that the role of the Sun God is also very important. The Celts acknowledged that the Sun God passed through death to rebirth just as the Goddess waxed and waned through her lunar cycles. In Wicca the God of fertility is also thought to have two personas. The Oak King, the God of the Waxing Year,

Midwinter celebration at
the winter solstice.

Lammas, or loaf mass – a time
for harvesting the grain.

Handfasting – a contemporary witch's wedding.

represents expansion and growth, and is associated with the time of the year when the days grow longer. The Holly King, the God of the Waning Year, represents withdrawal and rest, and is linked with the time when the days grow shorter.

GERALD GARDNER AND THE RISE OF MODERN WITCHCRAFT

The British Witchcraft Act of 1604 was not finally repealed until 1951. Before this, books advocating witchcraft rituals could not be published in the United Kingdom. One of the principal figures associated with the emergence of modern witchcraft, Gerald Gardner (1884–1964) published a volume titled *High Magic's Aid* in 1949, but it was disguised as a work of fiction.

Gardner had come to magic late in life. Born at Blundellsands, near Liverpool, he was of well-to-do Scottish descent. Gardner had some interesting ancestors, including Vice-Admiral Alan Gardner, commander-in-chief of the Channel fleet against Napoleon in 1807, and Grissell Gairdner, who was burnt as a witch in Newburgh, Scotland, in 1610.

By 1936 Gardner had made a fortune as a rubber planter in Malaya. On his retirement, Gardner and his wife settled in the New Forest area of Hampshire, and, just before the outbreak of the Second World War, he made contact with a group of local occultists headed by 'Brother Aurelius' and Mrs Mabel Besant-Scott, daughter of the well known Theosophist Annie Besant. Calling themselves

Gerald Gardner with Aleister Crowley's walking stick at a witchcraft exhibition, 1951. Gardner met Crowley in Hastings in 1946.

the Fellowship of Crotona, they held theatrical performances claimed as 'Rosicrucian' in character. Some members of the Fellowship had links with an established witchcraft coven, and secret sabbat meetings were held at that time in the New Forest.

Gardner soon became an enthusiastic devotee of witchcraft. He claimed that he had been initiated in 1939 by 'Old Dorothy' Clutterbuck. Doreen Valiente was able to establish that 'Old Dorothy' was the daughter of Thomas St Quintin Clutterbuck, a captain of the 14th Sikhs. The antiquity of her witches' coven, of course, could not be proven, and 'Old Dorothy' herself was hardly the crone her name suggests. Like Gardner, she was well-to-do, and when she died in 1951 her estate was valued at more than £60,000.[8]

In 1940 Gardner and 'Old Dorothy' were involved in a major ritual on Lammas Day in the New Forest, directed against Hitler's threatened invasion of England. Covens from the south of England gathered for 'Operation Cone of Power', chanting against Hitler and his generals, and telepathically trying to implant the thoughts, 'You cannot cross the sea…. You are not able to come.'[9]

Gardner described his experiences in the New Forest coven in *High Magic's Aid*. Then, following a campaign by British spiritualists, the last of the Witchcraft Acts was repealed in 1951, and the so-called Old Religion was allowed to come forth from the shadows. Gardner's first non-fiction book on the Craft, *Witchcraft Today*, was released in 1954, followed by *The Meaning of Witchcraft* in 1959. These supported the view, now widely disputed, that modern witchcraft was a surviving remnant of the organized pagan religion that existed in England during the medieval witchcraft persecutions. Gardner's wish was that witchcraft would reclaim its place as an authentic, Nature-based spiritual tradition. Gardner maintained that witchcraft should be accessible to a broader public, and believed that its future rested with the young, perhaps even leading to a revival of the old pagan ways. And, although Gardner would not live to see it, Wicca has positioned itself at the very centre of the contemporary occult revival.

In 1946 Gardner and his friend Arnold Crowther called on Aleister Crowley, who had retired to lodgings in Hastings. Crowther had met Crowley during his wartime travels, and it was he who arranged for the two occultists to meet. The encounter is significant because modern ceremonial magic, as developed by Mathers and Crowley in the Golden Dawn, and the coven-based witchcraft of the New Forest were now crossing paths – perhaps for the first time. Gardner and Crowley had several discussions before Crowley died in December the following year.

Crowley made Gardner an honorary member of his sexual magic order, the Ordo Templi Orientis, and Gardner began using quotations from Crowley's writings in his rites. It is also likely that substantial sections of Gardner's magical credo were written by Crowley and then fused with the rituals from a witch's book of spells.

Other aspects of Gardnerian witchcraft, however, are quite likely Gardner's own, such as the tendency for witches to work naked, or 'sky-clad'. Gardner was an enthusiastic naturist, and Doreen Valiente said he had 'a deep-rooted belief in the value of going naked when circumstances favoured.' For him 'communal nakedness, sunshine and fresh air were natural and beneficial, both physically and psychologically.'[10] Gardner may have taken the idea of ritual nudity, however, from the 1889 book *Aradia: Gospel of the Witches*, written by Charles G. Leland, the American folklorist. Leland said he first learned about Aradia, daughter of the Roman Moon goddess Diana, from a hereditary Etruscan witch called Maddalena while he was visiting Italy. Leland's text includes details of Diana's role as Queen of the Witches, and also mentions that devotees of Diana were instructed to perform their rituals naked as a sign of personal freedom.

While Gardner's approach to nudity seems to have been wholesome enough, other less appealing sexual practices found their way into his witchcraft. According to Francis King in *Ritual Magic in England*, 'Gardner was a sado-masochist with both a taste for flagellation and marked voyeuristic tendencies. Heavy scourging was therefore incorporated into most of his rituals, and what Gardner called the "Great Rite" was sexual intercourse between the High Priest and the High Priestess while surrounded by the rest of the coven.'[11] Crowley had included coded allusions to similar practices in his *Book of Lies* and in his *Magick in Theory and Practice*.

Gardner's Neopaganism, however, was more respectful to women than Crowley's cult of the Whore of Babalon, and a significant modifying factor seems to have been provided by Doreen Valiente, who was initiated by Gardner into his coven in 1953. She felt that some of the Crowleyian material was either too 'modern' or inappropriate. Much of this was written out of the ceremonial procedures between 1954 and 1957, as Gardner and Valiente worked together preparing the rituals that would form the basis of the 'Gardnerian tradition'.

Following the repeal of the Witchcraft Act, Gardner left the New Forest coven in 1951 to start his own. He then moved to Castletown on the Isle of Man, where a Museum of Magic and Witchcraft had already been established by the occult enthusiast Cecil Williamson. Gardner bought the museum, became the 'resident witch', and added his own collection of ritual tools. While the Museum attracted considerable media attention, so too did the publication of Gardner's later books. The publicity following *Witchcraft Today* led to the rise of new covens across Britain. Gardner was dubbed Britain's Chief Witch, but this was a title he did not seek or use himself. According to those who knew him well, Gardner was not attracted to the pursuit of power or fame.

Every witch creates and maintains a personal Book of Shadows. As anthropologist Dr Lynne Hume has noted, the idea for this is attributed to Gardner. Doreen Valiente believed that he only used this term after he published *High Magic's Aid*. 'Material from Gardner's Book of Shadows…comes from various sources including Rudyard Kipling, Charles Leland, the Key of Solomon, the Order of the Golden Dawn and Aleister Crowley. It contains rituals for all Wiccan occasions and is meant to be handcopied by each witch after she or he has been initiated.'[12]

Wiccan high priestess Doreen Valiente, photographed by Ron Cook, her partner. The tree behind her was known as 'the Naked Man', and was a meeting place for witches in the New Forest.

Doreen Valiente's ritual altar with Goddess and God figures, and Gerald Gardner's own Book of Shadows open at the First Degree Oath. Photographed by Stewart Farrar, early 1980s.

Gerald Gardner at Castletown Museum, Witches' Mill, Isle of Man (opposite). Photographed by Stewart Farrar.

In 1963 Gardner met Raymond Buckland, an Englishman who had moved to the USA. Gardner's high priestess, Monique Wilson – also known as Lady Olwen – initiated Buckland into the Craft. and it was Buckland who would introduce Gardnerian witchcraft to the United States.[13]

Gardner died at sea, on the way back to England from a trip to Lebanon, on 12 February 1964, and was buried the next day in Tunis. He bequeathed his museum to Monique Wilson, who ran it with her husband for a short time and then sold it to the Ripley organization. Nevertheless, Gardner would have been content to know that witchcraft was to become the dominant tradition in international Neopaganism.

THE INFLUENCE OF ALEX SANDERS

Gardner and Alex Sanders (1916–88) are regarded as the two most influential figures in the early phase of the witchcraft revival. Sanders even has an entire Wiccan tradition named after him – the Alexandrian witches (a play on his name) are descended from his initiatory covens in the late 1960s and early 1970s. This period was undoubtedly his heyday, for he was by then much in the public eye, and with his wife Maxine, provided witchcraft with a certain ceremonial glamour.

By his own account Sanders was born in Manchester in 1916.[14] He would later help revive the worship of the lunar Goddess, and it is clear that his mother, sister and grandmother played a formative role in his upbringing, his often drunken father being much less significant. His mother was a cleaner, his father an itinerant musician. According to his biographer, June Johns, the family had to struggle to make ends meet, and Sanders was raised on bread-and-dripping.

It was his Welsh grandmother, Grandma Bibby, who would determine his occult career. One day when he was seven he came upon her naked, 'with wrinkled belly and match-stick thighs', engaged in a ritual in her kitchen. Sanders recalls that 'a number of curious objects surrounded her. These were swords, a black-handled knife, a sickle-shaped knife and various bowls lying around on the floor: other odd objects lay on a large Welsh dresser.'[15]

Frightened, he was sworn to secrecy by his grandmother and told he would be initiated. She ordered him to remove his clothes, step into the magical circle, and bend over with his head between his thighs. She nicked his scrotum with the sickle-knife, drawing blood. 'You're one of us now,' she told him. Later, she explained that she came from a line of witches dating back to the fourteenth-century Welsh chieftain Owain Glyn Dwr (Owen Glendower), who had worshipped the Great Goddess and kept the ancient Celtic traditions alive.

Over the next few years, a strong bond developed between Sanders and his grandmother. She instructed him in making love potions and good luck charms,

Maxine and Alex Sanders presiding at the First Degree Initiation of Janet Farrar in 1970, photographed by Stewart Farrar.

and also showed him the ceremony of 'drawing down the moon'. Sanders learnt how to write his own personal Book of Shadows.

When Grandma Bibby died in 1942, Sanders burnt her Book of Shadows, as is the custom when a witch 'passes over', but he retained her black-handled knife, her ceremonial sword and other ritual items. She had initiated him into the third degree, which included token sexual intercourse with her – an act symbolizing the union of the fertility goddess and her consort. Sanders now had an occult pedigree, but by his own admission, Sanders initially engaged in ritual magic to attain prosperity and sexual success – and in his case it appeared to work. He was taken up by a wealthy couple who for several years treated him as their son, and his friends were a frivolous group of promiscuous party-goers. But this phase passed. He resolved to develop several witchcraft covens in the Manchester area and to continue the work passed on to him by his grandmother.

It was at this time that Sanders met Maxine Morris, a young woman raised as a devout Roman Catholic and educated at the local convent. Her mother was a committed Christian, but Maxine herself had had childhood visions of merging with the earth and sky, and Sanders was convinced that she was a natural witch. Although they were not initially drawn together, they gradually realized a shared purpose. They married in 1967, moved to Notting Hill Gate in west London, and established a new coven together. A few years earlier Sanders had been endorsed by a group of 1,623 practising Wiccans as 'King of the Witches', and Maxine was soon to become known as the 'Witch Queen'. Sanders was becoming a media celebrity. There were television appearances, late-night talks on the radio, the biography by June Johns (1969), record albums of his rituals and even a film, *The Legend of the Witches*, based loosely on his pagan activities.

Sanders had gained a third-degree initiation from his grandmother, whereas Gardner had only received a first degree from Old Dorothy. It is a distinction which still rankles in some occult circles when witchcraft pedigrees are discussed, for both Sanders and Gardner continue to retain a substantial Neopagan following and questions of 'authenticity' and 'lineage', as always, produce rivalry.

Sanders and his wife separated in 1973. Maxine Morris continued running her coven in London with a new consort and a low-key public presence. Sanders, meanwhile, drifted towards semi-retirement and moved to Bexhill in Sussex, where he lived until his death in 1988.

Issues of lineage and authenticity resurfaced with the death of Alex Sanders, and several respected witches in Britain let it be known that they did not promote the public witchcraft endorsed by Sanders and his group. The influential English witch, Patricia Crowther – whose husband had introduced Gerald Gardner to Aleister Crowley in 1946 – was one of those who objected to Sanders' public style. Patricia Crowther had been initiated by Gardner on the Isle of Man in June 1960, and later established a coven with her husband in Sheffield. She took the initiation of High Priestess in October 1961, and was considered by many to be Gardner's natural successor. When we discussed the issue of occult secrecy in the mid-1980s, she told me that she was strongly opposed to witches who 'break their oaths' and release too much information to the public. For her, the 'old school' of witches – including Doreen Valiente, Lois Bourne and Eleanor Bone – were authentic, whereas many of those who had gone public had not been properly initiated.[16]

JANET AND STEWART FARRAR

The issue of how much authentic Wiccan lore could be revealed to the public would be addressed by Janet and Stewart Farrar, both of whom had been initiated in Alex Sanders' coven.[17] By the late 1970s the Farrars had assumed a leading role in London's Neopagan community, and they wrote several major works on Neopaganism, including *Eight Sabbats for Witches*, *The Witches' Way*, *The Witches' Goddess* and *The Witches' God* – all published in the United States as well as in Britain. The Farrars strongly influenced Neopagan thought and practice on both sides of the Atlantic. The rituals, spellcraft and conjurations described in their books, a working guide to witchcraft, provide the sort of information Patricia Crowther believes should remain restricted to the inner circle.

Janet Farrar (née Owen), born in 1950, was raised in East London in a strictly Anglican family. She began to drift away from Christianity in adolescence, and was later briefly involved in Transcendental Meditation. After working as a model, she became a secretary in the Beatles' London office. Around this time Janet visited Alex and Maxine's coven in Notting Hill Gate. She was impressed by Wicca as a spiritual path, and decided to join the circle, and it was here that she met Stewart. He had a very different background. Born in Essex in 1916, he had been raised as a Christian Scientist, but later became an agnostic. He studied journalism at University College, London, during the 1930s, served as an anti-aircraft gunnery instructor in the Second World War and later worked for several years as an editor for Reuters. He also produced several drama scripts for BBC Radio before becoming a feature writer for the weekly magazine *Reveille* in 1969. It was as a journalist that Stewart Farrar was invited to the Sanders' coven – to write about a Wiccan initiation – but he was converted instead to Neopaganism.

Despite the thirty-four years' difference in age, Janet Owen and Stewart Farrar were drawn together as magical partners, and in December 1970, a few months after their initiations, they left Sanders' group to form a coven of their own. They

Janet and Stewart Farrar in Ireland, 1984.

married five years later in a traditional Wiccan handfasting ceremony, and in 1976 moved to Ireland, where they established a new coven. Stewart Farrar died on 7 February 2000, but Janet Farrar has continued as a strong advocate of practical Wicca. She married fellow Wiccan practitioner Gavin Bone in May 2001, and continues to tour and lecture internationally.

Janet Farrar maintains that the essential aim of witchcraft is a spiritual fusion of male and female polarities, and the restoration of the sacred bond with Nature: 'Once a woman realizes her own psychic potential she becomes fully mature and can reunite man with herself in a way that mankind hasn't seen for aeons. We don't want to *replace* a male-dominated culture with a female-dominated one. We want to make the two work in perfect harmony. The world needs an injection of the pagan outlook, relating to the earth, relating to the environment, relating to our fellow creatures. Culture, religion and society have been male-dominated for over two thousand years, and life is out of balance. We need to recover the feminine aspect – the Goddess.'[18]

The broader concept of Goddess worship has also established itself as a major Neopagan influence. This extends beyond the structure of coven-based witchcraft, and its rituals are less bound by the Wiccan three-fold initiation. Many Goddess-worshippers do not refer to themselves as witches at all, for, in its broadest definition, this form of Neopagan belief is a universal feminist religion, drawing on mythologies from many ancient cultures. And while Wicca has characteristically British roots, reflecting Celtic influences, Goddess worship first emerged in the American feminist movement as a spiritual perspective clearly at odds with mainstream, patriarchal religion.

In her book *Changing of the Gods: Feminism and the End of Traditional Religions* (1979), Naomi Goldenberg writes of creating a 'powerful new religion' focused on the worship of the Goddess.[19] Around the same time influential thinker Mary Daly was talking of a new feminist witchcraft in which woman's nature could be considered as innately divine. For Neopagan women it would not be a matter of *reflecting* the goddess so much as *being* the goddess,[20] and this was a sacred potential in which all women could share. As Mary Farrell Bednarowski and Barbara Starret observed in 'Women in Occult America', 1983: 'Feminist witchcraft elevates woman's nature above man's nature in its life-giving abilities…. Feminist witches describe themselves as committing a 'political act' when they replace the Father with the Mother: the image of the Mother does not lose its old connotations of earth, intuition, nature, the body, the emotions, the unconscious etc. But it also lays claim to many of the connotations previously attributed to the father symbol: beauty, light, goodness, authority, activity, etc. The feminist witch claims both sun and moon, both heaven and earth, and she invokes the goddess in herself and in other women in her efforts to make it possible.'[21] This is a feminist concept of self-empowerment. For over twenty years American feminist Goddess worshippers have focused on 'sisterhood', and for some devotees this means a Goddess tradition excluding men.[22]

A leading advocate of this position is Z (pronounced Zee) Budapest. Z Budapest has even developed a 'self-blessing ritual' – a means of 'exorcising the patriarchal policeman, cleansing the deep mind, and filling it with positive images of the strength and beauty of women'.[23] Zsuzsanna Budapest was born in Hungary in 1940, the daughter of a psychic medium and Tarot-card reader. At the age of nineteen, Z left Vienna, where she had been studying languages, to study German literature at the University of Chicago. She worked in theatre in New York before moving to Los Angeles in 1970, where she opened a now legendary occult shop, the Feminist Wicca, on Lincoln Boulevarde in Venice. This served as a 'matriarchal spiritual centre', dispensing candles, oil, incense, herbs, jewelry and

High Priestess of the Dianic mysteries, Z. Budapest in Berkeley, California, 1984.

Tarot cards. Soon there were groups of Neopagan women meeting for ceremonies on the equinoxes and solstices – Z proclaimed that 'feminist spirituality had been born again'.[24]

Among her friends was Miriam Simos, a Jewish woman who had rejected traditional Judaism and Buddhism as 'male authoritarian'. After graduating from UCLA and studying feminism, Simos heard about Z's centre, and was interested in its public rituals for the goddess Diana. Now known by her magical name, Starhawk, she formed her own group in San Francisco and has written several key books, including *The Spiral Dance* (1979), *Dreaming the Dark* (1982) and *The Pagan Book of Living and Dying* (1997).

Meanwhile, on 10 February 1975, Z was arrested and charged with fortune-telling after giving a Tarot reading to an undercover policewoman. Before her trial, she announced that her supporters would be burning two thousand candles 'on altars throughout the city'. Fortune-telling was forbidden under the municipal code unless performed by a religious leader. Z, therefore, under the First Amendment, claimed exempt status as High Priestess of the Susan B. Anthony #1 Coven – a group named after a controversial nineteenth-century suffragette. She described herself as the 'first witch to go on trial for her beliefs in three hundred years'. The trial resulted in a $300 fine and a probation order forbidding Z to read Tarot cards. She turned instead to teaching classes in the Tarot, divination and witchcraft.

Influential feminist and Goddess worshipper, Starhawk, drumming at Twin Peaks, San Francisco.

Interviewed by journalist Cheri Lesh shortly after the trial, Z explained that Wicca was not an inverted form of Christianity, but represented the remnants of a much older, matriarchal system of worship that recognized the feminine as the creative force in Nature.[25] Z spoke of the bloody transition from a matriarchal to a patriarchal society, when warriors ravaged the great Queendoms of Anatolia, Sumer and Thrace, and fragmented the 'Great Goddess' into a number of minor deities. It is hardly surprising, therefore, that Z's Dianic worship excludes men altogether. The women's mysteries, in her view, must be kept pure and strong, and, as she told me when I interviewed her for a television documentary in 1985: 'We have *women's* circles. You don't put men in women's circles – they wouldn't be women's circles any more.'[26]

Z Budapest's friend Starhawk is less confrontational in her eloquent advocacy of Goddess mythology. A psychotherapist and teacher, she was a founding member of an organization in San Francisco called Reclaiming: A Center for Feminist Spirituality and Counseling. In the mid-1980s she taught at Matthew Fox's postgraduate Institute at Holy Names College in Oakland, exploring the common ground between her own Neopaganism and Fox's renegade Roman Catholic-based, Creation-centred spirituality.[27] She was featured in the film productions *Goddess Remembered* and *The Burning Times,* and remains one of the leading advocates of the Goddess tradition in America.

RESPONDING TO THE GODDESS

There are many ways to approach the Goddess whose sacred presence is at the very heart of Wicca. For Starhawk, the encounter with the Goddess should be based on personal *experience*, and not on religious belief: 'In the Craft, we do not *believe* in the Goddess – we connect with Her; through the moon, the stars, the ocean, the earth, through trees, animals, through other human beings, through ourselves. She is here. She is within us all. She is the full circle: earth, air, fire, water and essence – body, mind, spirit, emotions, change. The Goddess is first of all earth, the dark, nurturing mother who brings forth all life. She is the power of fertility and generation; the womb, and also the receptive tomb, the power of death. All proceeds from Her, all returns to Her.'[28]

Some Wiccans stress the all-encompassing nature of the Great Goddess, while others acknowledge an innate dynamism between the female and male polarities in the mythic universe. The Golden Dawn magician Dion Fortune – who in many ways anticipated feminist ideas in contemporary Wicca – believed that all goddesses are manifestations of the One Great Goddess, the universal feminine spirit of Nature. Margot Adler has similarly claimed that many Wiccans regard the Goddess as essentially One – a view she herself endorses, but she has also acknowledged that others distinguish between the Goddess of the moon, earth and sea, and the God of the woods, hunt and animal realm – a type of 'duotheism'.[29] Vivianne Crowley, British Wiccan priestess and writer, says, however: 'All Gods are different aspects of the one God and all Goddesses are different aspects of the one Goddess...ultimately these two are reconciled in the one divine essence.'[30] Starhawk also makes this point: 'For women, the Goddess is the symbol of the inmost self, and the beneficent, nurturing, liberating power within woman.... For a man, the Goddess, as well as being the universal life force, is his own, hidden, female self.'[31]

A Wiccan tract, passed informally among covens in Australia, interprets this idea in this way:

Neopagan spokesperson and author Margot Adler in New York, 1984.

> *Silence preceded everything. And within the silence was the natural spark of life, inherent in all things, the creative magical current which was both male and female, equal with each other.... Man and woman came together, became one in sexual union, with the spirit of magic within them. He was the Lord incarnate upon the Earth, and She was the Great Earth Mother.*[32]

DRAWING DOWN THE MOON

Drawing Down the Moon is central to Wiccan practice. The High Priest invokes the Goddess into the High Priestess in the opening ceremony:

I invoke Thee and beseech Thee, O Mighty Mother of all life and fertility.
By seed and root, by stem and bud, by leaf and flower and fruit, by life and Love
do I invoke Thee to descend into the body of this thy servant and High Priestess.[33]

This may be preceded by the 'five-fold kiss', an act of psycho-spiritual arousal performed by the High Priest: 'First he ceremonially kisses her from the feet up to the crown of her head by way of the knees, womb, breasts and lips. Next he visualizes links between the chakras (energy centres) of his own body with those of the priestess — beginning at the base of her spine and working up. When the two are connected...and the energy is flowing between them, he envisages the form of the Goddess behind the priestess. Then the Goddess is asked to "descend into the body" of the priestess. It is not unknown for other participants in the ceremony to see changes in the priestess as she becomes inspired, filled with the Goddess.'[34] Vivianne Crowley has described the experience: 'There was a stillness and silence within me. Then the flow of the power came, down through my crown chakra,

Drawing Down the Moon, the central ritual in Wicca, when the High Priestess embodies the Goddess.

down to my feet and out into the circle. She had come. I was far away, deep into samadhi; that state of consciousness whereby there is no longer any "I and other", "this and that", "far and near", only a sense of oneness with the universe.'[35]

The High Priest then addresses the coven:

> Listen to the words of the Great Mother; she who of old was called among men Artemis, Astarte, Athene, Dione, Melusine, Aphrodite, Cerridwen, Dana, Arianrhod, Isis, Bride, and by many other names.

The High Priestess as the Goddess incarnate now utters the Charge:

> Whenever ye have need of anything, once in the month, and better it be when the moon is full, then shall ye assemble in some secret place and adore the spirit of me, who am Queen of all witches. There shall ye assemble, ye who are fain to learn all sorcery, yet who have not won its deepest secrets; to these will I teach things that are yet unknown. And ye shall be free from slavery; and as sign that ye be really free, ye shall be naked in your rites; and ye shall dance, sing, feast, make music and love, all in my praise. For mine is the ecstasy of the spirit, and mine is also joy on earth; for my law is love unto all beings. Keep pure your highest ideal; strive ever towards it; let naught stop you or turn you aside. For mine is the secret door which opens up the Land of Youth, and mine is the cup of the wine of life, and the Cauldron of Cerridwen, which is the Holy Grail of immortality. I am the gracious Goddess, who gives the gift of joy unto the heart of man. Upon earth, I give the knowledge of the spirit eternal; and beyond death, I give peace, and freedom, and reunion with those who have gone before. Nor do I demand sacrifice; for behold, I am the mother of all living, and my love is poured out upon the earth.

The High Priest:

> Hear ye the words of the Star Goddess; she in the dust of whose feet are the hosts of heaven, and whose body encircles the universe.

The Goddess addresses the coven through the High Priestess:

> I who am the beauty of the green earth, and the white Moon among the stars, and the mystery of the waters, and the desire of the heart of man, call unto thy soul. Arise and come unto me. For I am the soul of Nature, who gives life to the universe. From me all things proceed, and unto me all things must return; and before my face, beloved of Gods and men, let thine innermost divine self be enfolded in the rapture of the infinite. Let my worship be within the heart that rejoiceth; for behold all acts of love and pleasure are my rituals. And therefore let there be beauty and strength, power and compassion, honour and humility, mirth and reverence within you.

And thou who thinkest to seek for me, know that seeking and yearning shall avail
thee not unless thou knowest the mystery; that if that which thou seekest thou findest
not within thee, thou wilt never find it without thee. For behold, I have been with
thee from the beginning; and I am that which is attained at the end of desire.'[36]

THE MAGIC CIRCLE AND THE CONE OF POWER

Wiccan ceremonies take place in a magic circle, a symbol of sacred space, inscribed upon the floor of a room set aside as the 'temple', or marked on the earth at a designated meeting place, for example, in a grove of trees or on the top of a sacred hill. The earth is swept with a ritual broom for purification, the circle is drawn with a stick or with chalk, and the four elements are ascribed to the four directions:

> Earth in the North (symbolizing the physical body)
> Air in the East (thoughts and communication)
> Fire in the South (energy and will)
> Water in the West (emotions and feelings)

The altar is traditionally placed in the North. Metaphysical beings known as the 'Lords of the Watchtowers' are believed to govern the four quarters and are invoked in rituals for blessings and protection. The centre of the circle represents Spirit — a resolution of the four elements and a true sense of unity.

In Wicca the magic circle has added significance, for it is a symbol of the womb of the Goddess and represents containment, totality and a sense of transcendent wholeness. Margot Adler calls the sacred circle a 'microcosm of the universe', and Starhawk says that it 'exists on the boundaries of ordinary space and time; it is "between the worlds" of the seen and unseen...a space in which alternate realities meet, in which the past and future are open to us.'[37]

Wiccans also build what they call 'the cone of power' — a vortex of collective magical energy. To do this, coven members run clockwise around the circle holding hands, at the same time focusing their attention on the central altar candle. Often this is accompanied by 'the Witches' Rune', a chant written by Gerald Gardner and Doreen Valiente, which has become international. It begins:

> *Eko, Eko Azarak*
> *Eko, Eko Zamilak*
> *Eko, Eko, Cernunnos*
> *Eko, Eko, Aradia*
> *Darkesome night and shining moon*
> *East, then South, then West, then North;*
> *Hearken to the Witches' Rune —*

And includes the lines:

Queen of heaven, Queen of hell,
Horned hunter of the night —
Lend your power unto the spell,
And work our will by magic rite!
By all the power of land and sea,
By all the might of moon and sun —
As we do will, so mote it be;
Chant the spell, and be it done!

THE TOOLS OF WITCHCRAFT

On the altar are placed the communion wine, an altar candle, and the witch's personal tools and 'weapons'. As with the Golden Dawn, certain magical implements define the nature of Wiccan ritual.

Sword

This is a symbol of power, sometimes used to cast the circle, and is a potent symbol of protection. The sword of the High Priest rests on the ground before the altar.

Athame

This is a double-edged black-handled knife — sometimes with symbols on its hilt — used to direct magical power, and sometimes to cast the magic circle. It should have an iron blade representing the will and an ebony handle representing steadfastness. A white-handled knife called a boline may also be on the altar, but its use is purely utilitarian.

Dagger

This is employed for invoking and banishing spirits associated with the element Air.

Cup or Chalice

This is associated with the element Water and is a symbol of the womb of the Goddess. When inserted into a chalice filled with liquid, the sacred marriage of the God and Goddess is symbolized. The cup is also used for the ritual wine.

Wand

Used to direct the will and to summon and control spirits. It must be held with both hands, with its point away from the body, and is made from willow, birch, hazel, oak or elder.

Altar in a witches' coven.
A sculpture of the Goddess
takes pride of place, and
a chalice, lamp and candle
are also to be seen.

Thurible

This is the brass container for incense which stands on three legs or hangs
from three chains. It is carried around the edge of the circle to purify it with
the elements of Fire and Air.

Pentacle or Disc

It is a symbol of the element Earth, and made of copper. It is used to call
earth spirits and sometimes also to cast the magic circle by rolling the disc
around the circumference. It also serves as a receptacle for the 'mooncakes'
eaten in communion at the close of the ritual.

Candelabra

Depending on the lunar cycle or the nature of the ritual, the three-pronged
holder will hold a white candle (the Goddess as maiden), a red candle
(as mother) or a black candle (as crone). The black candle represents age
and wisdom and is not symbolic of the 'black arts'.

Scourge

Intended primarily as an aid to spiritual purification in initiation ceremonies,
it is sometimes used for mild forms of self-flagellation and only rarely for
punishing offenders within the coven.

Altar Cloth

Placed on this, usually black or white, are containers for the salt and water
used to purify the circle with the elements Earth and Water.

Francesca Howell, Wiccan
High Priestess, casting the
magical circle outside Boulder,
Colorado, 2001. A member of
the Eco-Wiccan movement, she
specializes in earth-healing.

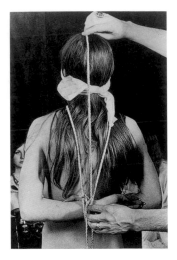

Janet Farrar photographed by Stewart Farrar at her First Degree Initiation, 1970. The inititiate is ritually bound by a cord, sometimes the cingulum itself.

Book of Shadows

The witch's personal collection of rituals, spells, herbal remedies and other details of occult lore is placed on the altar.

Images

Small figurines of the Goddess and the God appropriate to the specific ritual may be placed on the altar.

Besom

Broom fashioned from six different woods (birch, broom, hawthorn, hazel, rowan and willow) and used to clean the ritual area.

Cauldron

A female symbol. Made of cast iron, it has three legs, representing the three faces of the Goddess, and is used for ceremonial fire during indoor rituals.

In Wiccan ceremonies it is common for witches to work sky-clad, or naked, though in some groups robes are worn at all times. The most common ritual attire is a black hooded robe, large enough to allow for movement and dancing. High Priests and High Priestesses are often robed during major initiations, and may choose to wear a symbolically coloured cord, the cingulum, around the waist. This cord is traditionally 3 ft 6 in. long, to ensure that a witches' circle of at least 9 ft in diameter can easily be measured, and may also be used when candidates are ritually bound during initiation ceremonies.

THE NATURE OF EFFECTIVE RITUAL

In all magical religions – from ancient shamanism to contemporary Wicca – those performing a ritual believe that what they are doing is not simply theatrical, but accords with a sacred, inner reality. For a time the participant will feel caught up in a mystical drama. This is participating in a mystery, a transformative experience – engaging with the sacred nature of the Cosmos itself.

Selena Fox, a Wisconsin-based witch, divides rituals into three parts – preparation and orientation; the work or focus of the ritual itself; the closure and assimilation. Wiccans believe that sacred energy must be 'grounded' at the close of a ritual, enabling participants to return to the 'real' world. Sometimes a group will share 'cakes and wine' as part of the closure and there will be a parting blessing:

> *The circle is open but never broken*
> *Merry meet, merry part, and merry meet again.*

The circle is open but
never broken....

WICCA AND THE GODDESS

Chapter Eleven
Contemporary Satanism

If we are to understand contemporary satanism, we must explore the origins and philosophy of both the American Church of Satan and its successor, the Temple of Set, for they occupy a central position in the world of contemporary black magic. However, as will become evident, the Church of Satan is based primarily on hedonistic indulgence or pleasures of the flesh, the Temple of Set on metaphysical revelations from an ancient Egyptian spirit. The Church of Satan was always in one sense an offshoot of Californian show-business — a form of institutionalized party revelry. The Temple of Set, on the other hand, continues to explore a much broader esoteric domain, and is based on philosophical responses to the magical universe.

ANTON LAVEY AND THE CHURCH OF SATAN

From the very beginning, the Church of Satan was conceived as a religion of self-indulgence. Its founder, Anton LaVey (1930–97) was a carnival performer and musician, and his new religion was intended to shock conservative mainstream America out of its complacency and moral double standards. LaVey was known to his followers as the 'Black Pope', and made himself intentionally sinister, sporting a pointed beard, and wearing a black cloak and inverted pentagram. A close friend of Sammy Davis Jnr, he also later claimed a romantic involvement with both Marilyn Monroe and Jayne Mansfield. LaVey made Jayne Mansfield High Priestess of his church when she came to visit, but she herself maintained that this meeting was only in fun, and was at the suggestion of a publicist. As an orchestrator of occult extravaganzas, LaVey had no peer.

According to his main biographer, Blanche Barton, Anton Szandor LaVey was born in Chicago on 11 April 1930, and was of French, German, Russian and Romanian descent and also had Gypsy blood. The family moved to the San Francisco Bay Area shortly after he was born. He was attracted to the occult from an early age, and learnt about vampires from his Romanian maternal grandmother. He immersed himself in occult and fantasy literature, such as Bram Stoker's *Dracula* and the popular magazine *Weird Tales*. At the age of twelve he was familiar with medieval magical *grimoires* and the writings of Albertus Magnus. As a child, LaVey regarded school as a place 'to escape from', and at sixteen left his home in

Oakland to join the Clyde Beatty Circus as a cage boy, feeding and watering the big cats. Within a year he was handling eight lions and four tigers all at once – and frequently performing alone with the cats in the big cage.

Blanche Barton says that LaVey travelled with the Beatty Circus through California, Oregon, Washington, Nevada, Arizona and New Mexico before leaving at the end of the circus season in October 1947. He then worked in the Pike Amusement Park in Long Beach, California, playing a steam calliope,[1] and later played either a calliope or a Wurlitzer or Hammond organ for travelling shows on the Pacific coast. It was here that he was struck by Christian hypocrisy: 'On Saturday night I would see men lusting after half-naked girls dancing at the carnival, and on Sunday morning when I was playing the organ for tent-show evangelists at the other end of the carnival lot, I would see these same men sitting in the pews with their wives and children, asking God to forgive them and purge them of their carnal desires.'[2]

LaVey was inspired by his first wife to study criminology at San Francisco City College, and for a brief period was a photographer with the San Francisco Police Department. He saw 'people shot by nuts, knifed by friends, kids splattered in the gutter by hit-and-run drivers. It was disgusting and depressing.'[3] He concluded that violence was a part of the divine and inscrutable plan of God, and he turned away from God altogether as a source of inspiration and benevolence. LaVey went back to playing the organ, immersing himself further in his study of the occult and parapsychology. Soon he was holding weekly classes on esoteric topics, attended

American film star Jayne Mansfield with Anton LaVey in San Francisco in 1966.

by a diverse range of people, including novelist Stephen Schneck and avant-garde film producer Kenneth Anger. The Magic Circle met in his tightly shuttered house at 6114 California Street, and he gave lectures on vampires, werewolves, haunted houses, extrasensory perception and zombies. LaVey also lampooned the Catholic Church with a 'Black Mass' which involved desecrating the Host, using an inverted cross and black candles, and reciting prayers backwards.[4]

LaVey was fascinated by Sir Francis Dashwood's eighteenth-century Hellfire Club, which met in the ruins of an abbey at Medhenham on the Thames. Members of the British establishment had enjoyed evenings of debauchery with blasphemous hymns and orgies, conducted in chambers excavated beneath a hill. LaVey decided that the Magic Circle could provide a modern equivalent. In a typical act of bravado, LaVey shaved his head and announced the formation of the Church of Satan on the most demonic night of the year, Walpurgisnacht – associated with the ascendancy of the Powers of Darkness. LaVey declared 1966 to be Year One, Anno Satanas – the first year of the reign of Satan. The Age of Fire had begun.

Anton Szandor LaVey had no peer as an orchestrator of occult extravaganzas.

LaVey made the pronouncement: 'Satanism is the only religion in which a person can "turn on" to the pleasures around him without "dropping out" of society.' This was an emphatic rephrasing of the hippie dictum, 'Turn on, tune in and drop out,' then being advocated by counterculture guru Timothy Leary. LaVey was opposed to any notion of drug-based escapism: instead he emphasized sensual indulgence and personal empowerment. LaVey believed, essentially, that Man is God and God is Man. The ceremonies conducted in the Church of Satan would become a means for channelling magical power into a full expression of human carnal desire.

At 6114 California Street, the ritual altar room was completely black, with an inverted pentagram mounted on the wall above the fireplace. This particular pentagram represented the Sigil of Baphomet, a symbol purportedly adapted from the Knights Templars in the fourteenth century. Services began and ended with satanic hymns and a ritual invocation to Satan. A naked woman – a symbol of lust and self-indulgence – was used as an 'altar'.

Here is an account of a typical ceremony at the Church of Satan: 'A bell is rung nine times to signal the beginning of the service, the priest turning in a circle counterclockwise, ringing the bell to the four cardinal points. The leopard-skin cover is removed from the mantlepiece, revealing the nude body of the female volunteer altar for the evening. The purification is performed by one of the assistant priests, who sprinkles the congregation with a mixture of semen and water, symbolic of creative force. LaVey then takes a sword from its sheath, held by Diane, his wife and high priestess, and invokes Satan in his cardinal manifestations. Satan, in the South, represents Fire; Lucifer in the East, is symbolic of Air; Belial, in the North, represents Earth; and Leviathan, in the West, is his watery aspect. The officiating priest then drinks from the chalice, which is filled with any liquid he may desire, from lemonade to 100-proof vodka, making a symbolic offering to Satan. The chalice is then placed on the pubic area of the girl-altar, where it stays for the remainder of the evening.'[5]

The rituals themselves would vary from week to week, but invariably involved some form of personal wish-fulfilment: 'Members of the congregation are led forward into the center of a circle formed by the hooded priests and are asked what they desire. Accompanied by eerie organ music, the high priest touches the member's head lightly with a sword, in a kind of knighting gesture, and asks the Devil to grant the man's request. The member and the priests focus all their emotional powers on that which has been named. The request might be for material gain, for the acquiring of a mate, for the acquisition of a physical or emotional quality. Whatever the wish, the purpose of the ritual is to have the participant focus his powers inward, to enable him to visualize and achieve his objective. After each member of the congregation goes through this process and all are returned to their seats, the proceedings are brought to a close, the bell being run nine times clockwise, while the organ plays the satanic hymns.'[6]

LaVey believed in celebrating Christian 'sins' as virtues and formulated the following satanic statements as the quintessence of his approach:

> Satan represents indulgence instead of abstinence.
> Satan represents vital existence instead of spiritual pipe dreams.
> Satan represents undefiled wisdom instead of hypocritical self-deceit.
> Satan represents kindness to those who deserve it instead of love wasted on ingrates.
> Satan represents vengeance instead of turning the other cheek.

Satan represents responsibility to the responsible instead or concern for psychic vampires.

Satan represents man as just another animal...who, because of his 'divine spiritual an intellectual development' has become the most vicious animal of all.

Satan represents all of the so-called sins as they all lead to physical, mental or emotional gratification.

Satan has been the best friend the Church has ever had, as he has kept it in business all these years. [7]

LaVey also developed what he called the Eleven Satanic Rules of the Earth, which were effectively a guide to negotiating one's path through the 'human jungle':

Do not give opinions or advice unless you are asked.

Do not tell your troubles to others unless you are sure they want to hear them.

When in another's lair, show him respect or else do not go there.

If a guest in your lair annoys you, treat him cruelly and without mercy.

Do not make sexual advances unless you are given the mating signal.

The past and present High Priest of the Temple of Set, Dr Michael Aquino, photographed in 1984. He was the Temple of Set's first leader in 1975, and resumed the role in 2002.

Do not take that which does not belong to you unless it is a burden to the other person
  and he cries out to be relieved.

Acknowledge the power of magic if you have employed it successfully to obtain your desires.

If you deny the power of magic after having called upon it with success, you will lose all
  you have obtained.

Do not complain about anything to which you need not subject yourself.

Do not harm little children.

Do not kill non-human animals unless attacked or for your food.

When walking in open territory, bother no-one. If someone bothers you, ask him to stop.

If he does not stop, destroy him.[8]

LaVey's Rules combine parental authoritarianism with a streetwise wariness and a capacity for physical and magical confrontation. On one level LaVey was presenting a challenge to the conventional Christian mores of Middle America, but, while there was no place in his credo for humility, weakness, or 'turning the other cheek', he did not regard either himself or his Church as specifically anti-Christian. For him Christianity was simply irrelevant. It did not address humanity's basic emotional needs, it denied man's basic carnal nature, and placed its devotees in a position of dependence on a God who apparently had 'little concern regarding any suffering'. LaVey also had no illusions about vows of poverty as a means of gaining spiritual redemption. For him magic was essentially about power – and wealth was power. LaVey reserved the right to channel the funds of the Church of Satan for any purpose he saw fit. It was this that eventually led to a split in the Church leadership.

THE BIRTH OF THE TEMPLE OF SET

By 1975 it was clear that all was not well within the Church of Satan. In the words of LaVey's colleague Michael Aquino – editor of the newsletter *The Cloven Hoof* – the Church was now starting to attract far too many 'fad-followers, egomaniacs and assorted oddballs whose primary interest in becoming Satanists was to flash their membership cards for cocktail-party notoriety'.[9] At the same time, LaVey was finding that he couldn't survive as a full-time magician on the ten-dollar annual fee levied for Church membership, and it was this realization that brought about a crisis.

Early in 1975, LaVey announced in the newsletter that, forthwith, all higher degrees of initiation were available for contributions in cash, real estate or valuable objects of art. The effect, according to Aquino, was shattering: 'If there had been a single unifying factor that had brought us to Satanism, it was the Church's stand against hypocrisy. So when we learned of this policy, our reaction to it was that

The Temple of Set, like other magical orders, has revived the ancient Egyptian pantheon. Set, seated, holds an ankh. The other deity has a scarab's head. The Egyptian word for the sacred scarab *kheper* also represents 'becoming', and is associated with the Setian expression *xeper*, 'I have come into being'.

Anton LaVey was betraying his office, betraying everything that he had worked for, for so many years.'[10]

There was no way of dismissing the leader – the Church of Satan to all intents and purposes was vested in him. The only alternative was for the priesthood to leave. In June 1975 key members of the priesthood resigned from the Church of Satan taking many other members with them, at the same time making it clear that they were not leaving the priesthood itself. 'In fact,' says Aquino, 'we had a sacred responsibility to take it with us.'

Michael Aquino, a graduate from the University of California at Santa Barbara, with a strong interest in comparative religion and philosophy, had joined the Church of Satan in 1969.[11] He was now a Priest of the fourth degree and the senior member of the splinter group. However it was clear that new guidelines were required from Satan himself. On the evening of 21 June 1975, in a ritual magic ceremony, Aquino summoned the Prince of Darkness, 'to tell us what we may do to continue our Quest'. The result, according to Aquino, was an act of automatic writing, 'a communication from a god to a human being'.

In a document known as *The Book of Coming Forth by Night*, Satan now revealed himself as the ancient Egyptian god Set, and named Aquino as LaVey's replacement. Aquino was described in the script as the successor to Aleister Crowley, and Magus, fifth degree, of the new Aeon of Set. Gone were all references to the

Christian Devil. A new name was bestowed on both Church and deity:

Reconsecrate my Temple and my Order in the true name of Set. No longer will I accept the bastard title of a Hebrew Fiend.

There were also other instructions for the new magical epoch:

When I came first to this world, I gave to you my great pentagram, timeless measure of beauty through proportion. And it was shown inverse, that creation and change be exalted above rest and preservation.
With the years my pentagram was corrupted, yet time has not the power to destroy it. Its position was restored by the Church of Satan, but its essence was dimmed with a Moorish name, and the perverse letters of the Hebrews, and the goat of decadent Khar. During the Age of Satan I allowed this curious corruption, for it was meant to do me honour as I was then perceived.
But this is now my Aeon, and my pentagram is again to be pure in its splendour. Cast aside the corruptions, that the pentagram of Set may shine forth. Let all who seek me be never without it, openly and with pride, for by it shall I know them. Let the one who aspires to my knowledge be called by the name Setian...[12]
The Word of the Aeon of Set is Xeper — 'become'.

A NEW DIRECTION

Aquino maintains that this revelation led the priesthood of the former Church of Satan into completely new areas of enquiry: 'The founders of the Temple of Set knew very little about Egyptology and we had to go and find out who Set was, and

Drawing of the Tomb of Tansart in Thebes, 1835–40. In Ancient Egypt the rising sun was equated with the scarab, pushing its ball of dung, out of which it was believed that its offspring emerged, as the sun emerged from the east. The evening sun was represented by the ram-headed Horus.

why something like this should be happening.' The usual understanding was that Osiris was the benevolent father-god and his evil brother Set murdered him. 'In our research we discovered that...the initial identity of Set had been that of the god of night, of the darkness, as opposed to the god of the day, the sun. Set symbolized the *isolated psyche*, the spark of life within the self, a creative force in the universe rather than an enemy figure, an inspiration for the individual consciousness.'[13]

The magical word *xeper* would also become central to the philosophy of the Temple of Set. Pronounced *khefer*, it translated as 'I have come into being'. The Temple of Set took the scarab, symbol of the sun god in his aspect as the lord of rebirth, and the dawning sun itself as representing immortality and infinite potential. In a recent statement exploring the significance of *xeper*, senior member of the Temple of Set, Don Webb, has written that this word 'generates the Aeon of Set, and is the current form of the Eternal Word of the Prince of Darkness. To know this word is to know that the ultimate responsibility for the evolution of your psyche is in your hands. It is the Word of freedom, ecstasy, fearful responsibility, and the root of all magic.'[14]

Webb describes *xeper* as 'the experience of an individual psyche becoming aware of its own existence and deciding to expand and evolve that existence through its own actions'. And since the Temple of Set reveres the magical potential of the individual, the focus of the entire organization reflects this – all Setians are on an individual magical journey, and where this will take them is essentially up to them.

While there are various initiatory degrees within the Temple of Set, there are no prescribed rituals or dogmas, and no specific vows. According to Lilith Sinclair, Aquino's wife and fellow priestess in the Temple of Set, the rituals in the Church of Satan used to be presented 'on a very self-indulgent, materialistic level', and Satan himself was 'more a symbol than an actual reality', but in the Temple of Set her personal contact with the Prince of Darkness has been 'a very quiet, serene, beautiful touching of minds'. She emphasizes that there is no pact signed in blood, as popular folklore would have it, but instead a type of private vow: 'It's done on an individual basis, and it's something that I myself wanted to do.' While most forms of mysticism and Neopagan religion advocate the final surrender of the ego in a state of transcendence, in the Setian philosophy, awareness of the personal self is maintained at all times. When communicating with Set, says Lilith, 'You retain your individuality...but at the same time you are linked with the essence of the Prince of Darkness. It's a natural exchange and flow of energy, of mind awareness.'[15]

During the later years of the Church of Satan, Anton LaVey and his wife Diane tired of holding meetings solely in their own home and decided to sponsor other branches of the Church – both in San Francisco and in other cities across the nation. Known as Grottos, these branches were established as far afield as

Louisville, Kentucky, Santa Cruz, San Jose, Los Angeles, Denver, Dayton, Ohio, Detroit, Washington, DC, and New York – and were mostly centred around charismatic individuals intent on spreading the Satanic doctrine. LaVey had called himself High Priest of Satan and there were five initiatory degrees: Apprentice Satanist I°, Witch or Warlock II°, Priest of Priestess of Mendes III°, Magister IV°, and Magus V°. Even within these grades, however, the satanic quest was considered something *personal* – a developing relationship between the individual and the Prince of Darkness.

PYLONS OF THE TEMPLE OF SET

The Temple of Set maintains a comparable structure of initiatory degrees, although the Grottos have now been replaced by 'Pylons'. A key to the thinking behind this term is in Aquino's privately published volume on the Church of Satan (1983): 'Humanity is like a tall building. It needs stage after stage of scaffolding. Religion after religion, philosophy after philosophy; one cannot build the twentieth floor from the scaffolding of the first.'[16] A 1998 statement from the Temple of Set also makes it clear that the reference to Pylons derives from the massive fortified gateways of the temples of ancient Egypt.[17] The concept of Pylons is much more substantial than that of Grottos, and the intent is clearly more serious, although the core attitude remains the same: man is God, or a potential God. 'The mission of the Temple of Set is to recreate a tradition of self-deification.'[18]

The Temple of Luxor showing a pylon, obelisk and colossal statues of Ramses II. The image of a pylon as 'a narrow gateway within' has influenced the Setian philosophy. Lithograph by David Roberts, London, 1846.

The Temple of Set has authorized the establishment of Pylons in a number of towns and cities across the United States, as well as in Australia, Britain, Germany and Finland – although the extent of its membership is not publicly revealed.[19] Just as Grottos could only be established by second-degree members of the Church of Satan, Pylons are similarly sponsored by a senior Setian – in this case a third-degree member known as a Sentinel. Pylon meetings are generally held in members' homes, and their purpose is to 'provide a focus for the initiate, a place to internalize knowledge'.[20] The Temple of Amen-Ra at Luxor is referred to by way of illustration: '…the gateway presents a passage to the outside world, a narrow gateway within, and serves as a secure wall to the persons within. This is a good metaphor for what a Pylon should be…. The gateway to Pylons is narrow; it is easily guarded by one man or woman. The role of the Sentinel is a guardianship role.'[21] The Setian commitment itself, however, remains essentially a private and internal process: 'The gateway to your own initiation is in your heart, but often hidden there by circumstance and habit. External gateways are symbols you can use in making your rites of passage. Most of the rites of passage you need in your life, you will have to create yourself. Pylons are one such gateway. Real initiation doesn't come from texts, it passes from mouth to ear.'[22]

Nevertheless, the Temple of Set recognizes initiatory degrees and has a structure similar to that of the Church of Satan. There are different orders within the Temple dedicated to different types of magical research. One of these is the Order of the Trapezoid, whose particular focus is the rune magic of northern Europe – work associated with senior Temple scholar Dr Stephen Flowers. In 1996, Don Webb, (who subsequently ascended to the emeritus grade – Ipsissimus VI°) assumed the role of High Priest, or Magus V°. In 2002 he retired from this role, being replaced in 2002 by Anton LaVey's youngest daughter High Priestess Zeena Schreck, a Magistra IV° of the Temple.[23] She, however, resigned after six weeks, and Michael Aquino replaced her. He is also an Ipsissimus VI°.

THE SETIAN PERSPECTIVE

As the first High Priest of the Temple of Set, Aquino remains its principal formulator, and the Temple reflects his intellectual background. Aquino divides the manifested universe broadly into three levels of reality. In the everyday world – the co-called 'natural order' – we observe cause and effect, and the scientific method and technology are based on this. At another level, exemplified by the writings of Plato, whom Aquino admires, is philosophic thought. This is characterized by the processes of deduction and induction: the power of reason buttressed by observable fact. And beyond this is the world of magical reality. According to Aquino, there is a spiritual and psychic dimension to the human condition, and this transcends the more mundane levels of existence.

Where he differs from Christians, mystics and pagans – whom for this purpose he groups together – is in his belief that the psychic dimension *separates* mankind from the rest of Nature. For him, mystics and occultists alike are generally content to subsume their selfhood in the flow of cosmic consciousness – essentially an act of surrender. Christians, meanwhile, are oppressed with feelings of guilt, and find themselves endorsing 'hackneyed moral standards' in an effort to appease God. For Aquino, Satanism is unique because it advocates personal behaviour that is self-determined: 'All conventional religions, including the pagan ones, are simply a variation on the theme of reunion and submergence of the self within the natural universe. So from our point of view, it really makes no difference whether you pray to a Father god or to a Mother goddess – or to an entire gaggle of gods and goddesses! You are still wishing for their acceptance. You are waiting for them to put their arms around you and say: "You belong. You are part of us. You can relax. We will take care of you. We approve of you. We endorse you." The satanist, or black magician, does not seek that kind of submergence of the self. We do not seek to have our decisions and our morality approved or validated by any higher god or being. We take responsibility unto ourselves.'[24]

This, of course, begs the question of how the satanist stands in relation to Set, who is presumably regarded as a being on a higher plane of existence. According to Aquino, 'We do not pray to the Devil or Satan or Set. We have no desires or wishes that we expect to be granted by some sort of divinity. We consider Set to be our activating force and the entire notion of good and evil is something which is determined by human beings themselves. We cannot pass the responsibility to *any* god, whether it is a so-called benevolent god or a so-called evil god.' [25]

Those who have explored the different self-development and transpersonal movements will recognize here the self-actualizing philosophy in a different form.[26] As Werner Erhard, founder of *est* (Erhard seminar training), emphasized in his workshops and seminars, we should all learn to take responsibility for our own being, and in so doing we are then able to create our own reality. Others within the personal growth movement have similarly emphasized that we should 'own our own lives' and become independent psychic powers in a universe essentially of our own making — all of which implies that man has the potential to become a god. However, Lilith Sinclair expresses this position more emphatically: 'We regard ourselves very highly because we feel we are superior beings. We feel that we are gaining the knowledge of a deeper universe.'

Both Aquino and Webb endorse this view. According to Aquino, the Temple of Set has introduced a new philosophical epoch — a 'state of mental evolution', and Webb: 'If we want to participate in the cultural revolution/evolution of the New Cycle, the best method is to transform ourselves. To actively seek, every day, those experiences and perform those deeds that lead to wisdom. If the magician transforms himself or herself, the actions of the magician lead to a transformation of the world around them. If one becomes as a god, one's words and deeds will have the effect of gods.' [27]

NAZIS, DEATH AND NECROMANCY

The Temple of Set advocates the *deification* of its individual members. This brings with it the associated mythology of the *spiritual illuminati* — a doctrine of the elect that some have associated with mystical fascism. It comes as no surprise that Aquino has acknowledged a strong attraction to certain aspects of the former German Nazi regime.

Links between Setian philosophy and the magical practices of the esoteric Nazi group led by Heinrich Himmler are difficult to trace, but are there, nevertheless. Although Aquino states clearly that many aspects of the Nazi regime are repugnant to him, he is also convinced that the Nazis were able to summon an extraordinary psychic force which was misdirected but need not have been. Associated with the Setian quest for the *super* man, or *initiated* man, is the implication that, as a

The Nazi leader Heinrich Himmler, whose magical order, the Ahnenerbe, sought personal immortality. Setians similarly seek to transcend death.

god, the magical adept would gain the means to live forever – becoming a bright star in the firmament.

In the newsletter *Runes*, Aquino comments that 'the successful magician must develop and ultimately master the ability to make himself the *constant*, and everything else *variable*, subject to his Will' (my italics).[28] This means the magician 'moves gradually towards an existence in which time becomes your servant and not your master', and will also, 'enable you to conquer death.'

Aquino quotes from the classic of Egyptian thought, *Her-Bak*, which includes a sage's answer to the young priest Her-Bak's inquiry about life and death: 'What is life? It is a form of the divine presence. It is the power, immanent in created things, to change themselves by successive destructions of form until the spirit or activating force of the original life-stream is freed. This power resides in the very nature of things.... It is the spiritual aim of all human life to attain a state of consciousness that is independent of bodily circumstance.'

Aquino believes that the Nazis tried to transfer the life-consciousness from the individual to the state, but that members of Himmler's esoteric group understood the process on a deeper level: 'Most Nazis were able to achieve [the transfer of consciousness] only in a mundane sense – in a kind of ecstatic selflessness created and sustained by propaganda. But the "monk-knights" of the pre-war SS could disdain, even willingly embrace, the death of the individual human body because the consciousness had been transferred to a larger life-form – that of the Hegelian state – and individual sacrifice towards the strengthening of that life-form would actually contribute towards one's immortality. All of the individual-death references in the SS, such as the *Totenkopf* insignia and ritual pledges of "Faithfulness unto death" were in fact arrogant affirmations of immortality.'[29]

This led to a magical ceremony undertaken by Aquino in a chamber in Wewelsburg Castle, beneath the Marble Hall used by Himmler's magical order – the Ahnenerbe. The castle is located in German Westphalia, on the site of ancient Saxon fortifications. In 1815, the North Tower was nearly destroyed by lightning, and the castle fell into neglect. In 1933 the SS acquired Wewelsburg as its inner sanctum, and Himmler began reconstruction. One of his innovations was to build a circular chamber known as the Marmorsaal (Marble Hall) to replace the original chapel. According to Aquino, it was inspired by the Hall of the Grail created by Alfred Roller, on Hitler's instructions, for the 1934 production of *Parsifal* at Bayreuth.

Set in the red Italian marble floor is a dark green marble disc from which extend twelve rune-motifs. The design as a whole, while usually categorized as a 'solar symbol', is actually a secret magical sigil from an esoteric order, the Westphaelischen Femgerichte, also known as the Vehm. As such, the room was an ideal meeting place for the Ahnenerbe, who believed they were part of the same magical tradition.

It is clear that Aquino sees the inner group of priests and priestesses of the Temple of Set as the magical successors to the Ahnenerbe and Vehm. It was beneath the Marble Hall, in a secret chamber known as the Hall of the Dead, that he performed another ritual invocation to the Prince of Darkness in 1982. We have no details for there are aspects of the Setian doctrine that are secret. We do know, however, that during the ceremony Aquino confirmed his belief that magically *man stands apart from the universe*. In his own words: 'The Wewelsburg working asserts that Life is conceptually contrary to Nature…and "unnatural" in its very essence.'[30]

For Aquino, the essential task of the magical initiate is to evolve to god-like proportions, subjecting the 'natural' universe to his will. Man owes his special status on earth to 'the deliberate intervention of a non-natural intelligence [known as Set] and the respect accorded to the Prince of Darkness is simply an acknowledgment that he inspires man to strive ever higher in his quest for dominance.' Included in this pursuit is the attempt to conquer death. Whereas most mystics believe they must surrender their individuality to the godhead – *Nirvana, Sunyata, Ain Soph Aur* – Aquino maintains that this is ill-advised: 'We would simply say that

The Hall of the Grail, created by Alfred Roller for the 1934 production of *Parsifal* at Bayreuth. According to Michael Aquino, it inspired Himmler's Marmorsaal at Wewelsburg Castle.

what they have is a sort of sublimated death-wish of the self and that we, unlike them, do not want to die.'[31]

The key to Michael Aquino's philosophy of cheating death is also contained in the *Runes* newsletter. This involves manipulating the animating force in living things. Aquino believes that the psyche is neither dependent on, nor imprisoned by, the body, and that the mind of the magician is capable of reaching out 'towards the limitlessness of its conscious existence'. This is what *xeper* really means. For the master Setian, the conscious universe literally has no boundaries. Aquino developed this idea from a statement contained in *The Book of Lucifer* in Anton LaVey's *Satanic Bible:* 'If a person has been vital throughout his life and has fought to the end for his earthly existence, it is this ego which will refuse to die, even after the expiration of the flesh which housed it…. It is this…vitality that will allow the Satanist to peek through the curtain of darkness and death, and remain earthbound.'[32] The broader implication is that the satanist can meddle with life-forces governing the principles of birth, death and creation – manipulating the processes of Nature for his own ends.

THE SYMBOLISM OF BLACK MAGIC

Members of both the Church of Satan and Temple of Set have described themselves as 'black magicians', and yet their idea of *black magic* is clearly different from that prevailing in the popular imagination. For most people, the idea of black magic involves harmful intent, intended to do serious injury to another person or group of people, or to damage property – that is, basically destructive. This is not, however, how the Setians themselves regard their magical orientation. Leon Wild, editor of *The Ninth Night* – an Internet journal committed to Setian principles – has recently drawn a clear distinction between what he calls 'the myth of Satanic crime' and the core *raison d'etre* of the black magician. In his view, legitimate satanists do not kill or injure people or animals, do not engage in rape or human sacrifice, do not burn or desecrate the churches of other religions, and do not interfere with burial grounds – even though they are frequently accused of all these things.[33]

There are psychopaths in all walks of life, many of whom are attracted to the self-empowering philosophies presented by the occult traditions. Many such people – Charles Manson and his followers included – have committed terrible crimes through their deranged advocacy of the black arts. So we are obliged to ask whether all 'black magicians' are necessarily psychopaths or deviants.

There can be little doubt that for the first nine years of its existence the Church of Satan was an organization dedicated to licentious self-indulgence, advocating uninhibited revelry in 'sin' rather than a full-blown engagement in 'evil'. Nevertheless, its anti-Christian antics are hard to take seriously, offensive though they must

Vignette from the Papyrus of Herubes, c. 1000 BCE, showing the night voyage of the sun. The serpent lord of the netherworld, Apepi, tries to swallow the sun, but is attacked by Set. Setians believe Set, lord of the night, is the symbol of dynamic force for change, and that darkness does not represent evil but infinite human potential.

have been to many practising Christians. The Temple of Set presents a more cerebral and philosophical perspective. Aquino's interest in Himmler's esoteric practices provides very strong cause for concern, but the appeal seems to be associated with notions of immortality and superhuman aspirations rather than with flagrant evil.

For many contemporary black magicians, the so-called 'left-hand path' in magic would seem to mean something else altogether. Leon Wild distinguishes between *white* magic – which tends finally towards the sublimation of egoic awareness in an act of transcendence – and *black* magic, which is based on 'the acceptance and exultation of the Self.'[34] Here the Setian practitioner is proclaiming the aspiration of the human being as a potential god – an aspiration that could be seen simply as an arrogant assertion or a vain deceit. Satanists and Setians alike, however, make no secret of the fact that they believe that man has limitless potential and may even attain conscious immortality. For them the exploration of this sacred potential is a rational goal which carries its own justification.

Don Webb has written: 'The tradition of spiritual dissent in the West has been called Satanism...[and is] a rationally intuited spiritual technology for the purpose of self-deification. We choose as our role model the ancient Egyptian god Set, the

archetype of Isolate Intelligence, rather than the somewhat limiting Hebrew Satan, archetype of the Rebel against cosmic injustice. As part of our practice we each seek the deconstruction of the socially constructed mind, so we begin in rebellion. We do not worship Set – only our own potential. Set was and is the patron of the magician who seeks to increase his existence through expansion. [Embarking on the path of] Black Magic is to take full responsibility for one's actions, evolution and effectiveness.'[35]

Setians regard the image of Set – the Egyptian God of the Night – as a dynamic force for change. He is the 'separator' or 'isolator' – the God who 'slew' stasis (represented by Osiris) and overcame chaotic mindlessness (represented by Apepi). In this context Set represents the elimination of obsolete thought patterns and social conditioning – a 'dethroning of those internal gods that we have received from society'. To this extent the Setian approach is one of open rebellion against the status quo. As Don Webb explains in his essay on the sacred word *xeper*, the nature of the magical quest, as he sees it, is 'to become an immortal, potent and powerful Essence'.[36] Webb and his fellow Setians seek an infinite future, opened to them through the magical will. For these magicians darkness does not represent evil but infinite human potential.

Chapter Twelve
The Archaic Revival

In his *Ritual of the Mark of the Beast* Crowley proclaims: 'I am a God…very God of very God; I go upon my way to work my will…. I am Omniscient, for naught exists for me unless I know it. I am Omnipotent, for naught exists save by Necessity my soul's expression through my will to be, to do, to suffer the symbols of itself. I am Omnipresent, for naught exists where I am not, who fashioned space as a condition of my consciousness of myself.'[1] Here Crowley is doing what many magicians have done in different periods of history. The magician who imitates the god, becomes the god — *as above, so below*. Margot Adler, a leading American Neopagan, confirms this: 'The fundamental thing about the magical and pagan religions is that ultimately they say, "Within yourself you are the god, you are the goddess — you can actualize within yourself and create whatever you need on this earth and beyond." '[2]

Part of this thinking has to do with the basic concept in spiritual humanism that each individual has deep within their being a divine potential. However, there is only a slight shift of emphasis between acknowledging this and asserting: 'I have become the god.' The first viewpoint is a statement of connection, the second a statement of dominance and arrogance. The idea that we all have within us a sacred potential has much to commend it. One can trace its origins back to Gnosticism itself, Carl Jung (1875–1961) has echoed it, and this is a framework of the psyche widely endorsed by practising magicians and occultists.

CARL JUNG AND THE MYTHIC UNCONSCIOUS

Jung believed that deep within the psyche, beyond the biographical and sexual components of the unconscious mind, one could find mythic 'archetypes' that provided the impetus for visionary and religious experience. According to Jung, these archetypes transcended personal and cultural variables and manifested themselves in numerous symbolic forms around the world, having a profound impact on those visionaries fortunate enough to encounter them firsthand in dreams, mystical visions, or acts of creative inspiration.

Jung believed that divinity is not external to humanity, but lies within as an aspect of our 'humanness' that we all share and can access. After parting company with Freud — whose view of the unconscious was essentially biological — Jung increasingly stressed that the sacred depths of the psyche provided the origin of all religious and mystical experiences. To this extent he was advocating an essentially Gnostic approach to spiritual knowledge. For Jung, the encounter with the archetypes was not simply an act of grace bestowed by God. One could facilitate the process of spiritual awareness oneself – through dreamwork and visualization, as well as through such techniques as meditation and yoga.

Jung recognized that the unconscious mind seemed to contain a storehouse of imagery much vaster than the repressions of the individual ego, and that, to a certain extent, the unconscious appeared to act independently of the conscious mind. He also discovered that there were motifs within dreams that did not seem to be a part of the individual psyche. It was the study of these symbols that led him to formulate the concept of the 'collective unconscious': 'There are many symbols that are not individual but collective in their nature and origin. These are chiefly religious images; their origin is so far buried in the mystery of the past that they seem to have no human source. But they are, in fact, "collective representations" emanating from primeval dreams and creative fantasies. As such, these images are involuntary spontaneous manifestations and by no means intentional inventions.'[3]

Jung believed that these motifs were a symbolic expression of 'the constantly repeated experiences of humanity', derived from observations about Nature that had become embedded in the psychic patterns of the whole species. Jung provides this example of how an archetype is formed: 'One of the commonest and at the same time most impressive experiences is the apparent movement of the sun every

Lakota shaman, He Who Walks with Coals of Fire, gives himself to the Sun during the Sun Dance. Carl Jung believed that natural phenomena, such as the daily path of the sun, give rise to the archetypes of the 'collective unconscious'.

According to Jung, archetypes, symbolized by angels and archons, 'seize hold of the psyche with a kind of primeval force'. Here a winged Babylonian hero engages with two beasts.

day. We certainly cannot discover anything of this kind in the unconscious, so far as the known physical process is concerned. What we do find, on the other hand, is the myth of the sun hero in all its countless modifications. It is this myth and *not the physical process* that forms the archetype.'[4] Jung came to regard the archetype as an anthropomorphic rendition of a force in Nature. Its potency arose from the fact that the observation of the sun's movement was one of the universal experiences, and was a power beyond human manipulation. The sun therefore became an object of mystical veneration — one of a number of archetypes with which to identify in religious or ritual acts of transcendence.

Naturally, different cultures would conceive of the sun-hero in different forms — for example, as Apollo-Helios in classical Greece and Rome, or as Ohrmazd in ancient Persia. However, Jung regarded all these cultural variations as patterns on a theme — common to all was the archetype itself. And there was another side to this: 'The "primordial images" or archetypes, lead their own independent life...as can easily be seen in those philosophical or gnostic systems which rely on an awareness of the unconscious as the source of knowledge. The idea of angels, archangels, 'principalities and powers' in St Paul, the archons of the Gnostics, the heavenly hierarchy of Dionysius the Areopagite, all come from the perception of the relative autonomy of the archetypes.'[5] Furthermore, said Jung, an archetype 'seizes hold of the psyche with a kind of primeval force'.[6]

Jung saw the deepest regions of the psyche as profoundly spiritual, and he gradually took the view that the essential aim of personal development was *individuation* — the process of moving towards a wholeness of being by integrating the conflicting contents and archetypal processes of the unconscious. Jung regarded the self as the totality of the personality, and that it included all the aspects of the psyche. He considered the self a central archetype, personified symbolically by a circle or mandala, representations of wholeness. Self-realization, or individuation, simply meant 'becoming oneself' in a true and total sense.

'The Philosophical Tree',
an image (above) from Jung's
Alchemical Studies, 1967, and
a mandala created by one
of his patients (below) with
egg, snake, protective wings
and eyes. Jung regarded
the mandala as a symbol
of integration and
wholeness.

The self included the *persona*, the face we present to the world, and the *ego*, which included all the conscious contents of personal experience. Jung also believed that men and women should accommodate opposite gender polarities within their consciousness – he called these the *anima* for men and the *animus* for women – and he talked of the *shadow*, an embodiment of memories repressed from consciousness. The shadow would often appear in dreams as a dark, repellent figure. Jung argued, however, that if material from the shadow was acknowledged and allowed back into consciousness, much of its frightening nature would disappear. Dealing with the dark side of the psyche remains an important aspect of all Jungian forms of psychotherapy.

Jung described the process of personal growth in his essay 'The Relations Between the Ego and the Unconscious' (1928): 'The more we become conscious of ourselves through self-knowledge, and act accordingly, the more the layer of the personal unconscious that is superimposed on the collective unconscious will be diminished. In this way there arises a consciousness which is no longer imprisoned in the petty, oversensitive, personal world of objective interests. This widened consciousness is no longer that touchy, egotistical bundle of personal wishes, fears, hopes and ambitions which always has to be compensated or corrected by unconscious countertendencies; instead, it is a function of relationship to the world of objects, bringing the individual into absolute, binding and indissoluble communion with the world at large.'[7]

Jung's impact on contemporary forms of spiritual practice has been considerable. His concept of the collective unconscious has encouraged many to look at myths, fables and legends for insights into the human condition, and also to relate the cycles of symbolic rebirth, found in many of the world's religions, to the process of personal individuation.

Another aspect of Jung's approach is his emphasis on *individual* transformation. According to Jung, we are responsible for our own spiritual destinies. This is a profoundly Gnostic attitude – quite different from the spiritual message of most forms of Western institutional religion. According to Jung, the archetypes of the collective unconscious provide spiritual milestones along the awe-inspiring pathway that leads to the reintegration of the psyche – and where this journey takes us depends on each individual.

Many of Jung's principal ideas resonate strongly with Western magical and esoteric traditions, where there are also themes of personal spiritual growth through self-knowledge, initiation and rites of passage. We find the polarities of the *animus* and the *anima* reflected in the second of the three Wiccan initiations, and also in the mythic imagery of alchemy – indeed, Jung himself was fascinated by such correlations with alchemy. The concept of Jungian individuation, too, is mirrored

Jung was interested by the reflection of the polarities of *animus* and *anima* in the imagery of alchemy. The alchemical androgyne is a metaphor for the fusion of opposites and the transcendence of duality. This miniature is from *Splendor Solis*, a German manuscript, 16th century.

by the magical journey through the archetypes found on the Kabbalistic Tree of Life, with Tiphareth — symbolic of spiritual rebirth and wholeness — at their centre. Occultists have long sought to explore the visionary potentials of their inner being, and their invocations and visualizations are meant to call the gods forth into consciousness. In a mythic sense, magic is essentially about stealing the fire from heaven and then integrating it with the flame within.

THE RISE OF SACRED PSYCHOLOGY

Following the development of the personal growth movement from the late 1960s onwards — based substantially on the self-actualizing ideas of the American psychologist Abraham Maslow (1908–70) — many people in the spiritual counterculture became increasingly attuned to the idea of an inner mythology — of the God or Goddess within. One of those who continued the direct legacy of Carl Jung and who also served as a spiritual mentor to many in the personal growth movement was the American writer and teacher, Joseph Campbell (1904–87).

He had visited Jung in Zurich in 1953 and was enthusiastic about Jung's interpretation of the universal themes in world mythology. He was a distinguished scholar in his own right, producing a number of authoritative but accessible studies on Oriental, indigenous and Western mythology, and many insightful essays on the symbols of comparative religion.

Campbell's special skill was his ability to relate the themes of mythology to the human condition. In his seminars at Esalen Institute and elsewhere he would explain: 'Mythology helps you identify the mysteries of the energies pouring through you.... Mythology is an organization of images metaphoric of experience, action, and fulfilment of the human spirit in the field of a given culture at a given time.'[8] He also rejected fundamentalist concepts of creator gods, regarding them as archetypes of one's inner being. According to Campbell, 'Your god is a manifestation of your own level of consciousness. All of the heavens and all of the hells are within you.'[9]

Campbell remained primarily a scholar and a teacher during his long career, and probably would not have considered himself part of the 'personal growth movement' — even though he knew many of its key figures. And yet one aspect of Campbell's credo has had enormous impact, and is widely quoted in alternative mystical circles: 'Follow your bliss.' Campbell was reinforcing the idea that we should all follow what he called a 'path with heart', a path that defines our place in the cosmos and on this earth. Campbell was not alone in articulating this view, but he helped endorse it, and since his time there has been a substantial resurgence of interest in the role that mythology can play in modern life. Several key figures in the personal growth movement, among them American advocates Dr Jean Bolen and Dr Jean Houston, have helped develop Campbell's approach and have played a prominent role in exploring practical and inspirational ways of introducing archetypal mythic realities into everyday consciousness.

Dr Bolen is a Jungian psychiatrist and the author of such works as *Goddesses in Everywoman* (1985), *Gods in Everyman* (1989) and *The Tao of Psychology* (1982). For many years she has supported the view that all individuals can apply the archetypal energies of the gods and goddesses in their everyday lives. Bolen was strongly influenced by the women's movement in the 1960s and taught a course on the psychology of women at the University of California's San Francisco campus. She is now Clinical Professor of Psychiatry at the University of California Medical Center, and believes, like Jung, that myths are a path to the deeper levels of the mind: 'Myth is a form of metaphor. It's the metaphor that's truly empowering for people. It allows us to see our ordinary lives from a different perspective, to get an intuitive sense of who we are and what is important to us.... Myths are the bridge to the collective unconscious. They tap images, symbols, feelings, possibilities and patterns – inherent, inherited human potential that we all hold in common.'[10]

Although myths sometimes seem to have an archaic quality removed from the everyday world, Bolen argues that mythic awareness can provide a real sense of meaning in day-to-day life: 'If you live from your own depths – that is, if there is an archetypal basis for what you're doing – then there's a meaningful level to it that otherwise might be missing.... When people "follow their bliss" as Joseph Campbell says, their heart is absorbed in what they're doing. People who work in an involved, deep way are doing something that matters to them just to be doing it, not for the paycheck, not for someone saying to them: "What a good job you're doing."'[11]

Despite her Japanese ancestry, Jean Shinoda Bolen, identified with the goddesses of ancient Greece. She told journalist Mirka Knaster in 1989 that the goddesses most reflected in her life were those three representing the 'independent, self-sufficient qualities in women': Artemis, Goddess of the Hunt, embodied her family's moves around the United States in the 1940s to avoid detention in a US concentration camp; Athena, Goddess of Wisdom, seemed there in her decision to train as a doctor; and Hestia, Goddess of the Hearth, epitomized her love of 'comfort in solitude'. As a writer and lecturer, however, she has also felt drawn to Hermes as an archetype of communication. Bolen insists that we can all embody both the gods *and* goddesses in our lives, not just the archetypes of our own gender. And, most significantly, she sees such mythic attunement as opening out into greater, planetary awareness. Bolen echoes the sentiments of Wiccan devotees Margot Adler and Starhawk: 'The current need is a return to earth as the source of sacred energy. I have a concept that I share with others that we're evolving into looking out for the earth and our connection with everybody on it. Women seem more attuned to it, but increasingly more men are too. I believe that the human psyche changes collectively, when enough individuals change. Basically, the point of life is to survive and evolve. To do both requires that we recognize our planetary community and be aware that we cannot do anything negative to our enemies without harming ourselves.'[12]

Dr Houston, also a leading advocate of Goddess psychology, takes much the same position and is similarly attuned to the new 'Gaia consciousness'. 'The Earth is a living system,' she says. 'That is why women are now being released from the exclusivity of a child-bearing, child-rearing role. This is also a time when the Earth desperately needs the ways of thinking and being that women have developed through thousands of years.' Houston is the former president for the Association of Humanistic Psychology, but her talents also extend into many forms of creative expression. An award-winning actress in Off-Broadway theatre, she has developed

Healing the Wounded King, Italian School, *c.* 1380–1400, the legend of the Holy Grail. American psychologist Jean Houston believes that mythic cycles describe the sacred journey of personal transformation.

training programmes in spiritual studies that include the enactment of themes from the ancient Mystery traditions. Her methods include visualization, chanting, storytelling and rituals — and she believes strongly that myths can shape and transform consciousness. In an interview published in *Magical Blend* in 1988 she explained her own role: 'My task is to evoke people into that place of identifying the god or goddess or archetype that is personal to them and allowing that being to speak for them.'[13]

Houston is especially interested in those myths that describe sacred journeys of transformation, and in such archetypes as Parsifal and the Holy Grail, St Francis of Assisi, Odysseus, Christ, Isis and Osiris – for all seek spiritual renewal. 'Myths may be the most fundamental patterns in human existence. They're source patterns, I think, originating from beneath us, behind us, in the transpersonal realm…yet they are the key to our personal and historical existence. That's why I often say they're the DNA of the human psyche.'[14]

She also reminds us that not only mythologically, but also quite literally, our origins are in the cosmos: 'Earlier peoples saw archetypes in Nature and in the starry Heavens – in the Sun, the Moon, the Earth, the vast oceans – implicitly realizing our descent from these primal entities. Everyone and everything derives from the stars – those fiery solar generators of the primary elements of beingness. The sediments of Earth make up our cells, and the briny oceans flow through our veins and tissues. Our ancestors storied this deep knowing into tales of the community of Nature: the marriage of Heaven and Earth; the churning of the ocean to create

Huichol shaman don Jose Rios (Matsuwa) of El Colorin, Municipio del Nayar, Nayarit, Mexico, during the Ceremony of the Drum.

the nectar of life; the action of the wind upon the waters to bring form out of chaos. In these mythic tellings, our forerunners located higher reality and its values in the larger community – in the things of this world, shining reflections of the community of archetypes. They clearly perceived that the pattern connecting both world and archetype was the essential weave that sustains all life.'[15]

It is precisely because myths and archetypes are so primal and help define our relationship with the cosmos, that they are of such vital importance today. For Houston our own era – gripped by a sense of existential crisis – is characterized not simply by a sense of 'paradigm shift' but by a 'whole system transition, a shift in reality itself'. We live in a time of a 'radically changing story', and sacred psychology – with its lessons of transformation and renewal – will play a vital role in this transition. For Jean Houston the characteristic hallmarks of the age are an increasing sense of 'planetization', the rebirth of the archetypal Feminine, the emergence of new forms of science, new understandings of the potential for extending human capacities and the 'ecology of consciousness', and an emergence, overall, of a global spiritual sensibility.[16]

During the early 1980s Houston began to use a variety of experiential techniques to take participants into mythic states of being. One of these was to invite 'shapeshiftings' by relaxing and indentifying with different god and goddess identities, thereby helping attempting to acquire archetypal perceptions. This could involve, for example, meditating on such figures as the Great Mother, the Wise Old King, the Young Redeemer, the Trickster or the Divine Child. Houston now believes that visualizations in themselves, while helpful, are not enough. It may well

be that some sense of personal conflict is required to spark the quest. Personal growth, she feels, can often flow from a sense of being 'wounded' – a feeling of being abandoned or hurt in some way. 'God', she says, 'may reach us through our affliction…we can be ennobled and extended by looking at this wounding in such a way that we move from the personal particular to the personal universal.'[17]

The Shaman's Quest, wool and beeswax painting, by Huichol Ramón Medina. An anthropologists' account of Medina's leap over a waterfall may have inspired a Carlos Castaneda narrative.

THE REDISCOVERY OF SHAMANISM

As part of the quest to understand the universal wisdom traditions, shamanism has now been incorporated within the personal growth movement as a visionary approach to the cosmos. Shamanism first attracted widespread attention during the late 1960s and early 1970s – largely through the writings of South American author Carlos Castaneda (1925–98). For many devotees of the new spiritual awareness of the Western counterculture, Castaneda, and his 'teacher' – Yaqui shaman don Juan Matus – were the first point

Huichol ceremony in north-
central Mexico welcoming
home pilgrims from Wirikuta,
the Sacred Land of the peyote,
the place of the mythological
origin of their people.

of contact with the shaman. Even after his death, Castaneda's influence and fame continues to spread.[18] Casteneda's later works are now regarded substantially as 'fiction', but his early writings appear to have had some sort of authenticity.

Only sketchy details of Casteneda's personal history are known, but it has been established that between 1959 and 1973 he took a series of degree courses in anthropology at the University of California, Los Angeles. Although his real name was thought to be Carlos Arana, or Carlos Aranha, and he came from either Lima, São Paulo or Buenos Aires, he adopted the name Carlos Castaneda when he acquired United States citizenship in 1959. The following year, he apparently travelled to the American south-west to explore the indigenous use of medicinal plants. As the story goes, a friend introduced him to an old Yaqui Indian in Arizona, don Juan Matus, who was said to be an expert on the hallucinogen peyote.

Don Juan said he was a *brujo*, a sorcerer or one who cures by means of magical techniques. Born in Sonora, Mexico, in 1891, he spoke Spanish 'remarkably well' but appeared at first to be unimpressed with Castaneda's self-confidence. He indicated, however, that Castaneda could come to see him again, and an increasingly close relationship developed as the young academic entered into an 'apprenticeship' in shamanic magic.

Carlos Castaneda found many of don Juan's ideas and techniques strange and irrational. The world of the sorcerer contained mysterious, inexplicable forces that he was obliged to accept. The apprentice sorcerer would begin to 'see' whereas previously he had merely 'looked'. Eventually he would become a 'man of knowledge'. According to Castaneda's exposition of don Juan's ideas, the familiar world we perceive is only one of a number of worlds. It is a description of the relationship between objects that we have learned to recognize as significant from birth, reinforced by language and the communication of mutually acceptable concepts. This world is not the same as the world of the sorcerer. His universe is a vast and continuing mystery which cannot be contained within rational categories and frameworks.

In order to transform the perception from ordinary to magical reality, the apprentice must learn how to 'not do' what he has previously 'done'. He must learn how to transcend his previous conceptual categories, and for a moment freeze himself between the two universes, the 'real' and the 'magically real'. To use don Juan's expression, he must 'stop the world'. From this point onwards, he may begin to *see*, to acquire a knowledge and mastery of the mysterious forces operating in the environment which most people close off from their everyday perception.

'Seeing' said don Juan, could often be brought about by hallucinogenic drugs — among them *mescalito* (peyote), *yerba del diablo* (Jimson weed, or datura) and *humito* (psilocybe mushrooms). Through these, the *brujo* could acquire a magical ally, who could grant further power and the ability to enter more readily into 'states of non-ordinary reality'. The *brujo* would become able to see the 'fibres of light' and energy patterns emanating from people and other living organisms, encounter the forces within the wind and sacred water-hole, and isolate as visionary experiences — as if on film — the incidents of one's earlier life and their influence on the development of the personality. Such knowledge would enable the *brujo* to tighten his defences as a 'warrior'. He would know himself, and have complete command over his physical vehicle. He would also be able to project his consciousness from his body into images of birds and animals, thereby transforming himself into a myriad of magical forms and shapes while travelling in the spirit-vision. [19]

While Castaneda's books have been attacked by critics like Weston La Barre and Richard de Mille for containing fanciful and possibly concocted elements, it is likely that the early volumes are based substantially on shamanic tradition — even if some of the material has been borrowed from elsewhere. One of Castaneda's friends, the anthropologist Barbara Myerhoff, was studying the Huichol at the same time that Castaneda was claiming to be studying Yaqui sorcery, and she introduced Castaneda to Ramon Medina, a Huichol shaman. An incident, described in Castaneda's book *A Separate Reality* (1971) tells of don Genaro, don Juan's shamanic

American anthropologist Joan Halifax, whose work has contributed so much to the revival of interest in shamanism, believes: 'The veil is now being lifted off many of the traditions that have kept the teachings a secret.'

friend, leaping across a precipitous waterfall and clinging to it by magical 'tentacles of power'. This may have been borrowed from the observations of Myerhoff and another noted anthropologist, Peter Furst, who watched Ramon Medina leaping like a bird across a waterfall cascading over slippery rocks three hundred metres – nearly a thousand feet – below. Medina was exhibiting the balance of the shaman in 'crossing the narrow bridge to the other world'. Myerhoff told Richard de Mille how validated she felt when Castaneda told her that the sorcerer don Genaro could do similar things. It now seems that Castaneda was like a mirror – his own accounts reflected borrowed data from all sorts of sources. The rapid running, 'the gait of power', for example, was likely to have come from accounts of Tibetan mysticism, and there were definite parallels between don Juan's abilities and accounts in other anthropological, psychedelic and occult sources.[20]

Even in death, Castaneda remains controversial. While Castaneda's brand of shamanic sorcery was always elusive, however, a more accessible approach to practical shamanism was being introduced to the personal growth movement by an American anthropologist whose academic credentials were never in question – Dr Michael Harner.

A former visiting professor at Columbia, Yale and the University of California, Harner is now Director of the Foundation for Shamanic Studies in Mill Valley, California. Born in Washington, DC, in 1929, Harner spent the early years of his

American anthropologist
Michael Harner has helped
to revived interest in
shamanism in the West.

childhood in South America. In 1956 he returned to do fieldwork among the Jivaro of the Ecuadorian Andes, and between 1960 and 1961 visited the Conibo of the Upper Amazon in Peru. His first period of fieldwork was conducted as 'an outside observer of the world of the shaman', but his second endeavour – which included his psychedelic initiation among the Conibo – led him to pursue shamanism firsthand. In 1964 he returned to Ecuador to experience the supernatural world of the Jivaro more completely.

Harner made contact with his Jivaro guide Akachu at the former Spanish settlement of Macas. They ventured northwards, crossing the Rio Upano and entering the forest. It was here that he told Akachu that he wished to acquire spirit-helpers, known to the Jivaro as *tsentsak*. Harner offered gifts to Akachu, and was told that that the first task was to bathe in the sacred waterfall. Later he was presented with a magical pole to ward off demons. Then, after an arduous journey to the waterfall, Harner was led into a dark recess behind the wall of spray – a cave known as 'the house of the Grandfathers' – and here he had to call out, attracting the attention of the ancestor spirits. He now had his first magical experiences: the wall of falling water became a torrent of liquid prisms. 'As they went by,' says Harner, 'I had the continuous sensation of floating upward, as though they were stable and I was the one in motion.... It was like flying inside a mountain.'

Deeper in the forest, Akachu squeezed the juice of some psychedelic datura plants he had brought with him and asked Harner to drink it that night. Reassuring him, Akachu told him he was not to fear anything he might see, and if anything frightening did appear, he should run up and touch it. That night was especially dramatic anyway – with intense rain, thunder and flashes of lightning – but after a while the effects of the datura became apparent. Harner was aware of a luminous, multicoloured serpent writhing towards him. Remembering his advice from Akachu, Harner charged at the visionary serpent with a stick. Suddenly the forest was empty and silent, and the monster had gone. Akachu later explained that this supernatural encounter was an important precursor to acquiring spirit-helpers. And his triumph over the serpent had confirmed that he was now an acceptable candidate for the path of the shaman.

Harner believes, as the Jivaro do, that the energizing force within any human being can be represented by a 'power animal'. One of the most important tasks of the shaman is to summon the power animal while in trance, and undertake visionary journeys with the animal as an ally, exploring the 'upper' and 'lower' worlds of the magical universe. The shaman also learns techniques of healing which usually entail journeys to the spirit world to obtain sources of 'magical energy'. This energy can then be transferred to sick or *dis*-spirited people in a ceremonial healing rite.[21]

After living with the Conibo and Jivaro, Michael Harner undertook further fieldwork among the Wintun and Pomo in California, the Lakota Sioux of South Dakota and the Coast Salish in Washington State. The techniques of applied shamanism which he now teaches in his workshops, and which are outlined in his book *The Way of the Shaman* (1980), are a synthesis from many cultures, but they are true to the essence of the tradition. 'Shamanism,' says Harner, 'takes us into the realms of myth and the Dreamtime...and in these experiences we are able to contact sources of power and use them in daily life.'[22]

Harner is now deeply committed to shamanic research, and trains tribal peoples in shamanic techniques that have disappeared from their own indigenous cultures. Several groups, including the Sami (formerly known as Lapps) and the Inuit (formerly known as Eskimo) have approached him to help restore sacred knowledge lost as a result of missionary activity or Western colonization. Harner and his colleagues at the Foundation for Shamanic Studies have been able to help them with what he calls 'core shamanism' – general methods consistent with those once used by their ancestors. In this way, he believes, 'members of these tribal societies can elaborate and integrate the practices on their own terms in the context of their traditional cultures', and shamanic knowledge can once again be restored to the indigenous traditions.

Chapter Thirteen
Technopagans and Digital Magic

Now, at the beginning of the twenty-first century, it has become possible to explore the unexpected and fascinating connection between the ancient spiritual tradition of shamanism and the technological world of computers and cyberspace. For cyber-explorers like the late Terence McKenna (1946–2000), who believed that archaic cultural forms and modern technology were not only compatible but synergistic, a fusion of this sort presented no problems. McKenna was both a shamanic adventurer and an internationally recognized spokesperson for the metaphysics of cyberspace. For him the shamanic tradition was essentially about 'externalizing the soul' – making tangible both the human spirit and 'the Logos of the planet'. He also believed that computer networks like the World Wide Web, could take us into a global collective consciousness.

McKenna's original interest was in central Asian shamanism. During the late 1960s he went to Nepal to learn the Tibetan language and to study indigenous Bon-Po shamanism. He lived for a time in both India and the Seychelles before deciding to visit regions of the world where shamanism was still practised. This took him to several islands in Indonesia – including Sumatra, Sumba, Flores, the Moluccas and Ceram – and later to South America, where he observed native shamanic practices first-hand.

In the upper Amazon basin (Colombia, Peru and Ecuador) shamans make extensive use of *ayahuasca*, a psychedelic drink made from the tree-climbing forest vine *Banisteriopsis caapi*. Taking this sacrament allows the shaman to enter the supernatural realm, to have initiatory visions, and to make contact with ancestors and helper-spirits. McKenna was interested in the fact that from a biochemical view, *ayahuasca* appeared to resemble psilocybin, the active principle in the sacred mushrooms used by shamans in the highlands of central Mexico. He also believed – and this is where he entered the realm of anthropological controversy – that the intake of psilocybin by early humans living in the African grasslands may have led to the origins of human language. Psilocybe mushrooms produce a mystical state where the soul 'speaks' to the mind. These mushrooms grow prolifically in cattle dung, and McKenna argued that the entry of psilocybin into the food chain in Africa between fifteen and twenty thousand years ago and the subsequent domestication of cattle, may have led to the first Palaeolithic religion – that of the Great Horned

Cyberspace explorer Terence McKenna believed that shamanism provided a pathway to the 'mind' of the planet.

Banisteriopsis caapi, a tree-climbing forest vine found in the Upper Amazon basin. Shamans use this plant to make the psychedelic drink *ayahuasca*.

Psilocybe mushrooms. For Terence McKenna they provided the key to hearing the inner voice of the Logos.

Goddess.[1] He also maintained that psilocybin itself has a unique part to play in human culture: 'Under the influence of psilocybin there is an experience of contacting a speaking entity – an interiorized voice that I call the *Logos*. If we don't go back to Hellenistic Greek terminology then we are left with only the vocabulary of psychopathology. In modern times to hear "voices" is to be seriously deviant.... And yet if we go back to the Classical literature the whole goal of Hellenistic esotericism was to gain access to this thing called the *Logos*. The Logos spoke the Truth – an incontrovertible Truth. Socrates had what he called his *daimon* – his informing "Other". And the ease with which psilocybin induces this phenomenon makes it, from the viewpoint of a materialist or reductionist rooted in the scientific tradition, almost miraculous.'[2]

For McKenna the psilocybin experience was central to understanding the origins of spiritual awareness, and was also linked to the development of ancient religious structures: 'What I think happened is that in the world of prehistory all religion was experiential and it was based on the pursuit of ecstasy through plants. And at some time, very early, a group interposed itself between people and the direct experience of the "Other". This created hierarchies, priesthoods, theological systems, castes, rituals, taboos. Shamanism, on the other hand, is an experiential science which deals with an area where we know nothing.... So the important part of the Human Potential Movement and the New Age, I believe, is the re-empowerment of ritual, the rediscovery of shamanism, the recognition of psychedelics and the importance of the Goddess.'[3]

Taking this further, McKenna maintained that, as with those South American and Mexican shamans who use visionary sacraments respectfully, psychedelics put the individual literally in touch with the 'mind' of the planet: 'I take very seriously the idea that the Logos is real, that there is a guiding Mind – an Oversoul – that inhabits the biome of the planet, and that human balance, dignity and religiosity depend on having direct contact with this realm. That's what shamanism is providing. It was available in the West until the fall of Eleusis and the Mystery traditions – to some people – but then was stamped out by barbarians who didn't realize what they had destroyed.'[4] Shifting now to the present post-industrial era – admittedly, a very great leap in time – McKenna believed that there was a parallel between the Oversoul of the planet and the emerging consciousness permeating cyberspace via the medium of the Internet. According to McKenna, the new cyberculture has forced us to re-examine our linear thinking and our relationship to the cosmos.

In an interview with cultural critic Mark Dery, published in 1997, McKenna explained that in his view the future of humanity lies in its capacity to embrace a technological, or scientific, shamanism: 'I expect to see the coming decades transform the planet into an art form; the new man, linked in a cosmic harmony that transcends time and space:... I believe in what I call a forward escape, meaning that you can't go back and you can't stand still, so you've got to go forward, and technology is the way to do this. Technology is an extension of the human mental world, and it's certainly where our salvation is going to come from; we cannot return to the hunter-gatherer pastoralism of 15,000 years ago.'[5] According to McKenna, these new techno-shamanic directions would be essentially metaphysical, because they would take us beyond notions of linear progress: 'My position is that all of history involves making the Logos more and more concrete. In the same way that McLuhan saw print culture as replacing an earlier eye-oriented manuscript culture, my hope is that the cyberdelic culture is going to overcome the linear, uniform bias of print and carry us into the realm of the visible Logos...what these new technologies are doing is dissolving boundaries.'[6]

TECHNO-VISIONARY REALITIES

So how does the shamanic perspective relate to the world of cyberspace? How does the world of cyberculture challenge our notions of rational and linear thinking? The word cyberspace was coined by William Gibson, who used it in his 1984 novel *Neuromancer*. Gibson described a scenario where 'console cowboys' could put on their cyberspace helmets and project their awareness into three-dimensional 'virtual' environments. Here Gibson was anticipating that the human imagination would create its own perceptual 'realities' within a technological setting.

Less than twenty years after the publication of Gibson's novel, the realm of virtual reality had already established itself as a valuable tool in such fields as architecture and medicine. Meanwhile, the Internet is rapidly becoming the preferred means of communication around the planet, and ventures into cyberspace are an everyday occurrence. This has interesting philosophical connotations. In *The Pearly Gates of Cyberspace* (1998), science writer Margaret Wertheim argues that the Internet is providing us with a new concept of space that did not exist before – the interconnected 'space' of the global computer network.[7] And, as she points out, this is a very new phenomenon. During the early 1980s few people outside the military and academic field of computer science had network access, but in the next decade there will be close to one billion people online. This has sprung up from nothing in twenty-five years, making it surely the fastest-growing territory in history. It is the actual nature of the cyberspace experience that Wertheim finds so fascinating. When one person communicates with another online there is no sense of physicality, for cyber-journeys cannot be measured in a literal sense. 'Unleashed into the Internet,' she says, 'my "location" can no longer be fixed purely in physical space. Just "where" I am when I enter cyberspace is a question yet to be answered, but clearly my position cannot be pinned down to a mathematical location.' So all we can really confirm about the nature of cyberspace is that it involves a form of digital communication where information is relayed back and forth from one computer site to another, and where people share the outpourings of each other's minds.

As many Internet enthusiasts have discovered, the world of cyberspace is also a realm where fantasy personas can be created in *virtual* reality – where human beings can interact with each other in ways limited only by their imagination. Individuals can pose as members of the opposite sex, as fantasy beings – even as dark and evil gods – and this has become a central feature of role-play on the Internet. The Internet has become an extension of the human psyche, a forum for both its realities and its fantasies. From an esoteric or mystical perspective, though, what is so intriguing about this interplay between technology and the human imagination is that here we are dealing with the equation: *As I imagine, so I become* – and this is the very essence of magic.

TECHNOPAGANS AND DIGITAL MAGIC

It comes as no surprise that Neopagans and occultists of all descriptions have been quick to embrace the Internet. For many, the World Wide Web provides a pathway into the mythic conjurings of the world-at-large – an enticing and increasingly seductive means of engaging with the global imagination. The relationship between Neopagans and technology appears to have its roots in the American counterculture itself, for it is now widely acknowledged that today's computer ethos owes a substantial debt to the psychedelic consciousness movement. The conservative *Wall Street Journal* even ran a front-page article in January 1990 asking whether virtual reality was equivalent to 'electronic LSD'.[8]

It would seem that the somewhat unlikely fusion between pagans and cyberspace arose because technopagans are capable of being both technological and mystical at the same time. As cyber-punk novelist Bruce Sterling has written: 'Today, for a surprising number of people all over America, the supposed dividing line between bohemian and technician simply no longer exists. People of this sort may have a set of windchimes and a dog with a knotted kerchief 'round its neck, but they're also quite likely to own a multimegabyte Macintosh running MIDI synthesizer software and trippy fractal simulations.'[9]

The American psychedelic culture of the late 1960s and early 1970s was essentially about experiencing the psyche through mind-altering drugs – the word 'psychedelic' itself literally means 'mind revealing' – and this consciousness exploration would have a direct impact on the rise of the new technology. According to Mark Dery, Timothy Leary regarded the personal computer phenomenon as a clear vindication of the counterculture: 'It's well known,' he told Dery, 'that most of the creative impulse in the software industry, and indeed much of the hardware, particularly at Apple Macintosh, derived directly from the sixties consciousness movement.... [Apple co-founder] Steve Jobs went to India, took a lot of acid, studied Buddhism, and came back and said that Edison did more to influence the human race than the Buddha. And [Microsoft founder Bill] Gates was a big psychedelic person at Harvard. It makes perfect sense to me that if you activate your brain with psychedelic drugs, the only way you can describe it is electronically.'[10]

What Mark Dery calls the 'cyberdelic wing' of the computer movement clearly has its roots in the 1960s counterculture, and Wiccan computer buff Sara Reeder remembers the early years well: 'Silicon Valley and the modern Wiccan revival

For Timothy Leary, photographed here in 1967 with his fingers in a chanting position, computer technology became the LSD of the 1990s.

literally took root and grew up alongside each other in the rich black clay surrounding San Francisco Bay…both blossomed in the 1960s – the Valley through the miracle of the space program, the Pagan community by way of Haight Street's prominence as the worldwide Counterculture HQ.'[11]

At this time, Timothy Leary was urging his followers to 'turn on, tune in and drop out' on LSD, a psychedelic synthesized from ergot. A generation later, he would switch his allegiance to the computer generation, announcing that 'the PC is the LSD of the 1990s'. 'What is so intriguing about our own era is that the human quest for knowledge and understanding in the last twenty-five years has seen an amazing blend of shamanic techniques, psychedelic drugs and the international global boom in resurrecting the pre-Christian, pagan, totemic and Hindu traditions. At the same time, with these computers…you have a situation where you can walk around in realities of your own construction. So we are very much on a threshold. I don't want to put any limits on what I'm saying, but here we have ancient techniques merging with the most modern. Computers give us the ways to communicate with the basic language of the universe – which is *quanta-electronic*. Matter and bodies are just electrons that have decided to come together, buzzing around with information.'[12]

Stewart Brand, formerly of the Merry Pranksters (who 'tripped' around the US with Ken Kesey in his psychedelic bus) and creator of the *Whole Earth Catalogue* in the 1960s, also became an icon of the cyberdelic movement. Brand has been credited with creating the computer hacker subculture as the direct result of an article he published in *Rolling Stone* magazine in 1972.[13]

According to Dery, these psychedelic roots have left their mark, and the 'cyberdelic' phenomenon now encompasses a cluster of subcultures – 'among them Deadhead computer hackers, "ravers" (habitués of all-night electronic dance parties known as "raves"), technopagans and New Age technophiles. Cyberdelia reconciles the transcendentalist impulses of sixties counterculture with the infomania of the nineties. As well, it nods in passing to the seventies, from which it borrows the millenarian mysticism of the New Age and the apolitical self-absorption of the human potential movement.'[14]

Cyberculture enthusiast Erik Davis has a similar view, describing technopagans as 'a small but vital subculture of digital savants who keep one foot in the emerging technosphere and one foot in the wild and woolly world of Paganism'.[14] Meanwhile, for Douglas Rushkoff, author of *Cyberia: Life in the Trenches of Hyperspace* (1994), 'the Neopagan revival incorporates ancient and modern skills in free-for-all sampling of whatever works, making no distinction between occult magic and high technology. In the words of one Neopagan, "The magic of today is the technology of tomorrow. It's all magic. It's all technology." '[16]

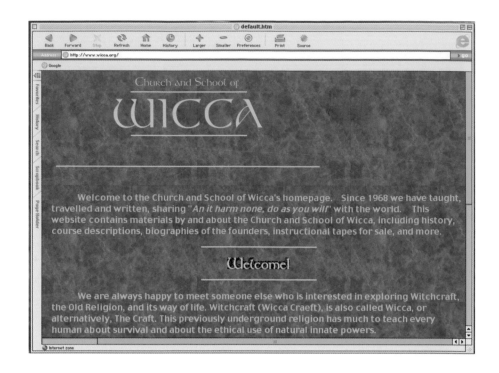

Wiccan groups moved quickly to explore the benefits of the Internet. These Wiccan web-pages reflect the Neopagan enthusiasm for cyberspace technology.

Neopagans generally regard technology and magic as interchangeable. Ever pragmatic, they seem to be primarily concerned with what works. If technology is effective in producing something physically useful, and if rituals and magical incantations can produce a specific spiritual or psychological outcome, for many Neopagans this means they are compatible. According to Erik Davis, 'it is this pragmatic hands-on instrumentality that allows some Pagans to powerfully reimagine "technology" as both a metaphor and a tool for spiritual work.'[17]

An urban Neopagan witch named Green Fire told Douglas Rushkoff: 'High technology and high magic are the same thing. They both use tools from inner resources and outer resources. Magic from the ancient past and technology from the future are really both one. That is how we are creating the present; we're speeding up things, we are quickening our energies; time and space are not as rigid as they used to be.... Those of us who know how to work through time and space are using our abilities to *bend* time and space into a reality that will benefit people the most.... We humans are all shape-shifters. We just learn to access our DNA codes. It's very computer-oriented. We are computers; our minds are computers, our little cells are computers. We are bio-organic computers.'[18]

Californian Neopagan Tom Williams writes, 'Far from being seen as the tool of the oppressor, technology harnessed with the proper spiritual motivation can be a blast of liberation.... Take up the athame, the wand and the light-sound machine, the cup and the pentacle and the oscilloscope and the computer. Dedicate them to the service of the Life Force, to the Unio Mystica and to the praise of the

Great Mother and weave their power together into ritual, song and the sacred accomplishment of the Great Work!'[19]

For Michael Hutchison – author of the bestseller *Mega Brain Power: Transform Your Life with Mind Machines and Brain Nutrients* (1994) – 'consciousness technology' is coming to the aid of humanity in an unexpected way: 'To some it may seem odd and paradoxical that machines – the synthetic, hard, material devices of this electronic temporal reality – may serve as gateways to the spirit, tools of transcendence. But in fact this fusion of spirituality, or the "inner quest" , and science, "the external quest" , is the central force of the emerging new paradigm.'[20]

Many Neopagan groups use computer technology and the Internet to announce seasonal rites, celebrations, workshops and conferences, and also to provide information on pagan rites of passage, including handfastings (weddings), child-blessings and funerals. The London-based Pagan Federation, established in 1971, uses the Internet to promote Neopaganism, Druid, Wiccan, Odinic, Northern, Celtic, Eco-magic and women's spirituality groups, and its American counterparts, like the Church of All Worlds, Circle Sanctuary and the Church of Wicca, do the same for their equivalent memberships. Pagans also communicate with each other through 'newsgroups' – discussion forums where they can chat in real time about magical ceremonies, spells and the occult powers of herbs. Jem Dowse also makes the point that new pagans who happen to live in the American Bible Belt make use of this new technology to access like-minded people without fear of repercussions.[21]

Some technopagans try to extend the scope of their digital magic still further, by conducting rituals over the Internet, and even establishing 'virtual' shrines in cyberspace. Sara Reeder explains that 'while Christians and other mainstream religions ignored the Net for years – their members had an established network of churches and clergy to turn to – we became the first religious movement to depend heavily on it for growth and cohesion. And cyberspace, in turn, became the first mass Pagan gathering place since ancient times.' For her, computer technology does not affect the poetry of the ritual experience: 'Our rituals have always taken place in the realm of the imagination, so we can make effective ritual anywhere we can exercise our love for poetry and storytelling. I've led online rituals for thirty in chat rooms that allowed us to talk to each other two lines at a time; some of them were as memorable and powerful as any I've attended in person.... As VRML and other technologies open the sensual band with, allowing us to share songs, images, and even virtual bodies to the mix, cyberspace ritual will allow us to open up our private dreamscapes, and share our internal visions with each other in much more intimate ways. The traditional Neo-Pagan focus on individual creativity, combined with our emphasis on poetry and fluid ritual forms, may well make us the first to pioneer online altars and sacred sites, once more setting the example for other religions to follow.'[22]

DARK ARCHETYPES

While many Neopagan responses to cyberspace are innovative and essentially positive, there is an underbelly – a darker realm which feeds on fear and powerlessness in a rapidly changing world. One of the archetypes that embodies these feelings most strongly is that of the Alien – the space-entity created by H. R. Giger, which featured in the Oscar-winning film of the same name and which has since become an icon of the cyberculture. Giger now has an impressive website on the Internet, and an increasing sphere of influence. Mark Dery has noted that 'cyberpunk bands such as Cyberaktif and Front Line Assembly routinely cite him as an inspiration. The highest tribute is paid by modern primitives who emblazon themselves with Giger's slavering, mace-tailed Alien – a cyberpunk rite of passage.'[23]

Many of Giger's most surreal artworks are now on permanent display at his museum in Castle St Germain in Gruyères, Switzerland, which opened in June 1998. The paintings draw strongly on the left-hand path of Western magic as well as on fantasy and horror fictions, as in his extraordinary *The Necronomicon* of 1978. There is an unquestionable potency – even a macabre beauty – in his biomechanoid creations, but his nightmare fusions of the human and the mechanical also breathe a sense of *no escape* – a sense that we are all trapped in a virtual hell of our own making. Perhaps this is an portent of our times.

There is no doubt that, in terms of his art, Giger is a magician – conjuring dramatic visions that propel us into the darker recesses of the psyche. His paintings have been praised by such visionary artists as Ernst Fuchs and Salvador Dalí, and display a magical calibre rarely seen in modern art. Giger is also linked in spirit with earlier masters of the visionary, such as Hieronymus Bosch and Lucas Cranach.

Hans Ruedi Giger was born in 1940 in the small Swiss town of Chur, which he describes as an 'unbearable' place of 'high mountains and petty bourgeois attitudes'. Growing up there, he had nightmares, and would imagine 'gigantic bottomless shafts bathing in pale yellow light'. In his *Necronomicon*, Giger writes that, 'on the walls, steep and treacherous wooden stairways without banisters led down into the yawning abyss', and the cellar in his family house gave rise to the image of 'a monstrous labyrinth, where all kinds of dangers lay in wait for me'. Time and again, the figures in his paintings seem trapped and tormented in gruesome, tortuous tunnels, and there is no apparent escape.

While he has studied the works of Aleister Crowley, like many other cyberspace enthusiasts, he is not a magician in the conventional sense. He does not perform rituals, engage in invocations, or summon spirits. But one could hardly find a better temple of the black arts than the Spell Room at the H. R. Giger Museum, where the walls display several of his most powerful paintings and murals. It would seem that, when the thin veil across Giger's psyche is slightly drawn aside, tempestuous visions of evil and alienation come forth. It is almost as if the dark gods were emerging from his nightmares.

THE FUTURE OF MAGIC

So what are the implications of this strange new world of magical cyberspace, and where are the magical undercurrents in contemporary Western culture taking us? Is there a search for new mythologies to define our future?

It seems to me that devotees of the various magical traditions in the West may find themselves gravitating in two quite different directions. The first focuses primarily on the sacred dimensions of Nature, and engages in a magic of the Earth and Cosmos. This is the option chosen by practitioners of Wicca and Goddess worship. The other path advances still further into the archetypal realms of cyberspace and virtual reality as their myriad potentials unfold. And although technopaganism seeks to embrace both dimensions, I think that the main pathways within Western magic will increasingly diverge — a fundamental choice will be made between Nature and technology.

Since the time of the Renaissance, and especially during the last hundred years, magic has focused on the quest for personal transformation. Occultists of all persuasions invoke their gods and goddesses as archetypes of the divine potential they seek within themselves. As Austin Spare wrote, this is the magical act of stealing fire from heaven. Can this fire of sacred inspiration be found both within the natural world and also in the furthest reaches of cyberspace?

Many magical devotees will feel powerfully drawn towards the new technology in all its diversity. Sacred shrines and archetypal symbols will find ever more convincing graphic expression on the Internet becoming magical doorways in their own right — the cyberspace equivalent of the Magic Theatre in Hermann Hesse's novel *Steppenwolf* (1927). The explorers entering these doorways will engage further in virtual worlds, blending technological motifs with mythic archetypes to produce fusions we can only begin to envisage. Perhaps this magic will produce the Giger-visions of the future — where elements of the mechanistic world merge with what is human, creating bizarre permutations of cyber-magical mythology. The cyber-shamans of the future will have to integrate these new sacred images within themselves in order to make sense of it all, for if they fail to do this they will risk engulfing their psyches in a whirlpool of virtual magical imagery.

Other magical practitioners will choose to identify only with the mythic archetypes of the past – but those with a resonance for the present. The modern magical revival has already seen not only a return to medieval esotericism and the mythic traditions of the Celts, as well as a renewed interest in the ancient gods and goddesses, but there has also been a very specific resurgence, in certain quarters, of traditions like Odinism and Druidry, and the magic of the various shamanic cultures around the world. In many cases this return to an archaic past brings with it a thirst for authentic simplicity – for rituals that embrace the earth, sun, moon

Swiss visionary artist H. R. Giger, creator of the Alien.

and sky as they are found in the real world, and not in the virtual realms of cyberspace. For this reason many magical devotees will restrict their use of the new technology to the exchange of information. Andrew Siliar, a Neopagan from Arizona, makes this point in a letter published in the Wiccan journal *Green Egg*: 'Paganism is a Nature religion, rooted deep in the Earth, honoring the Gods and Goddesses, feeling the heartbeat of the Mother Earth, loving and honoring all of Her creatures. And now we have this wonderful new technology, along with computer graphics. We can link up with other people on-line, and now we can be techno-witches, and cyber wizards.... I'm sorry, but that doesn't sound like much of a Nature Religion to me anymore.... I need no online link to let me feel the power of the Goddess, I just touch the Earth and connect.'[24]

So the future may present us with two quite different traditions – natural magic and techno-cybermagic – along with all the assorted mythologies they will bring in their wake. For many, nevertheless, the magical quest will remain an eclectic journey to self-knowledge and transcendence, enabling each individual to find a sense of sacred meaning in his or her own way. The compelling attraction of magic will be that it is both Life-affirming and Nature-affirming – that it honours the cycles of the seasons and the gods and goddesses of Creation, and also honours the sacred connection between humanity and the Universe as a whole.

Li 1, from an edition of
hand-coloured photogravure
prints by H. R. Giger, 1974.
Do Giger's visionary art-forms
provide a glimpse into
the mythologies of
the future?

Notes

Short titles are given for publications listed in full in the Bibliography.

Introduction
1 see Gareth Knight, *A History of White Magic*, p. 15.

Chapter 1 pp. 10–31
1 Abbé Henri Breuil, 'The Paleolithic Age', in René Huyghe (ed.), *Larousse Encyclopedia of Prehistoric and Ancient Art*, 1962, p. 30.
2 Joan Halifax, *Shaman: the Wounded Healer*, p. 6.
3 Ibid, p. 14.
4 Ralph Linton, *Culture and Mental Disorders*, p. 124.
5 Halifax, *Shaman*, p. 14.
6 Waldemar Bogoras, *The Chukchee*, 1909, p. 421.
7 See H. S. Sullivan, *Conceptions of Modern Psychiatry*, pp. 151–2.
8 Mircea Eliade, *Shamanism*, p. 13.
9 Mircea Eliade, *Birth and Rebirth*, p. 102.
10 Eliade, *Shamanism*, p. 120.
11 Ibid, p. 88.
12 A. P. Elkin, *Aboriginal Men of High Degree*, p. 20.
13 Ibid, pp. 142–43.
14 Ibid, p. 143.
15 W. A. Lessa and E. Z. Vogt (eds), *Reader in Comparative Religion*, p. 389.
16 Eliade, *Shamanism*, p. 198.
17 Halifax, *Shamanic Voices*, p. 183.
18 H. L. Roth, *The Natives of Sarawak and British North Borneo*, vol. 1, p. 281.
19 Sue Ingram, 'Structures of Shamanism in Indonesia and Malaysia', p. 127.
20 Larry G. Peters, 'The Tamang Shamanism of Nepal', p. 171.

Chapter 2 pp. 32–45
1 Fritz Graf, *Magic in the Ancient World*, p. 6.
2 Gideon Bohak, *Traditions of Magic in Late Antiquity*.
3 Geraldine Pinch, *Magic in Ancient Egypt*, p. 163.
4 Bohak, *Traditions of Magic in Late Antiquity*.
5 Marie-Louise Thomsen, 'Witchcraft and Magic in Ancient Mesopotamia' in Ankarloo and Clark (eds), *Witchcraft and Magic in Europe: Biblical and Pagan Societies*, p. 38.
6 Ibid, p. 40.
7 Ibid, p. 67.
8 J. S. Morrison, 'The Classical World' in Loewe and Blacker,(eds), *Divination and Oracles*, p. 99.
9 Graf, *Magic in the Ancient World*, p. 108.
10 Ibid, pp. 115–16.
11 Walter Burkert, *Ancient Mystery Cults*, p. 2.
12 Marvin W. Meyer (ed.), *The Ancient Mysteries*, p. 7.
13 Ibid, pp. 7–8.
14 John Pollard, *Seers, Shrines and Sirens*, p. 66.
15 See R. Gordon Wasson et al., *The Road to Eleusis*. Burkert, *Ancient Mystery Cults*, p. 108, believes that opium poppies rather than ergot may have caused the visionary hallucinations at Eleusis, but ergot poisoning has recently been linked to visionary aspects of medieval European witchcraft, so Wasson's hypothesis may well be credible.

Chapter 3 pp. 46–60
1 See Ioan P. Couliano, *The Tree of Gnosis*.
2 Ibid, p. 33.
3 See James M. Robinson, Introduction to *The Nag Hammadi Library in English*, p. 4.
4 Wallis Barnstone (ed.), *The Other Bible*, p. 627.
5 According to Robert M. Grant, Ptolemaeus was head of the Valentinian school in Italy and succeeded Valentinus around the year 160 CE .
6 Robert M. Grant (ed.), *Gnosticism*, p. 163.
7 Ibid, p. 163.
8 See Barnstone, *The Other Bible*, p. 669.
9 Quoted in Geo Widengren, *Mani and Manichaeism*, p. 26.
10 Ibid, p. 53.
11 From Plotinus, 'The Ascent to Union with the One', in A. H. Armstrong (ed.), *Plotinus*, p.137.
12 Admittedly, not all scholars agree on this point. The late Ioan P. Couliano believed that Scholem overstated the connection between the Kabbalah and Gnosticism (see Couliano's *The Tree of Gnosis*, p. 42 ff). , Scholem believed quite emphatically, however, that the Kabbalistic text *Bahir*, which predates the *Zohar*, makes it clear that the 'thirteenth century Kabbalists became the heirs of Gnostical symbolism' (*Major Trends in Jewish Mysticism*, p. 214).
13 Daniel C. Matt ,*The Essential Kabbalah*, p. 3.
14 Ibid, pp. 4–5.
15 G. Scholem, *Major Trends in Jewish Mysticism*, p. 209.
16 Ibid, pp. 218–19.
17 Ibid, pp. 215–16.
18 Steven A. Fisdel, *The Practice of Kabbalah* , p. 100.

Chapter 4 pp. 61–81
1 Joan O'Grady, *Heresy*, pp. 69–70.
2 Jeffrey Burton Russell, *Witchcraft in the Middle Ages*, p. 123.
3 Ibid, p. 175.
4 Ibid, p. 230.
5 Ibid, p. 127.
6 Rossell Hope Robbins, *The Encyclopedia of Witchcraft & Demonology*, Bonanza Books, New York 1981, p. 179.
7 Jeffery Burton Russell, *A History of Witchcraft*, p. 113.
8 Quoted in Peter Haining (ed.), *The Witchcraft Papers*, p. 139.
9 Rosemary Ellen Guiley, *The Encyclopedia of Witches and Witchcraft*, p. 60.
10 Russell, *A History of Witchcraft*, p. 103.
11 Guiley, *The Encyclopedia of Witches and Witchcraft*, p. 297.
12 See Linnda Caporael, 'Ergotism: The Satan Loosed in Salem?' *Science*, vol. 192, 2 April 1976.
13 Andrew McCall, *The Medieval Underworld*, pp. 17–18.
14 Henry M. Pachter, *Paracelsus: Magic Into Science*, p. 73.
15 Kurt Seligmann, *Magic, Supernaturalism and Religion*, p. 145.
16 Michael R. Best and Frank H. Brightman (eds), *The Book of Secrets of Albertus Magnus*, pp. xxiv–xxv.
17 Ibid, pp. 18–19.
18 Ibid, p. 31.
19 Ibid, p. 60.
20 Ibid, p. 61.
21 Frances Yates, *The Occult Philosophy in the Elizabethan Age*, p. 55.
22 A. M. Stoddart, *The Life of Paracelsus*, p. 269.
23 According to Henry M. Pachter, 'Trithemius approved of all efforts to use the hidden forces of God's nature, so long as no demons were called in. This was legitimate "white magic." ' (See Pachter, *Paracelsus: Magic Into Science*, p. 76.)
24 Paracelsus, *The Archidoxes of Magic*, 1975 edition, p. 115.
25 Ibid, pp. 94–95.
26 The 18 'Enochian Calls' received by Edward Kelley and John Dee were used by Aleister Crowley (1875–1947) as ritual conjurations in the Algerian desert with Victor Neuburg (see Chapter 9).
27 Quoted in Derek and Julia Parker, *A History of Astrology*, p. 136.

Chapter 5 pp. 82–95
1 Quoted in Wayne Shumaker, *The Occult Sciences in the Renaissance*, p. 202.
2 Ibid, p. 203.
3 Tobias Churton, *The Gnostics*, p. 104.
4 From W. Scott (trans.), *Hermetica vol.1.* quoted in C. and J. Matthews, *The Western Way*, p. 216.
5 Churton, *The Gnostics*, p. 113.
6 Ibid, p. 115.
7 Ibid, p. 112.
8 C. and J. Matthews, *The Western Way*, p. 218.
9 See Kurt Seligmann, *Magic, Supernaturalism and Religion*, pp. 82–83.
10 H. Stanley Redgrove, *Alchemy: Ancient and Modern*, pp. 10–11.
11 Quoted in M. Berthelot, *La Chimie au Moyen Age*, vol. 2, Paris 1893, p. 262.
12 E. J. Holmyard *Alchemy*, p. 22.
13 Cherry Gilchrist, *The Elements of Alchemy*, p. 7.
14 See A. E. Waite's compilation *The Hermetic Museum Restored and Enlarged*, 1893.
15 Cherry Gilchrist, *The Elements of Alchemy*, pp. 84–85.
16 See Titus Burckhardt, *Alchemy*, p. 75.

Chapter 6 pp. 96–115
1 Fred Gettings *Dictionary of Astrology*, p. 209.
2 Serge Hutin, *Astrology: Science or Superstition?*, p. 43.
3 The Vernal Point is the zero point of Aries in the zodiac.
4 See Fred Gettings, *Dictionary of Astrology*, p. 40.
5 Derek and Julia Parker, *A History of Astrology*, p. 27.
6 Ibid, p. 28.
7 Ibid, p. 15.
8 C. J. S. Thompson, *The Mystery and Romance of Astrology*, pp. 61–62.
9 Hutin, *Astrology*, pp. 58–59.
10 See Gettings, *Dictionary of Astrology*, p. 260.
11 See Henry Corbin, *History of Islamic Philosophy*, vol. 1.
12 Wayne Shumaker, *The Occult Sciences in the Renaissance*, p. 16.
13 Quoted in Derek and Julia Parker, *A History of Astrology*, p. 134.
14 see Hutin, *Astrology*, p. 98.
15 Richard Cavendish, *The Tarot*, p. 11.
16 Ronald Decker, Thierry Depaulis and Michael Dummett, *A Wicked Pack of Cards: The Origins of the Occult Tarot*, p. 28.
17 Ibid, p. 27.
18 See Stuart R. Kaplan *Tarot Classic*, pp. 8 and 35.
19 Fred Gettings, *The Book of Tarot*, p. 140.
20 Ishbel, *Ishbel's Temple of Isis Egyptian Tarot*.
21 See Stuart Kaplan, *Tarot Classic*, p. 47.

Chapter 7 pp. 116–126
1 Joseph Fort Newton, *The Builders*, pp. 17–18.
2 See Charles W. Heckethorn, *The Secret Societies of All Ages and Countries*, vol. 2, pp. 16–17.
3 Joseph Fort Newton, *The Builders*, p. 192.
4 Ibid, p. 211.
5 Ibid, p. 130.
6 Text quoted in Francis King, *Modern Ritual Magic*, pp. 15–16.
7 See Frances A. Yates, *The Rosicrucian Enlightenment*, p. 45.
8 Kurt Seligmann, *Magic, Supernaturalism and Religion*, p. 291.
9 See Yates, *The Rosicrucian Enlightenment*, pp. 52–53.
10 See Newton, *The Builders*, pp. 51–52.
11 Ibid, p. 53.
12 Ibid, p. 58.

Chapter 8 pp. 127–143
1 Quoted in Ellic Howe *The Magicians of the Golden Dawn*, p. 12.
2 Some members of the Golden Dawn itself also had their doubts about the authenticity of Anna Sprengel. See R. A. Gilbert, *Revelations of the Golden Dawn*, p. 30.
3 For detailed histories of the Golden Dawn, readers are referred to the excellent studies by Ellic Howe, Ithell Colquhuon, R. A. Gilbert and Mary K. Greer, listed in the Bibliography.
4 See Howe, *The Magicians of the Golden Dawn*, p. 127.
5 Ibid.
6 Francis King, *Modern Ritual Magic*, p. 97.
7 George Mills Harper, *Yeats's Golden Dawn*, p. 77. The full text of Yeats's essay is provided as an appendix in Harper's book.
8 W. B. Yeats was initiated into the grade of Adeptus Minor on 10 July 1912, eleven years after he had written his essay.
9 King, *Modern Ritual Magic*, p. 57.
10 For full details of the Golden Dawn rituals see Israel Regardie (ed.), *The Golden Dawn*, four volumes.
11 Mathers' manuscript *The Book of Correspondences* was circulated among senior Golden Dawn students in the 1890s. Ithell Colquhoun, author of a biography of Samuel Mathers, *Sword of Wisdom*, believes that Crowley and another Golden Dawn member, Allan Bennett, borrowed much of the material in *777* from their teacher. The Tarot listings in *777*, for example, are conventional, whereas Crowley derived his own symbolic meanings and re-arranged the correspondences to fit in with his own magical philosophy after leaving the Golden Dawn in 1900. Had the material in *777* belonged entirely to Crowley, this would not have been the case. Nevertheless, the inclusion of Harpocrates in this list as a deity linked to Kether reflects his own personal cosmology (see Chapter 9).
12 Franz Bardon, *The Practice of Magical Evocation*, p. 20.
13 Aleister Crowley, *Book Four*, 1972 edn, p. 42.
14 Dion Fortune, *Applied Magic*, pp. 56–57.
15 Some magical rituals in the Golden Dawn tradition utilize the **magic triangle**, but this symbol has a very different meaning from the circle (which symbolizes the Infinite). The triangle represents finite manifestation, a focus for that which already exists. Symbolic of the spiritual, mental and physical levels in all forms of creation, the triangle represents *evocation* – the calling forth of specific spirit-beings by spells or words of power. The magical talisman placed in the centre of the triangle incorporates the seal, or sign, of the spirit and provides the focus of the ritual. Some ritual magicians regarded the evoked spirits as their 'spirit familiars' or 'astral guardians'. Interested readers are referred to the practical writings and magical diaries of Aleister Crowley, and also Franz Bardon's seminal work, *The Practice of Magical Evocation*.
16 In the Golden Dawn the wand was originally ascribed to the element Fire, and the sword to the element Air, but, as Francis King and Stephen Skinner point out in *Techniques of High Magic* (p. 60), it makes more sense to switch these symbolic associations.
17 The magicians of the Golden Dawn utilized a visualization technique known as the Middle Pillar exercise to activate their inner awareness. This involved visualizing different spheres upon the central axis of the Kabbalistic Tree of Life, starting with Kether and culminating with Malkuth. These visualizations also included meditations on specific symbolic colours and the intoning of appropriate god-names. See Israel Regardie, *The Middle Pillar*
18 Quoted in Francis King (ed.), *Astral Projection, Magic and Alchemy*, 1971 edn, pp. 73–74.
19 See V. H. Soror, V. N. R, 'Of Skrying and Travelling in the Spirit-Vision' in Israel Regardie (ed.), *The Golden Dawn*, vol. 4, pp. 29–42; reprinted in King (ed.), *Astral Projection*, 1987, (revised and enlarged edn).
20 See King (ed.) *Astral Projection, Magic and Alchemy*, 1971 (first edn), p. 69.
21 Quoted in Israel Regardie (ed.), *The Golden Dawn*, vol. 4, 1940, p. 43. The god-name HCOMA is not a Kabbalistic god-name but derives from an 'angelic language' called Enochian, transcribed by Elizabethan occultists Dr John Dee and Edward Kelley and used in Golden Dawn rituals and visualizations (see n. 26 for Chapter 4).

Chapter 9 pp. 144–161
1 Aleister Crowley, *Magick in Theory and Practice*, privately published, Paris 1929, (republished in 1973 by Routledge & Kegan Paul, London), p. xv.
2 Ibid, p. xvi.
3 Ibid, p. xvii.
4 Ibid, p. 4.
5 Ibid, p. 4.
6 John Symonds, *The Great Beast*, p. 43.
7 The text of *The Book of the Law* is included as an appendix in John Symonds and Kenneth Grant (eds), *The Magical Record of the Beast 666*.
8 See Crowley, *Magick in Theory and Practice*, p. 12.
9 See Kenneth Grant, *The Magical Revival*, p. 20.
10 Crowley, *Magick in Theory and Practice*, p. 11.
11 see Grant, *The Magical Revival*, p. 45.
12 Ibid, p. 144.
13 Interested readers are referred to Colin Wilson's highly accessible account of Crowley's insatiable search for sexual partners in *Aleister Crowley: The Nature of the Beast*. Also of considerable interest is Lawrence Sutin's biography, *Do What Thou Wilt: A Life of Aleister Crowley*.
14 See Grant, *The Magical Revival*, p. 145.
15 See John Symonds and Kenneth Grant (eds), *The Confessions of Aleister Crowley*, p. 395. Crowley's mention of the A∴ A∴ refers to the Argenteum Astrum (or Silver Star), the magical order that he established in 1907.
16 Ibid, p. 396.
17 Ibid, pp. 399–400.
18 Ibid, p. 403.
19 Quoted in Gerald Suster, *The Legacy of the Beast*, p. 44.
20 See Symonds, *The Great Beast*, p. 122.

21 Quoted in Symonds, *The Magic of Aleister Crowley*, p. 35.
22 See Wilson, *Aleister Crowley*, p. 90.
23 Ibid, p. 91. Colin Wilson makes reference to an entry in Neuburg's magical diary which describes how Crowley on one occasion rebuked him by giving him thirty-two strokes of a gorse switch, drawing blood. 'He is apparently a homosexual sadist,' wrote Neuburg, 'for...he performed the ceremony with obvious satisfaction.'
24 See Aleister Crowley, *The Vision and the Voice*, 1972 edition, pp. 57–58.
25 See Symonds, *The Great Beast*, p. 138.
26 Ibid, p. 161.
27 Ibid, p. 163.
28 Quoted in Symonds, *The Great Beast,* p. 144.
29 Several Crowley biographers have noted the discrepancy between the date of Crowley's meeting with Theodor Reuss (May 1912) and the claimed date of publication of *The Book of Lies* (1913). In his book *Sexuality, Magic and Perversion* (1971, p. 94) Francis King suggests that the printed date of publication is incorrect in the first edition. Advertisements for Crowley's journal *The Equinox* printed in the back of *The Book of Lies* suggest a 1912 publication date.
30 See King, *Sexuality, Magic and Perversion*, p. 100.
31 Ibid, p. 337 – a quote from Loveday's personal account.
32 See Francis King (ed.), *The Secret Rituals of the O.T.O.*, p. 29.
33 John Symonds was fascinated by Crowley's phallic signature and notes in *The Great Beast*: 'Crowley had long identified himself with the penis, just as he identified his mistress – any mistress – with the vagina. He did not consider a woman as a person in her own right. Thus Leah Hirsig was "pure Yoni decorated by the rest of her." ' (From Crowley's magical record, 17 August 1920.) See Symonds, *The Great Beast*, p. 415. In 777, in a note about 'the will of women', he identifies their key roles as the mother, the wife and the whore.
34 See Sandy Roberston's fascinating collection of Crowleyian memorabilia, *The Aleister Crowley Scrapbook*, p. 125.
35 Suster, *The Legacy of the Beast*, p. 204.

Chapter 10 pp. 162–187
1 Bishop Latimer, 1552, quoted in the *Oxford Dictionary of English Folklore,* 'we run hither and thither to witches and sorcerers, whom we call wise men'.
2 For a full description of these initiations see Janet and Stewart Farrar, *The Witches' Way*.
3 Doreen Valiente, *An ABC of Witchcraft*, p. 108.
4 Quoted in James R. Lewis (ed.), *Magical Religion and Modern Witchcraft*, p. 62.
5 See Janet and Stewart Farrar, *Eight Sabbats for Witches*, p. 61.
6 Ibid, p. 82.
7 Lynne Hume, *Witchcraft and Paganism in Australia*, p. 123.
8 See Doreen Valiente, 'The Search for Old Dorothy', in Janet and Stewart Farrar, *The Witches' Way*, p. 283 ff.
9 See Valiente, *An ABC of Witchcraft*, p. 155; and Rosemary Ellen Guiley, *The Encyclopedia of Witches and Witchcraft*, p. 69.
10 Valiente, *An ABC of Witchcraft*, p. 156.
11 Francis King, *Ritual Magic in England*, p. 180.
12 See Lynne Hume, *Witchcraft and Paganism in Australia*, pp. 28–29. Hume also notes that 'Today's witch, however, is more likely to be handed a computer disc, or a printout of a computerised version of the coven's Book of Shadows, when the time is appropriate, usually after initiation.'
13 Guiley, *The Encyclopedia of Witches and Witchcraft*, p. 134.
14 Personal communication to the author. Several other writers, including June Johns, give Sanders' year of birth as 1926.
15 See *Man, Myth and Magic*, issue 40, London, 1973.
16 It must be noted, however, that Patricia and Arnold Crowther were not averse to media publicity themselves. They produced the first radio series in Britain dealing with witchcraft – *A Spell of Witchcraft* – for Radio Sheffield in 1971, and wrote *The Secrets of Ancient Witchcraft* (1974). After her husband's death in 1974, Patricia Crowther continued to appear on radio and television, and published several other books, including *One Witch's World* and *Lid Off the Cauldron* (1981).
17 Janet Owen (Farrar) was initiated by Alex Sanders, and Stewart Farrar by Sanders' wife Maxine, in 1970.
18 Personal interviews with Janet and Stewart Farrar, Drogheda, Ireland, December 1984, and with Janet Farrar in Sydney, Australia, March 2002.
19 Naomi Goldberg, *Changing of the Gods: Feminism and the End of Traditional Religions*, p. 190.
20 See Mary Daly, *Gyn/Ecology: the Metaethics of Radical Feminism*, p. 190.
21 See Mary Farrell Bednarowski, 'Women in Occult America', in Howard Kerr and Charles L. Crow (eds), *The Occult in America: New Historical Perspectives*, p. 190.
22 Judy Davis and Juanita Weaver, 'Dimensions of Spirituality', *Quest,* 1, 1975, p. 2.
23 See Carol P. Christ and Judith Plaskow (eds), *Womanspirit Rising: A Feminist Reader in Religion*, p. 272.
24 Personal communication to the author, December 1984.
25 Cherie Lesh, 'Goddess Worship: the Subversive Religion', *Twelve Together*, 1975.
26 Interview for the documentary *The Occult Experience*, produced for Channel 10, Sydney, in 1985, and released in the US on Sony home video.
27 Following his association with Starhawk, Matthew Fox came to the view that there was a connection between the 'Nature spirituality' in Wicca and the sense of 'wholeness-in-Christ' expressed in his own Creation spirituality. However, he was heavily criticised by the Roman Catholic authorities for this perception, Cardinal Joseph Ratzinger referring to Fox's book *Original Blessing* as 'dangerous and deviant'. See Ted Peters, *The Cosmic Self*, 126–27.
28 Starhawk, 'The Goddess', in Roger S. Gottlieb (ed.), *A New Creation: America's Contemporary Spiritual Voices*, pp. 213–14 .
29 Margot Adler, *Drawing Down the Moon*, revised edition, Beacon Press 1986, p. 35.
30 Quoted in Dennis D. Carpenter, 'Emergent Nature Spirituality' in James R. Lewis (ed.), *Magical Religion and Modern Witchcraft*, p. 57.
31 See Starhawk, 'The Goddess', in Roger S. Gottlieb (ed.), *A New Creation,* p. 221.
32 Quoted in Lynne Hume, *Witchcraft and Paganism in Australia*, p. 70.
33 See Aidan Kelly, *Crafting the Art of Magic*, p. 52 and also Janet and Stewart Farrar, *Eight Sabbats for Witches*.
34 See Graham Harvey, *Listening People, Speaking Earth*, p. 40.
35 See V. Crowley, ' The Initiation', in P. Jones and C. Matthews, (eds), *Voices from the Circle: The Heritage of Western Paganism*, pp. 77–79.
36 Quoted in Janet and Stewart Farrar, *Eight Sabbats for Witches*, pp. 42–43.
37 Quoted in James R. Lewis (ed.), *Magical Religion and Modern Witchcraft*, p. 62.

Chapter 11 pp. 188–205
1 According to some of his critics, elements of LaVey's background have been invented to make him appear more exotic than he actually was. In an article entitled 'Sympathy for the Devil' in *Rolling Stone* magazine, 5 September 1991, Lawrence Wright claimed that there was no evidence of LaVey's involvement with either the Beatty Circus or the San Francisco Police Department. More recently, LaVey's estranged daughter, Zeena LaVey Schreck and her husband Nikolas have stated in an article published on the Internet, entitled 'Anton LaVey, Legend and Reality', that LaVey's alleged gypsy heritage was concocted, and that claims of his romantic involvement with both Marilyn Monroe and Jayne Mansfield were also fictitious, although they acknowledge that Mansfield was a member of the Church of Satan (see http://www.churchofsatan.org/aslv.html). Meanwhile, Blanche Barton has defended the accuracy of her 'authorized biography', and so the controversy continues.
2 Blanche Barton, *The Secret Life of a Satanist: The Authorized Biography of Anton La Vey*, pp. 39–40.
3 Arthur Lyons, *The Second Coming: Satanism in America*, p. 173.
4 See Barton, *The Secret Life of a Satanist,* p. 78.
5 Lyons, *The Second Coming,* pp. 183–84.
6 Ibid., pp. 184–85.
7 Quoted in Barton, *The Secret Life of a Satanist,* p. 243.
8 Ibid., p. 244.
9 See Michael Aquino, *The Crystal Tablet of Set*, p. 23.
10 Personal communication to the author.
11 Michael Aquino has since received a doctorate in political science from this university.
12 See Michael Aquino, *The Crystal Tablet of Set*, p. 27.
13 Personal communication to the author.
14 Don Webb, 'Xeper: The Eternal Word of Set', Internet statement from the Temple of Set, 8 January 1999 (www.xeper.org).
15 Personal communication to the author.
16 See Michael Aquino, *The Church of Satan*, 1983, p. 68.
17 See Don Webb, 'The Pylon System', Internet statement from the Temple of Set, 25 November 1998, p. 3.
18 See Don Webb, 'The Black Beyond Black: The Temple of Set', undated statement on the Temple of Set website, p. 5.
19 Nevertheless, membership of the Temple of Set is probably in the hundreds rather than the thousands. Although there were claims that the Church of Satan had 50,000 card-carrying members, the initial San Francisco membership was only around 50, climbing to a nationwide peak of 300 by 1975 – and the Temple of Set began as a splinter group from the Church of Satan.
20 See Webb, 'The Pylon System', Internet statement from the Temple of Set, 25 November 1998, p. 2.
21 Ibid., p. 3.
22 Ibid., p. 4.
23 Schreck served as High Priestess of the Church of Satan during the 1980s before breaking away from her father and the Church of Satan. She is now based in Berlin.
24 Personal communication to the author.
25 Personal communication to the author.
26 See Nevill Drury, *Exploring the Labyrinth: Making Sense of the New Spirituality*, for an overview of the transpersonal and personal growth movements.
27 See Don Webb, 'Seven of the Many Gateways', in Leon D.Wild (ed.), *The Ninth Night*, vol. 1, no. 2, Sydney, June 1998, published on the Internet.
28 Michael Aquino, *Runes*, vol II: 6, San Francisco 1984.
29 Ibid.
30 See Aquino, *Runes*, vol. I: 2, San Francisco 1983.
31 Personal communication to the author.
32 See Anton LaVey, *The Satanic Bible*, p. 94.
33 Leon D. Wild, 'An Introduction to the Left Hand Path', *The Ninth Night*, vol. 1, no. 1, Sydney, June 1998, published on the Internet.
34 Ibid.
35 Webb, 'The Black Beyond Black', undated statement on the Temple of Set website, pp. 1, 4 and 10.
36 Don Webb, '*Xeper*: The Eternal Word of Set', Internet statement from the Temple of Set, 8 January 1999, p.2.

Chapter 12 pp. 206–221
1 Quoted in *Starfire: A Magazine of the New Aeon*, vol. 1 no. 3 , London 1989, p. 89.
2 Interview with the author for the television documentary *The Occult Experience*, New York, December 1984 (released in the US on Sony home video)
3 C. G. Jung, *Man and his Symbols*, pp. 41–42.
4 C. G. Jung, *Two Essays in Analytical Psychology*, p. 68.
5 Ibid, pp. 65–66.
6 Ibid, p. 70.
7 See C. G. Jung, 'The Relations Between the Ego and the Unconscious' (1928) in *Two Essays on Analytical Psychology.*
8 Quoted in Doiane K. Osbon (ed.), *Reflections on the Art of Living: A Joseph Campbell Companion*, p. 40
9 Ibid, p. 123.
10 See Mirka Knaster, 'The Goddesses in Jean Shinoda Bolen', in *East West*, March 1989, p. 45. An interesting interview with Bolen is also included in Alexander Blair-Ewart, *Mindfire: Dialogues in the Other Future*.
11 Knaster, 'The Goddesses in Jean Shinoda Bolen', in *East West*, March 1989, p. 44.
12 Ibid, p. 73.
13 See Richard Daab and Silma Smith, 'Midwife of the Possible; an Interview with Jean Houston', Part Three, *Magical Blend*, Fall 1988, p. 22.
14 See Alexander Blair-Ewart's interview with Jean Houston in *Mindfire*, p. 111.
15 Jean Houston, *The Hero and the Goddess*, p. 10.
16 Jean Houston, *The Search for the Beloved: Journeys in Sacred Psychology*, p. 13.
17 See Jean Houston, 'Myth and Pathos in Sacred Psychology', *Dromenon*, vol. 3, no. 2, Spring 1981, p. 33.
18 For a more detailed discussion of the debate surrounding Carlos Castaneda and Lynn Andrews, readers are referred to the chapter 'Two Controversies' in Nevill Drury, *The Elements of Shamanism*.
19 Castaneda's first four books have been his most influential: *The Teachings of Don Juan, A Separate Reality, Journey to Ixtlan* and *Tales of Power*.
20 See Richard de Mille's interview with Barbara Myerhoff in his fascinating book *The Don Juan Papers: Further Castaneda Controversies*, p. 336 ff.
21 When a person is 'dis-spirited', their animating force, or spirit, has departed. The role of the shaman is to retrieve it.
22 Personal communication to the author.

Chapter 13 pp. 222–233
1 See 'Magic Plants and the Logos: Terence McKenna in conversation with Alexander Blair-Ewart' in Alexander Blair-Ewart, *Mindfire: Dialogues in the Other Future*, p. 60 ff.
2 See 'Sacred Plants and Mystic Realities: an Interview with Terence McKenna' in, Nevill Drury, *Echoes from the Void*, p. 158 ff. This interview also appeared in Terence McKenna's anthology *The Archaic Revival*.
3 Ibid, pp. 159–60 and 166.
4 Ibid, p. 166.
5 Mark Dery, 'The Inner Elf' in Ashley Crawford and Ray Edgar (eds), *Transit Lounge: Wake-up Calls and Travelers' Tales from the Future*, pp. 94–95.
6 Ibid, p. 95.
7 Margaret Wertheim, *The Pearly Gates of Cyberspace*.
8 Howard Rheingold, *Virtual Reality*, p. 354.
9 Bruce Sterling, *The Hacker Crackdown: Law and Disorder on the Electronic Frontier*, p. 235.
10 Mark Dery, *Escape Velocity: Cyberspace at the End of the Century*, p. 28.
11 Sara Reeder, 'Children of the Digital Gods', in *Green Egg*, vol. 29, no. 129, Aug.–Sept. 1997, p. 15.
12 See 'Computers, Consciousness and Creativity: an Interview with Dr Timothy Leary' in Nevill Drury, *Echoes from the Void*, p. 172.
13 See Dery, *Escape Velocity*, p. 22.
14 'Frantic Life and Symbolic Death among the Computer Bums', quoted in Dery, *Escape Velocity*, p. 27.
15 Erik Davis, 'Technopagans: May the Astral Plane be Reborn in Cyberspace', *Wired*, July 1995, p. 128.
16 See Douglas Rushkoff, *Cyberia: Life in the Trenches of Hyperspace*, p. 143.
17 Erik Davis, 'TechnoPagans: The Roots of Digital Magick' in *Green Egg*, vol. 29, no. 129, Aug.–Sept. 1997, p. 41.
18 Rushkoff, *Cyberia*, pp. 145–46.
19 Tom Williams, 'Navigation Systems for the Spirit' in *Green Egg*, vol. 29, no. 129, Aug.–Sept. 1997, p. 39.
20 Michael Hutchison, *Mega Brain Power*, p. 431.
21 See Jem Dowse, 'Cyberpagans!' in *Pagan Dawn*, no. 119, Beltane 1996, p. 11.
22 Sara Reeder, 'Children of the Digital Gods',in *Green Egg*, vol. 29, no .129, Aug.–Sept. 1997, p.16.
23 Dery, *Escape Velocity*, p. 280.
24 Andrew Siliar, 'Cyber-Space Cadets' in *Green Egg*, vol. 29, no. 120, Aug.–Sept. 1997, p. 65.

Bibliography

Adler, M., *Drawing Down the Moon*, Viking Press, New York, 1979 (republished by Beacon Press, Boston, 1981, and revised 1986)
Alvarado, L., *Psychology, Astrology and Western Magic: Image and Myth in Self-Discovery*, Llewellyn, St Paul, Minnesota, 1991
Ankarloo, B. and Clark, S. (eds), *Witchcraft and Magic in Europe: Biblical and Pagan Societies*, Univ. of Pennsylvania Press, Philadelphia, 2001
Aquino, M., *The Church of Satan*, Temple of Set, San Francisco, 1983
—,*The Crystal Tablet of Set*, Temple of Set, San Francisco, 1983
—, *Runes* , vol II: 6, San Francisco, 1984
Armstrong, A. H. (ed.), *Plotinus*, Allen & Unwin, London, 1953
Ashcroft-Nowicki, D., *Highways of the Mind: the Art and History of Pathworking*, Aquarian Press, Wellingborough, 1987
—, *The Shining Paths: An Experiential Journey through the Tree of Life*, Aquarian Press, Wellingborough, 1983
Bardon, F., *The Practice of Magical Evocation*, Rudolf Pravica, Graz-Puntigam, Austria, 1967
Barnstone, W. (ed.), *The Other Bible*, Harper & Row, San Francisco, 1984
Barton, B., *The Secret Life of a Satanist: The Authorized Biography of Anton La Vey*, Feral House, Los Angeles, 1990
Best, M. R., and Brightman, F. H., *The Book of Secrets of Albertus Magnus*, Oxford Univ. Press, New York, 1973
Blacker, C., *The Catalpa Bow*, Allen & Unwin, London, 1975
Blair-Ewart, A. (ed.), *Mindfire: Dialogues in the Other Future*, Somerville House, Toronto, 1995
Bogoras, W., *The Chukchee: Memoirs of the American Museum of National History*, vol. xl, 1909
Bohak, G., *Traditions of Magic in Late Antiquity*, exhibition catalogue, Univ. of Michigan, Ann Arbor, Michigan, 1996
Bolen, J. S., *Goddesses in Everywoman*, HarperCollins, New York, 1985
—, *Gods in Everyman*, HarperCollins, New York, 1989
—, *The Tao of Psychology*, Harper & Row, New York, 1982
Bonner, J., *Qabalah*, Skoob Publishing, London, 1995
Bracelin, J. L., *Gerald Gardner: Witch*, Octagon Press, London, 1960
Breuil, A. H., 'The Paleolithic Age', in René Huyghe (ed.), *Larousse Encyclopedia of Prehistoric and Ancient Art*, 1962
Budapest, Z., *The Holy Book of Women's Mysteries*, Wingbow Press, Los Angeles, 1989
Budge, E. A. (ed.), *Lefefa Sedek:The Bandlet of Righteousness*, Luzac, London, 1929
Burkert, W., *Ancient Mystery Cults*, Harvard Univ. Press, Cambridge, Mass., 1987
Burckhardt, T., *Alchemy*, Penguin Books, Baltmore, 1971
Burland, C. A., *The Arts of the Alchemists*, Weidenfeld & Nicolson, London, 1967
Butler, W. E., *Apprenticed to Magic*, Aquarian Press, London, 1962
—, *Magic: Its Ritual, Power and Purpose*, Aquarian Press, London, 1952
—, *Magic and the Qabalah*, Aquarian Press, London, 1964
—, *The Magician: His Training and Work*, Aquarian Press, London, 1959
Campbell, J., *The Hero with a Thousand Faces*, Pantheon, New York, 1949
—, *The Inner Reaches of Outer Space: Metaphor as Myth and as Religion*, Harper & Row, New York, 1988
—, *Myths to Live By*, Viking Press, New York 1972; Souvenir Press, London, 1973
Case, P. F., *The Tarot*, Macoy Publishing Co., New York, 1947
Castaneda, C., *The Art of Dreaming*, HarperCollins, New York, 1993
Castaneda, C., *Journey to Ixtlan*, Simon & Schuster, New York, 1972
—, *A Separate Reality*, Simon & Schuster, New York, 1971
—, *Tales of Power*, Simon & Schuster, New York, 1974
—, *The Teachings of Don Juan*, Univ. of California Press, Berkeley, 1968
Cavendish, R., *The Tarot*, Michael Joseph, London, 1975
Christ, C. P., and Plaskow, J., (eds), *Womanspirit Rising: A Feminist Reader in Religion*, Harper & Row, San Francisco, 1979
Churton, T., *The Gnostics*, Weidenfeld & Nicolson, London, 1987
Colquhoun, I., *Sword of Wisdom*, Spearman, London, 1975
Corbin, H., *History of Islamic Philosophy*, vol. 1, Gallimard, Paris, 1964
Couliano, I. P., *The Tree of Gnosis*, HarperCollins, San Francisco, 1992
Crawford, A., and Edgar, R., (eds), *Transit Lounge: Wake-up Calls and Travelers' Tales from the Future*, Craftsman House, Sydney, 1997
Crowley, A., *Book Four*, Sangreal Foundation, Dallas, 1972 (first published in 1913)
—, *The Book of Lies*, Haydn Press, Devon, 1962 (first published London, 1913)
—, *The Book of Thoth*, Weiser, New York, 1969 (first published London, 1944)
—, *Magick in Theory and Practice*, privately published, Paris, 1929 (republished by Dover and Castle Books, New York, various editions)
—, *The Vision and the Voice*, Sangreal Foundation, Dallas, 1972 (first published London, 1911)
Crowley, V., *Wicca: the Old Religion in the New Millennium*, Thorsons, London, 1996
—, *A Woman's Kabbalah*, Thorsons, London, 2000
Crowther, P. & A., *The Secrets of Ancient Witchcraft*, University Books, Secaucus, New Jersey, 1974
Crowther, P., *Lid off the Cauldron*, Muller, London, 1981
—, *One Witch's World*, Hale, London, 1998
Daab, R., 'An Interview with Jean Houston', Berkeley, *Magical Blend* issues 18, 19 and 20, 1988
Daly, M., *Gyn/Ecology: The Metaethics of Radical Feminism*, Beacon Press, Boston, 1978
Davis, E., 'TechnoPagans: the Roots of Digital Magick', *Green Egg*, vol. 29, no. 129, Aug.–Sept. 1997
—, 'Technopagans: May the Astral Plane be Reborn in Cyberspace', *Wired*, July, 1995
Decker, R., Depaulis, T. and Dummett, M., *A Wicked Pack of Cards: The Origins of the Occult Tarot*, St Martins Press, New York, 1996
De Mille, R., *Castaneda's Journey*, Capra Press, Santa Barbara, 1976
—, *The Don Juan Papers: Further Castaneda Controversies*, Ross-Erikson, Santa Barbara, 1980
Dery, M., *Escape Velocity: Cyberculture at the End of the Century*, Hodder & Stoughton, London, 1996
Dowse, J., 'Cyberpagans !', *Pagan Dawn*, no.119, London, Beltane, 1996
Drury, N., *Echoes from the Void: Writings on Magic, Visionary Art and the New Consciousness*, Prism Press, Dorset, 1994
—, *The Elements of Shamanism*, Element, Dorset, 1989
—, *Exploring the Labyrinth: Making Sense of the New Spirituality*, Allen & Unwin, Sydney 1999; Continuum, New York, 1999
—, *The Occult Experience*, Hale, London, 1987
Edinger, E., *Ego and Archetype*, Penguin, London, 1973
Eliade, M., *Birth and Rebirth*, Harper & Row, New York, 1964
—, *Cosmos and History*, Harper & Row, New York, 1959
—, *The Sacred and the Profane*, Harper & Row, New York, 1961
—, *Shamanism*, Princeton Univ. Press, New Jersey, 1972
Elkin, A. P., *Aboriginal Men of High Degree*, Univ. of Queensland Press, St Lucia, Queensland, 1977
Farrar, J. & S., *Eight Sabbats for Witches*, Hale, London, 1981
Farrar, J. & S., *The Witches' Bible*, Magickal Childe, New York, 1985
—, *The Witches' Goddess*, Hale, London, 1987
—, *The Witches' Way*, Hale, London, 1984
Farrar, S., *What Witches Do*, Phoenix, Custer, Washington, 1983
Feinstein, D. and Krippner, S., *Personal Mythology*, Tarcher, Los Angeles, 1988
Feldman, D. H., *Qabalah: the Mystical Heritage of the Children of Abraham*, Work of the Chariot, Santa Cruz, California, 2001
Ferguson, J., *An Illustrated Encyclopaedia of Mysticism and the Mystery Religions*, Thames & Hudson, London, 1976
Fisdel Steven A., *The Practice of Kabbalah* , Jason Aronson Inc., Northvale, New Jersey, 1996
Fortune, D., *Applied Magic*, Aquarian Press, London 1962
—, *Psychic Self-Defence*, Rider, London, 1930
Fuller, J. O., *The Magical Dilemma of Victor Neuburg*, W. H. Allen, London, 1965
Furst, P. T. (ed.), *Flesh of the Gods*, Allen & Unwin, London, 1972
Galloway, B. (ed.), *Fantasy and Wargaming*, Patrick Stephens, Cambridge, 1981
Gardner, G. B., *High Magic's Aid*, Michael Houghton, London, 1949
—, *The Meaning of Witchcraft*, Aquarian Press, London, 1959
—, *Witchcraft Today*, Rider, London, 1954
Gettings, F.,*The Book of Tarot*, Triune/Trewin Copplestone Publishing, London, 1973
—, *Dictionary of Astrology*, Routledge & Kegan Paul, London and New York, 1985
Giger, H. R., *Necronomicon*, Big O Publishing, London, 1978 (repubished by Morpheus International)
—, *N. Y. City*, Ugly Publishing, Zurich, 1981
—, *Retrospektive 1964–1984*, ABC Verlag, Zurich, 1984
Gilbert, R. A., *Revelations of the Golden Dawn*, Quantum/Foulsham, London, 1997
Gilchrist, C., *The Elements of Alchemy*, Element Books, Dorset, 1991
Ginsburg, C., The *Kabbalah: Its Doctrines, Development and Literature*, Routledge & Kegan Paul, London, 1956
Gleadow, R., *The Origin of the Zodiac*, Atheneum, New York, 1968
Goldberg, N., *Changing the Gods: Feminism and the end of Traditional Religions*, Beacon Press, Boston, 1979
Gottlieb, R. S. (ed.), *A New Creation: America's Contemporary Spiritual Voices*, Crossroad, New York, 1990
Graf, F., *Magic in the Ancient World*, Harvard Univ. Press, Cambridge, Mass., 1997
Grant, K., *Hecate's Fountain*, Skoob, London, 1992
—, *The Magical Revival*, Muller, London, 1972
Grant, R. (ed.), *Gnosticism – an Anthology*, Collins, London, 1961
Gray, W. G., *Inner Traditions of Magic*, Weiser, Maine, 1984
Greer, M. K., *Women of the Golden Dawn*, Park Street Press, Rochester, Vermont, 1995
Guiley, R. E., *The Encyclopedia of Witches and Witchcraft*, Facts on File, New York, 1989
Haining, Peter (ed.), *The Witchcraft Papers* , Robert Hale, London 1974,
Halifax, J., *Shaman: the Wounded Healer*, Crossroad, New York, 1982; Thames & Hudson, London, 1984
—, (ed.), *Shamanic Voices*, Arkana, New York, 1991
Harner, M., *The Jivaro*, Univ. of California Press, Berkeley, 1984
—, *The Way of the Shaman*, Harper & Row, San Francisco, 1980
Harper, G. M., *Yeats's Golden Dawn*, Macmillan, London, 1974
Harvey, G., *Listening People, Speaking Earth*, Hurst, London, 1997
Harvey, G., and Hardman, C. (eds), *Paganism Today*, Thorsons, London, 1996
Heckethorn, C. W., *The Secret Societies of All Ages and Countries*, University Books, New York, 1966 (first published London, 1875, revised 1897)
Holmyard, E. J., *Alchemy*, Penguin Books, Harmondsworth, 1957
Houston, J., *The Hero and the Goddess*, Ballantine, New York, 1992
Houston, J., 'Myth and Pathos in Sacred Psychology', *Dromenon*, vol. 3, no. 2, Spring 1981
—, *The Search for the Beloved: Journeys in Sacred Psychology*, Crucible, Wellingborough, 1990
Howe, E., *The Magicians of the Golden Dawn*, Routledge & Kegan Paul, London, 1972
Hume, L., *Witchcraft and Paganism in Australia*, Melbourne Univ. Press, Melbourne, 1997
Hutchison, M., *Mega Brain Power*, Hyperion, New York, 1994
Hutin, S., *Astrology: Science or Superstition?* Bay Books, Sydney, 1972
Hutton, R., *The Triumph of the Moon*, Oxford Univ. Press, Oxford, 1999
Ingram, S., 'Structures of Shamanism in Indonesia and Malaysia', unpublished MA anthropology thesis, University of Sydney, 1972
Ishbel, *Ishbel's Temple of Isis Egyptian Tarot*, Llewellyn Publications, St Paul, Minnesota, 1989
Jamal, M., *Shape Shifters*, Arkana, New York and London, 1987
Johns, J., *King of the Witches: the World of Alex Sanders*, Coward-McCann, New York 1969
Jones, P. and Matthews, C. (eds), *Voices from the Circle*, Aquarian Press, London, 1990
Jordan, M., *Witches: An Encyclopedia of Paganism and Magic*, Kyle Cathie, London, 1996
Jung, C. G., *Man and his Symbols*, Dell, New York, 1968
—, *Memories, Dreams, Reflections*, Random House, New York, 1961
—, *Symbols of Transformation*, Bollingen Foundation, New Jersey, 1956
—, *Two Essays in Analytical Psychology*, Routledge & Kegan Paul, London, 1953
Kalweit, H., *Dreamtime and Inner Space*, Shambhala, Boston, 1988
Kaplan, A., *Meditation and Kabbalah*, Weiser, New York, 1982
Kaplan, S. R., *Tarot Classic*, Grossett & Dunlap, New York, 1972
Kelly, A., *Crafting the Art of Magic*, Llewellyn, St Paul, Minnesota, 1991
Kerr, H. and Crow, C. L. (eds.), *The Occult in America: New Historical Perspectives*, Univ. of Illinois Press, Urbana and Chicago, 1983
Kieckhefer, R., *Magic in the Middle Ages*, Cambridge University Press, Cambridge, 2000
King, F. (ed.), *Astral Projection, Magic and Alchemy*, Spearman, London, 1971
—, *Ritual Magic in England*, Neville Spearman, London, 1970 (republished as *Modern Ritual Magic*, Prism Press, Dorset, 1989)
—, (ed.),*The Secret Rituals of the O.T.O.*, C. W. Daniel, London, 1973
—, *Sexuality, Magic and Perversion*, New English Library, London, 1972
—, and Skinner, S., *Techniques of High Magic: A Manual of Self-Initiation*, C. W. Daniel, London, 1976
—, and Sutherland, I., *The Rebirth of Magic*, Corgi, London, 1982
Knaster, M., 'The Goddesses in Jean Shinoda Bolen', *East West*, March 1989
Knight, G., *A History of White Magic*, Mowbray, London and Oxford, 1978
Larsen, S., *The Shaman's Doorway*, Harper & Row, New York, 1976
Larsen, S. & R., *A Fire in the Mind: The Life of Joseph Campbell*, Doubleday, New York, 1991
LaVey, A. *The Satanic Bible*, Avon, New York, 1969
—, *The Satanic Rituals*, Avon, New York, 1972
Leary, T., *Chaos and Cyberculture*, Ronin, Berkeley, California, 1994
—, *Flashbacks*, Tarcher, Los Angeles, 1983
Lesh, C., 'Goddess Worship: the Subversive Religion', *Twelve Together*, Los Angeles, May 1975
Lessa, W. A., and Vogt, E. Z., (eds), *Reader in Comparative Religion*, Harper & Row, New York, 1972
Levi, E., *The History of Magic Rider*, London, 1913
—, *The Key of the Mysteries*, Rider, London, 1959
Lewis, J. R., (ed.), *Magical Religion and Modern Witchcraft*, State University of New York Press, Albany, 1996
Linton, R., *Culture and Mental Disorders*, Charles C. Thomas, Springfield, Illinois, 1956
Loewe, M., and Blacker, C., (eds), *Divination and Oracles*, Allen & Unwin, London 1981

Luhrmann, T. M., *Persuasions of the Witch's Craft*, Harvard Univ. Press, Cambridge, Mass., 1989
Lyons, A., *The Second Coming: Satanism in America*, Dodd-Mead, New York, 1970
Majidi, A., 'H. R. Giger: Night Visionary', *Manhattan's Entertainment Magazine*, vol. 1, issue 7, New York, Sept. 1998
Mathers, S. L., *The Book of the Sacred Magic of Abramelin the Mage*, De Laurence, Chicago, 1932
—, *The Greater Key of Solomon*, De Laurence, Chicago, 1914
—, *The Grimoire of Armadel*, Routledge & Kegan Paul, London, 1980
—, *The Lesser Key of Solomon*, De Laurence, Chicago, 1916
—, *The Kabbalah Unveiled* (translation of *Kabbala Denudata*), George Redway, London, 1887
Matt, D. C., *The Essential Kabbalah*, HarperCollins, New York, 1995
Matthews, C. and J., *The Western Way*, Arkana, London, 1994
McCall, A., *The Medieval Underworld*, Hamish Hamilton, London, 1979
McKenna, T., *The Archaic Revival*, HarperCollins, San Francisco, 1991
—, *True Hallucinations*, HarperCollins, San Francisco, 1993
Meyer, M. W. (ed.), *The Ancient Mysteries: A Sourcebook*, Harper & Row, San Francisco, 1987
Morrison, J. S., 'The Classical World', in Michael Loewe and Carmen Blacker (eds), *Divination and Oracles*, Allen & Unwin, London, 1981
Murray, M., *The Witch-Cult in Western Europe*, Oxford Univ. Press, New York and Oxford, 1971 (first published Oxford, 1921)
Newton, J. F., *The Builders*, Allen & Unwin, London, 1924
O'Grady, Joan, *Heresy*, Element Books, Dorset, 1985,
O'Hare, G., *Pagan Ways*, Llewellyn, St Paul, Minn., 1997
Osbon, D. K., (ed.), *Reflections on the Art of Living: A Joseph Campbell Companion*, HarperCollins, New York, 1991
Pachter, H. M., *Paracelsus: Magic into Science*, Collier Books, New York, 1961
Pagels, E., *The Gnostic Gospels*, Weidenfeld & Nicolson, London, 1979
Papus, *The Tarot of the Bohemians*, Rider, London, 1919
Paracelsus, *The Archidoxes of Magic*, Askin Publishers, London, 1975 (first edition 1656)
Parker, D. & J., *A History of Astrology* , Andre Deutsch, London, 1983
Patai, R., *The Hebrew Goddess*, Wayne State University Press, Detroit, 1990
Peters, L. G., 'The Tamang Shamanism of Nepal', in Shirley Nicholson (ed.), *Shamanism*, Quest Books, Whaton, Illinois, 1907
Peters, T., *The Cosmic Self*, HarperCollins, San Francisco, 1991
Pinch, G., *Magic in Ancient Egypt*, British Museum Press, London, 1994
Pollard, J., *Seers, Shrines and Sirens*, Allen & Unwin, London, 1965
Redgrove, H. S., *Alchemy: Ancient and Modern*, Rider, London, 1922
Reeder, S., 'Children of the Digital Gods', *Green Egg*, vol. 29, no. 129, Aug.–Sept. 1997
Regardie, I., *The Eye in the Triangle: An Interpretation of Aleister Crowley*, Falcon Press, Phoenix, Arizona, 1982
—, (ed.), *The Golden Dawn*, vols 1–4, Aries Press, Chicago, 1937–40 (republished in various editions)
—, *The Middle Pillar*, Aries Press, Chicago 1945 (republished in various editions)
—, *The Tree of Life: A Study in Magic*, Rider, London, 1932
Rheingold, H., *Virtual Reality*, Mandarin, London, 1992
Richardson, A., *Priestess: The Life and Magic of Dion Fortune*, Aquarian Press, Wellingborough, 1987
Robbins, R. H., *The Encyclopedia of Witchcraft & Demonology*, Bonanza Books, New York, 1981
Robertson, S., *The Aleister Crowley Scrapbook*, Foulsham, London, 1988
Robinson, J. M. (ed.), *The Nag Hammadi Library in English*, Harper & Row, San Francisco, 1977
Roszak, T., *Unfinished Animal*, Harper & Row, New York, 1975
—, *The Voice of the Earth*, Simon & Schuster, New York, 1992
Roth, H. L., *The Natives of Sarawak and British North Borneo*, vol. 1, University of Malaya Press, Singapore, 1968
Rushkoff, *Cyberia: Life in the Trenches of Hyperspace*, HarperCollins, San Francisco, 1994
Russell, J. B., *A History of Witchcraft: Sorcerers, Heretics and Pagans*, Thames & Hudson, London and New York, 1980
—, *Witchcraft in the Middle Ages,* Cornell University Press, Ithaca and London, 1972
Scholem, G., *Kabbalah*, Quadrangle, New York, 1974
—, *Major Trends in Jewish Mysticism*, Schocken, New York, 1961
—, *On the Mystical Shape of the Godhead,* Schocken, New York. 1997
—, *Origins of the Kabbalah*, Princeton University Press, New Jersey, 1990
Seligmann, K., *Magic, Supernaturalism and Religion*, Pantheon, New York, 1971 (first published as *The History of Magic*, Pantheon, New York, 1948)
Shumaker, W., *The Occult Sciences in the Renaissance*, University of California Press, Berkeley, 1979
Spare, A. O., *The Book of Pleasure*, privately published, London, 1913 (republished by 93 Publishing, Montreal, 1975)
Starhawk, *Dreaming the Dark*, Beacon Press, Boston, 1982
—, *The Spiral Dance*, Harper & Row, New York, 1979
Sterling, B., *The Hacker Crackdown: Law and Disorder on the Electronic Frontier*, Bantam, New York, 1992
Stevens, J., *Storming Heaven: LSD and the American Dream*, Atlantic Monthly Press, New York, 1987
Stoddart, A. M., *The Life of Paracelsus*, Rider, London 1915
Sullivan, H. S., *Conceptions of Modern Psychiatry*, Norton, New York, 1953
Suster, G., *The Legacy of the Beast*, Weiser, Maine, 1989
Sutin, L., *Do What Thou Wilt: A Life of Aleister Crowley*, St Martins Press New York, 2000
Symonds, J., *The Great Beast*, Mayflower, London, 1973
—, *The Magic of Aleister Crowley*, Muller, London, 1958
Symonds, J., and Grant, K., (eds), *The Confessions of Aleister Crowley*, Jonathan Cape, London 1969; Hill and Wang, New York, 1970
—, (eds),*The Magical Record of the Beast 666*, Duckworth, London, 1972
Taylor, F. S., *The Alchemists*, Paladin, London, 1976
Thompson, C. J. S., *The Mystery and Romance of Astrology*, Causeway Books, New York, 1973 (first published London, 1929)
Thomsen, M-L., 'Witchcraft and Magic in Ancient Mesopotamia' in Bengt Ankarloo and Stuart Clark (eds), *Witchcraft and Magic in Europe: Biblical and Pagan Societies* , University of Pennsylvania Press, Philadelphia, 2001
Valiente, D., *An ABC of Witchcraft, Past and Present*, Hale, London, 1984
—, *Witchcraft for Tomorrow*, Hale, London, 1978
Waite, A. E., *The Hermetic Museum Restored and Enlarged* , J.Elliott & Co., London, 1893
—, *The Holy Kabbalah*, University Books, New York, 1960 (first published London, 1929)
Walker, B., *Gnosticism: Its History and Influence*, Aquarian Press, Wellingborough, 1983
Walker, D. P., *Spiritual and Demonic Magic: From Ficino to Campanella*, Alan Sutton Publishing, Stroud, Glos, 2000 (first published Warburg Institute, London, 1958)
Wasson, R. G., et. al, *The Road to Eleusis*, Harcourt, Brace Jovanovich, New York, 1968
Wertheim, M., *The Pearly Gates of Cyberspace*, Norton, New York, 1998
Widengren, G., *Mani and Manichaeism*, Holt, Rinehart and Winston, New York, 1965
Wilby, B., (ed.), *The New Dimensions Red Book*, Helios, Cheltenham, 1968
Wild, L. (ed.), *The Ninth Night*, vol.1, nos. 1 and 2, Sydney, 1998
Williams, T., 'Navigation Systems for the Spirit', *Green Egg*, vol. 29, no. 120, Aug.–Sept. 1997
Wilson, C., *Aleister Crowley: the Nature of the Beast*, Aquarian Press, Wellingborough, 1987
Yates, Frances, *Giordano Bruno and the Hermetic Tradition,* Routledge & Kegan Paul, London, 1971
Yates, Frances, *The Rosicrucian Enlightenment*, Routledge & Kegan Paul, London, 1972; Shambhala Publications, Boulder, Colo., 1987
—, *The Occult Philosophy in the Elizabethan Age*, Routledge, London and New York, 2000 (first published Routledge & Kegan Paul, London, 1979)

Acknowledgments

Over the years many people have assisted me with my study of the Western magical traditions and I would like to thank them for contributing either directly, or indirectly, to the creation of this book. They include Stephen Skinner, who first introduced me to the study of the Kabbalah, and Dr Michael Harner, who deepened my knowledge of shamanism and taught me the technique of shamanic drumming. I have also been greatly influenced by key figures in the 'new consciousness' movement like Stanislav Grof, Timothy Leary, Jean Houston, John Lilly, Ralph Metzner and Joan Halifax – these people have helped define the new spiritual paradigms of our age. Metaphysical writers like Mircea Eliade, Arthur Machen, Lord Dunsany and Jorge Luis Borges have also impacted greatly on my work.

List of Illustrations

List of Illustrations

a = above, b = below, c = centre, l = left, r = right, t = top

Pages 2–3 Shaman Mongush Lazo, Tuva, south-central Siberia, February 2002. Photo Dimitry Beliakov.
4 *Love's Enchantment*, Flemish, 15th century. Museum der Bildenden Kunste, Leipzig.
9 Rembrandt van Rijn, *Faust in his Study,* etching, *c.* 1652–53.
11 Shaman Mongush Lazo, Tuva, south central Siberia, February 2002. Photo Dimitry Beliakov.
12a Sacrifice of a bison bull and prostrate shaman, drawing after cave painting, Lascaux, France, *c.* 13,000 BCE.
12b Disguised hunter, Les Trois-Frères, Ariège, France, drawing of a cave painting after Abbé Breuil, c. 13,000 BCE.
13 Gundestrup cauldron, detail, Denmark, 1st or 2nd century BCE. National Museet, Copenhagen.
14 Torres Straits Aboriginal fish headdress, Australia. British Museum, London.
15 Aborigines with personal totemic body markings, Central Australia. Haddon Collection, University Museum of Archaeology and Anthropology, Cambridge.
16a Shaman spirit-journey, Late Pueblo Style III, rock carving, Inkom, Idaho, drawing after Wellmann, 1979.
16b The Underworld, Ostiak-Samoyed, Siberia, from *Asia* magazine, 1926.
19 Tracks of the mythical emu, Aboriginal ground painting. Photo The Mountford Sheard Collection in the State Library of South Australia.
21a Drawing of Inuit shamans' flying race, from Knud Rasmussen, *Eskimo Folk Tales*, 1921.
21b Sedna, Mother of the Seas, stone-cut print, Inuit, 1961. Canadian Museum of Civilization, National Museums of Canada, Ottawa.
22 Siberian shaman healing ceremony, former USSR. Photo Joan Halifax.
23a Shaman and Anky-Kele, god of the seas, Chukchee, North Siberia, 1945, drawing after Lavrov.
23b Masked coyote dancer on a Mimbres funerary vessel, New Mexico, 1100–1250 CE. Colorado Springs Fine Art Center, Taylor Museum Collection.
24a Shaman's wooden mask, Nunivak, south Alaska, early 20th century. Thomas Burke Memorial Washington State Museum, University of Washington, Seattle.
24b Maya Lord's shamanic double (*way*), polychrome pottery vase, Tepeu culture, Altar de Sacrificios, Guatemala, 754 CE. Museo Nacional de Arqueologia y Etnologia, Guatemala City.
25 Female *machi* (shaman) on notched pole, Mapuche region of Chile. Photo Louis C. Faton.
26 Jaguar impersonator, back view of dancer, Matto Grosso, Brazil. The University Museum, University of Pennsylvania.
28 Grimoire (book of spells and astrology), Sumatra, Indonesia. British Museum, London.
29 The witch Rangda and dead child, Tjalonarog dance, Bali.
30 Masked dancer in seasonal Bon-Po/Buddhist ceremony, Tibet.
32 Circe and Odysseus, detail of Boetian black-figure skyphos (vase), Thebes. late 5th century BCE. Ashmolean Museum, Oxford.
33a Orpheus, Attic red-figure column krater (vase), by the Orpheus painter from Gela, *c.* 440 BCE. Photo J. Beazley.
33b Oracular head of Orpheus, with Apollo and scribe, Attic red-figure cup, *c.* 400 BCE. Corpus Christi College, Cambridge.
34 Bronze head probably of Pythagoras, copy of Greek original of *c.* 300 BCE, Villa dei Pisoni, Herculaneum. National Museum, Naples.
35 The Three Magi, mosaic (detail), Sant'Apollinare Nuovo, Ravenna, 5th or 6th century CE.
36a Drawing of *defixio*, Rome, late 4th century CE. From *Curse Tablets and Binding Spells from the Ancient World*, New York, 1992, edited by John G. Gager, copyright John G. Gager. Used by permission of Oxford University Press, Inc.
36b Female figurine with 13 needles (made after a recipe in *Papyri Graecae Magicae*, 2nd century CE) and found with a *defixio* in a clay pot, Egypt, 3rd or 4th century CE. Louvre, Paris.
37a Gnostic deity Abraxas, drawing. Nevill Drury.
37b Amulet with 'Abracadabra' inscription, British Museum, London.
38al Two amulets, *wedjat*, or 'eye of Horus', Egypt, *c.* 1000 BCE. British Museum, London.
38ar Detail of funerary text, Papyrus of Hunefer, Egypt, *c.* 1350 BCE. British Museum, London.
39ar Painted terracotta plaque of goddess Lilith, 'Bringer of Death', winged and holding symbols of justice, Mesopotamian, Syria, early 2nd millennium BCE. Photo Sotheby's, London.
39bl Prophylactic figurines for burial in walls and floors, Babylonian, Iraq. British Museum, London.
40 Bronze statue of Zeus from Dodona, *c.* 470 BCE. Staatliche Museen, Berlin.
41ar Pythia on tripod, Attic red-figure vase, 440 BCE. Staatliche Museen, Berlin.
41bl Apollo shooting at Python with tripod, silver stater (coin) from Croton, *c.* 420 BCE. Photo Hirmer.
42a Zeus and Typhon, drawing of a bronze relief, shield band panel from Olympia.
43a Mithras slaying the bull, sculpture, Rome, early 2nd century CE. British Museum, London.

238   LIST OF ILLUSTRATIONS

Index

Page numbers in *italics* refer to illustrations